On Rationality, Artificial Intelligence and Economics

On Rationality, Artificial Intelligence and Economics

Daniel Muller
BTB - Be The Bank, Tel Aviv, Israel

Fernando Buarque
University of Pernambuco, Recife, Brazil

Tshilidzi Marwala
University of Johannesburg, South Africa

World Scientific

NEW JERSEY • LONDON • SINGAPORE • BEIJING • SHANGHAI • HONG KONG • TAIPEI • CHENNAI • TOKYO

Published by

World Scientific Publishing Co. Pte. Ltd.
5 Toh Tuck Link, Singapore 596224
USA office: 27 Warren Street, Suite 401-402, Hackensack, NJ 07601
UK office: 57 Shelton Street, Covent Garden, London WC2H 9HE

British Library Cataloguing-in-Publication Data
A catalogue record for this book is available from the British Library.

ON RATIONALITY, ARTIFICIAL INTELLIGENCE AND ECONOMICS

ISBN 978-981-125-511-3 (hardcover)
ISBN 978-981-125-512-0 (ebook for institutions)
ISBN 978-981-125-513-7 (ebook for individuals)

For any available supplementary material, please visit
https://www.worldscientific.com/worldscibooks/10.1142/12801#t=suppl

Foreword

If you are reading this, you must be interested in rationality, artificial intelligence (AI), economics, or several of these topics. You have probably also opened the book, and have noticed that it contains formulas. Don't let this put you off. There are plenty of popular books on either rationality, AI, or economics. They will give you the story, and increase your interest. After reading these books, you will be able to join in the conversation at a cocktail party, or a Zoom hangout. You will probably end up buying another popular book from the same bestselling author. However, if you want to *benefit* from your knowledge of rationality, AI or economics, you have to work through the maths. You need this book.

Even if you master the content of this book, you haven't arrived yet. You will need access to software, and access to a market place or an environment where you can exercise your decision-making skills. This can be done from home, but I hope you find a tech company to work for, or start one yourself. You will also need a diversity of colleagues. A software engineer, an economist, a salesperson, a networker, a fundraiser. You need a communications person who can explain why you're so good at decision-making. You need a cleaner. You need a diverse group of colleagues, male and female, from several continents. Finally, you need somebody who has read this book. I hope this is you.

Rationality has a long history. Plato elevated rationality to a sophisticated abstract level. However, before Plato there have been thousands of hunters who rationally forecast where their prey would show up, and later thousands of farmers who rationally selected grains with a high yield to sow next year. With the decline of the ancient Greek empire, rationality had a bad time, but it survived. Some religions valued the law, and needed rationality to make this work. Later, rationality had a comeback in the

Age of Enlightenment. Greek philosophers were rediscovered, and the scientific method was developed. An industrial revolution happened, and from then on there was no way back for rational economic decision-making. Our modern world is still developing along the lines of decision-making initiated three hundred years ago. China's rapid development, for example, would be unthinkable without rational resource allocation.

AI is a baby compared to rationality and economics. Barely 75 years old. It's still having growth spurts. It can't make up its mind whether it's about imitating our brains, or about clever algorithms that can function without human embodiment. AI is a boom-and-bust world. We are experiencing an AI boom for the moment, but how long will it last? Face recognition and social network algorithms are being rejected. Self-driving car development is set back after every crash. Governments want to regulate AI, and risk throttling it. I have been working in AI for 34 years, and have seen difficult years as well as the current boom. I firmly believe that the enduring value of AI is in practical and easily understood algorithms. That are the sort of algorithms described in this book. When all the hype about AI will have gone once more, books such as this will still be read and used. They will still be understood because they use the universal language of mathematics. So take some time to work through the formulas in this book, and apply, or pass on, your knowledge. You are acquiring a skill that lasts.

Economics has always relied on rationality. The earliest writing was book-keeping. Ancient Mesopotamians were not just *writing* 5,500 years ago, they were also following rules of accounting and securing their income. Unfortunately, the book-keeping was not just of goods, but also of slaves. So right from the beginning of record keeping we see how economics and rationality can co-exist with the worst deviations of human behavior. Rational economic decision-making, assignment of value and utility maximization are not without risk. We need to understand the limitations. Let me explain how this book does this.

An important part of this book is about bounded rationality. This was proposed by Nobel Prize winner Herbert Simon. He realized that there is not just one type of rationality, and that our knowledge is not perfect. He did this work in the 1950s, and it is far from finished. Kahneman and Tversky have brought new ideas, but a lot more is needed to safeguard rationality, AI and economics, and ensure that they benefit humankind and do no harm. So, when you read this book, don't skip Chapter 2 on decision-making and rationality. Every book on economics or AI should have a chapter like that.

Books, even books with formulas, are written by people! I am fortunate to know the three authors of this book, and have got to know them, not as a group, but as three fascinating individuals. They come from three different continents, and represent the diversity we so desperately need in economics and AI. None of them is a career economist or a career AI researcher, but they have an incredibly rich, diverse and complementary background. They give us a new angle on rationality, AI and economics. This book is methodologically very strong. It's useful. It is lasting. Let's read it together.

Philippe De Wilde
Professor of Artificial Intelligence
University of Kent, UK

Preface

The humanity's current revolution (a.k.a. Fourth Industrial Revolution) is sending shock waves across all segments of society and has been deemed to be more profound and impactful to modern life than all the previous industrial revolutions combined. Computers are now ubiquitous and interconnected, and their use is growing steadily. They are also developing unprecedented levels of autonomy. Robots (including virtual ones) and machines with embedded Artificial Intelligence (AI) are becoming so common that simple activities such as driving the kids to school, making purchases, and most decisions in the workplace are no longer performed by humans alone. At the same time, intelligent systems can (sometimes they already are) take control of our freedom and hijack fragile democracies. This crossroads of opportunities/threats between flourishing societies and doomed places was the primary motivation for bringing the three authors together.

The mind-boggling implications of the new AI-fueled decision processes, apparently so overwhelming, are, unexpectedly, quite bounded. Thus, such decision processes demand careful reflection. This apparent paradox (among many others included in the book) motivated the authors to delve further in the underlining rationality of AI in Economics. All intelligent algorithms, the economics of such decisions, and their underscoring limitations are the underpinnings of this book.

The three authors share many things with each other: friendship, worries about the lack of reflection on the topic, a drive for improvement in the field of AI, and working in the top technical hubs of their respective countries. Despite these striking similarities, the authors could not come from more different backgrounds and upbringings. Daniel Muller was born in beautiful St. Petersburg, Russia (at the time of the USSR). An economist and AI researcher, he currently lives in the tech-hub of Tel-Aviv, Israel.

Fernando Buarque was born in Recife, Brazil. He is a computer scientist. After a decade away from Brazil, living in four countries, he is now back in Recife. Tshilidzi Marwala was born in the Limpopo province of South Africa and is an engineer. After a decade away from South Africa, living in three countries, he is back in Johannesburg to spread the importance of AI for a better future.

Daniel Muller, Tel-Aviv, Israel
Fernando Buarque, Recife, Brazil
Tshilidzi Marwala, Johannesburg, South Africa
December 2021

Acknowledgments

The authors would like to thank their universities for the unshakable support they have shown them (The Technion — Israel Institute of Technology, the Federal University of Pernambuco and the University of Johannesburg), their families for their patience, and their fellow countrymen for their inspirational resilience. They would also like to thank Emma Hutton for ensuring the use of good written English. And finally they would like to thank the publisher for the support and encouragement received. The high expectation the authors have of this book is that it will shed some light on the topics that are already so seminal to us all!

The authors dedicate this book to their beloved partners and kids (the ones who have already landed in this world and the forthcoming ones), as they undoubtedly break down all boundaries of rationality.

About the Authors

Daniel Muller is an Artificial Intelligence researcher, Economist, Engineer, Data Scientist, and industry practitioner. He received his PhD in Artificial Intelligence from the University of Johannesburg, supervised by Prof. Tshilidzi Marwala. He holds a Master of Science in Information Management Engineering, a Bachelor of Science in Industrial Engineering and Management (cum laude), and a Bachelor of Arts in Economics and Management from the Technion — Israel Institute of Technology. His research interests are multi-disciplinary, and they include Artificial Intelligence, Machine Learning, Economics, and Data Science but not limited to these. His current research focuses on automated action planning, sequential decision-making and rationality in Artificial Intelligence and Economic Systems. His industrial experience was acquired in the defense and finance industries through engineering, data science, and R&D leadership positions. Currently, he serves as Chief Technology Officer and Chief Information Officer in the Fintech company BTB — Be The Bank. He achieved the Outstanding Leadership Award in the Money 2.0 Conference, a leadership seal of recognition that acknowledges creativity and innovation in the finance world. Further information can be obtained at `https://www.linkedin.com/in/daniel-muller-in/` and `https://mullerdaniel.com/`.

Fernando Buarque de Lima Neto received his PhD in Artificial Intelligence from the University of London-Imperial College (2002). He is the head of the Computational Intelligence Research Group and Senior Associate Professor at the University of Pernambuco-Brazil, where he has supervised over 100 students in the PhD, MSc and

BSc final dissertations. He has authored over 220 scientific publications and holds visiting positions at Texas A&M University, University of Johannesburg, University of Münster — WWUU, and University of Exeter. He is Alexander von Humboldt Fellow (Germany), IEEE Senior Member (USA), and Life member of the Academy of Science (PE-Brazil). He visited the European Research Center for Information Systems (ERCIS in Münster-Germany) during his postdoctoral sabbatical leave in 2014, and the University of Florida-USA in 2019. His current research focuses on Computational Intelligence and Semiotics for Modeling/Simulations of complex optimization problems, and Intelligent Decision Support using Explainable AI. Presently, he is investigating how Responsible AI could be attained via rational processes for establishing flourishing societies. Prof. Buarque is also involved in spreading the use of AI for practical complex problems in industry. For that he coaches students and former students who want to venture into the business world of innovation. He has an extensive list of previously delivered workshops in Artificial Intelligence for advanced audiences in several universities and companies. Further information can be obtained at `http://fbln.me`, `https://www.linkedin.com/in/fernandobuarque/` and `https://www.researchgate.net/profile/Fernando-Lima-Neto`.

Tshilidzi Marwala is the President (Vice-Chancellor) of the University of Johannesburg (UJ). UJ has 50,000 students and 5,000 staff members. He was previously the Deputy Vice-Chancellor for Research and Internationalization, as well as the Dean of the Faculty of Engineering at UJ. Before then, he progressively held the positions of Associate Professor, Full Professor, the Carl and Emily Fuchs Chair of Systems and Control Engineering, and the SARChI Chair of Systems Engineering at the University of the Witwatersrand. Prior to that, he was a post-doctoral research associate at the Imperial College (London). He holds a Bachelor of Science in Mechanical Engineering (magna cum laude) from Case Western Reserve University (USA), a Master of Mechanical Engineering from the University of Pretoria, and a PhD in Artificial Intelligence from the University of Cambridge. Marwala is a Fellow of TWAS (The World Academy of Sciences for the Developing World), a Senior Member of the IEEE and a distinguished member of the Association for Computing Machinery (ACM). His research interests are multidisciplinary, and they include the theory and application of Artificial Intelligence to Engineering, Computer Science, Finance, Social Science, and Medicine. He has supervised 47 masters and 32 doctoral students to completion. He has published 23 books in artificial intelligence, one of these has been translated into Chinese, over 300 papers in journals, proceedings, book chapters, and magazines, and holds five patents. He has been a visiting scholar at Harvard University, University of California at Berkeley, University of Cambridge and Nanjing Tech University. His writings and opinions have featured in media such as *New Scientist*, *The Economist*, *Time*, CNN, BBC, Royal Society, Cambridge Union and Oxford Union. Further information can be obtained at `https://www.linkedin.com/in/tshilidzimarwala/?originalSubdomain=za` and `https://en.wikipedia.org/wiki/Tshilidzi_Marwala`.

Contents

Chapter 1

Introduction

1.1 The Rationale of the Book

This book examines rationality, artificial intelligence (AI) and economics. A rational agent can be defined as an agent that can accomplish its goal in a highly optimal manner. In classical economics, a rational agent is one that maximizes its utility. Utility is the measure of the usefulness of a particular goal. In this book we define a rational agent as one that optimizes its net utility rather than its nominal utility (i.e., not the overall output collected, but rather what is yielded after settlements and the net gain/loss due to the changing of the position). This book also explores how AI can be used to create a value rational agent that maximizes its net utility. Using net utility, rather than nominal utility, as a measure allows us to capture a broader context of the impact of a decision's possible achievement. This book applies the concepts of the net utility, AI and optimization to solving the St. Petersburg Paradox as well as planning problems.

Different AI methods and how they can be used in economics and planning are described and investigated in this book. We include a chapter with a wide outlook on AI which provides a brief account of its history and current context, an overview of major concepts in AI, and an integrative perspective that bridges classes of problems with families of intelligent algorithms. Additionally, we examine how AI may carry out optimizations that minimize the distance between the AI model and the observed data. Optimization algorithms can be categorized into local and global optimization methods. The local methods that are investigated in this book include the simplex method and conjugate gradient method. The global methods include Genetic Algorithms and simulated annealing.

We also investigate planning and decision-making problems through the lens of economics and rationality, with the aim of increasing the effectiveness of planning and domain-independent problem-solving processes, as well as increasing the overall rationality of sequential decisions in the decision-making process. We investigate the utility structure in planning and decision-making problems at the level of decisions and actions and sequences of decisions and actions. We present a framework with which to analyze the utility of decision actions over multi-valued variables and increase the accuracy and effectiveness of single actions as well as the overall impact of planning and sequential decision-action application in the decision-making process.

We present economic aspects of the decision-making process and provide cost-value, budget, and utility analyzes. We also investigate the role of utility and net utility value rational decision-making processes. We provide a closer inspection of the role of data, information, and knowledge in decision-making and action execution. This book goes on to conclude that the net utility concept more universally explains value than the nominal utility. The concept of net utility captures the dynamics and the exchange of values by considering the state difference before a decision (or action) is taken and the outcome state just after that decision (or action) is made. Furthermore, the concept of net utility considers the combined value of maximization of profit and minimization of cost (or negative utility) in the system.

We then use our observations from the economics, decision making and rationality fields to devise a theory of value rational decision planning. We start with the most fundamental question: What is the rationality of sequential decision making and planning processes? We then discuss the challenges of the sequential decision making and the action execution processes and provide observations of the information, costs and values involved in these processes. We propose a globally local prospective to rationalize the process of investment, built from sequences of rational and irrational decision-choices, actions under budget restrictions and utility functions over multivariate variables. We use net utility to provide the properties for optimality in planning and sequential decision making.

We specify a simple model representation language for Oversubscription planning (OSP), as well as providing the essential background on heuristic search methods and, in particular, on the landmarks and properties of optimal plans in OSP search methods. We also provide a framework for the online and offline analysis of the net utility of actions to determine the net utility polarity of actions in automated planning. We introduce an efficient way to define the net utility of an action based on an offline analysis of the problem structure and its utility setting. In this book we address the ambiguity of an action's net utility for actions that are applicable in several different original states.

1.2 The Core Contributions

1.2.1 *St. Petersburg Paradox*

We present the St. Petersburg Paradox and propose a resolution to it from a planning perspective. We also define the theorem of indifference. The famous St. Petersburg Paradox demonstrates that the theory of expected value does not capture the real-world economics of decision-making problems. Over the years, many economic theories have been developed to resolve the paradox and explain gaps in the economic value theory in evaluating economic decisions, the subjective utility of the expected outcomes, and risk aversion as observed in the St. Petersburg Paradox game. We use the concept of the relative net utility to resolve the St. Petersburg Paradox and provide a mathematical resolution for the St. Petersburg Paradox. We also put some of our observations on planning and sequential decision-making processes into practice in order to resolve the St. Petersburg Paradox. We propose a sequential event diagram that can be used to analyze the paradox from different perspectives. We define the break-even point and adopt the terms "dynamic reference point" and "incremental improvement of utility" from recent work on oversubscription planning [Muller and Karpas (2018a,b)]. We also provide a mathematical analysis of the paradox and propose a solution based on the means of expectation for an infinite sequence of events.

1.2.2 *Planning and Decision Making*

Problem-solving and planning are decision-making processes that consist of ordered decision choices and decision actions [Kriger and Barnes (1992); Marwala (2015)]. Instantaneous decision choices are the atomic units that compose a decision action. Decision-theoretic planning is an approach [Boutilier *et al.* (1999)] for solving sequential decision problems that results in a plan or a policy. If the environment is assumed to be deterministic, a course of actions is a plan that guarantees that a specific goal will be reached. A more flexible framework for a solution plan or policy is a course of action with an expected high utility that fits uncertainty scenarios and has more complicated target structures and reward dynamics represented in preferences value or utility functions. An optimized decision results in a global maximization of utility [DeGroot (2005); Berger (2013)]. Rational decision-making process comprises of rational decision actions, and the entire process is optimized in time and results in a global utility optimum [Grüne-Yanoff (2012); Marwala (2014, 2015)]. For the purpose of simplicity, decision actions will sometimes be referred to as actions in this work.

1.2.3 *Oversubscription Planning*

Oversubscription planning [Smith (2004)], or OSP, refers to achieving a state of high utility value, given a budget on the total action cost. This formulation allows us to handle situations with limited resources, that do not allow us to achieve all possible goals. This is in contrast to classical planning, in which the objective is to find a cheap plan that achieves your *all* goals. In optimal OSP and optimal classical planning, the tasks are further constrained to finding a path that achieves a state of maximum utility within budget limits, and, finding the cheapest path to achieving the goal, respectively.

Over the years, the theory and practice of classical planning has been studied and has advanced much more than OSP. Recent work [Mirkis and Domshlak (2013, 2014); Domshlak and Mirkis (2015); Muller and Karpas (2018a,b)] has made several contributions aimed at improving the scalability of OSP solvers. In particular, they developed a planner that exploits the standard landmark discovery tools of classical planning to solve OSP problems. They showed how the standard goal-reachability landmarks of certain classical planning tasks could be generated to represent the achievements of valuable facts from the original OSP task. These landmarks were compiled into the original OSP task to obtain an equivalent OSP task with a lower cost allowance, and thus with a smaller effective search space.

Recent work on the oversubscription planning problem [Muller and Karpas (2018a)] introduced the notion of *net utility of an action*, which allows for more detailed reasoning about achievements. The concept of the net utility of action takes the context of fact dependencies into account (in a specific state), as well as the context of previous variable assignments (in previous states along the plan) that were given away along the plan to achieve a *seemingly* valuable fact. The notion of an action's net utility will help us set a more accurate estimation of likely goal states in an OSP task and reduce the search space. It also eliminates assumptions about the utility of the initial state and defines a reference point to indicate improvement for any given state. This reference point is a set of propositions[1] with improved utility over propositions in a given state, for each state variable. A *gross positive* action is an action that improves the utility for at least one of the state variables, although possibly at the cost of the lower utility of other variables. An optimal plan must contain a gross positive action (that might have negative net utility), that achieves some valuable fact that is *maintained* until the end of the plan (which must be an action with positive net utility). With our focus on **improving** state-variables rather than on **collecting** valuable facts or goals, the investigation of planning tasks and their utility structure on the level of actions and sequences of actions allows us to handle OSP general additive utility functions over multi-valued variables. This approach focuses on *improving* sets of variables, which differs from previous approaches that attempted to *collect* valuable facts or goals and allowed us to handle general additive utility functions, rather than only non-negative utilities.

We introduce an efficient way to define the net utility of an action based on an offline analysis of the problem structure and its utility setting. Instead of calculating the net utility of an action in each state during the search, we perform a pre-processing step that include identifying and marking **only** the net positive actions that are candidates for terminating the search. When an action can be applied in many different states, the impact of the same action is relative to the original state in which the action is applied. Achieving the same outcome from different states can cause negative, positive or no change in total terms, depending on the context and the value of the origin state in which the action has been applied. In this work we address the ambiguity of an action's net utility for actions that are applicable in several different original states. To define the net utility of an action, a Simplified Action Structure (SAS) formalism [Bäckström and Klein (1991); Klein (1991)] is assumed, where, a specific precondition is specified for each effect of an action. SAS+ [Bäckström and Klein (1991); Bäckström and Nebel (1995)] representation of planning tasks allows for a more flexible representation of actions. In SAS+, the precondition list of an action specifies those state variables that must have a certain defined value in order to make the action applicable and that will be changed to

[1]We refer to an assignment of a single state variable to a specific value as a proposition or fact.

another value by the action. This representation allows for an incomplete precondition list, which in turn allows for a more compact representation of actions. At the same time, the obtained degree of freedom in state variables that are in the effects list of an action but not in the precondition list, results in an ambiguity regarding the net change in the utility that is caused by the action.

1.3 The Structure of the Book

The book is structured as follows: In Chapter 2 we discuss rationality and the decision-making process, and investigate the value rational decision process. Chapter 3 provides an overview of the main families of AI algorithms and the classes of problems that AI can solve. This serves to pave the way for the coming explanations on how non-natural intelligence (whatever form or shape) that equip current machines can evoke rationality in an automatic manner. Chapter 4 explores different optimization methods and evaluates how rational these methods are. In Chapter 5 we present economic aspects of the decision-making process and provide cost-value analyzes and show some hidden dimensions of values and costs. We continue to investigate the utility term and present the diamond-water paradox and types and dynamics of utility. We discuss the terms utility and net utility as well as positive and negative values of actions and decisions. We expand the discussion on rationality, decision-making, and actions concerning values, costs, and utility. Chapter 5 is also dedicated to providing a closer look at the role of data, information, and knowledge in decision making and action execution. In Chapter 6, we present the St. Petersburg Paradox and propose a resolution to it from a planning perspective and define the theorem of indifference. This chapter presents the expected utility theorem and defines the expected net utility theorem that helps us to solve the St. Petersburg Paradox. In this chapter we also provide a mathematical resolution for the St. Petersburg Paradox. In Chapter 7 we specify a simple model representation language for OSP, as well as providing the essential background on heuristic search methods and, in particular, on the landmarks and properties of optimal plans in OSP search methods. Chapter 8 is dedicated to the online and offline analysis of the net utility of actions to determine the net utility polarity of actions in automated planning. Finally, in Chapter 9 we conclude and discuss some promising directions for future work.

Chapter 2

Decision-Making and Rationality

This chapter explores decision-making and rationality. The decision-making process consists of ordered decision choices and decision actions. Instantaneous decision choices are the atomic units that device a decision action. A decision action can be rational or irrational. A decision action is rational if it results in a global optimum, is based on logical principles and is derived from complete relevant information. Furthermore, the decision-making process can be rational or bounded rational, where the bounds of rationality might be flexible.

2.1 Introduction

In this chapter, we discuss the value rational decision-making process. First, we present the rational and the bounded rational decision models. We then discuss the term of rationality in the decision-making process, the bounded and the flexible bounded rationality. We go on to lay out some of the bounds of rationality. Finally, we present some instrumental and value rational decision actions and discuss the effectiveness and efficiency of these actions. The discussion and conclusion on value rational actions and the decision-making process allows us to solve economic and AI planning and decision-making problems, as we show in the following chapters.

2.2 Decision-Making Process

Problem-solving and planning are sequential decision-making processes (illustrated in Fig. 2.1) that consist of ordered decision choices and decision actions [Kriger and Barnes (1992); Marwala (2015)]. Instantaneous decision-choices are the atomic units that form a decision-action. A course of actions make up a plan or policy designed to reach a solution. Without any loss of generality, a solution can be defined in terms of goals, states, profit or utility creation. Decision-theoretic planning is an approach [Boutilier *et al.* (1999)] to solving sequential decision problems that results in a plan or a policy. If a deterministic environment is assumed, a course of actions is a plan that guarantees that a specific goal will be reached. A more flexible framework for the solution plans or policies results in a course of actions with an expected high utility that fits the uncertainty scenarios and more complicated target structures and reward dynamics represented in preferences value or utility functions. An optimized decision results in a global maximization of utility [DeGroot (2005); Berger (2013)].

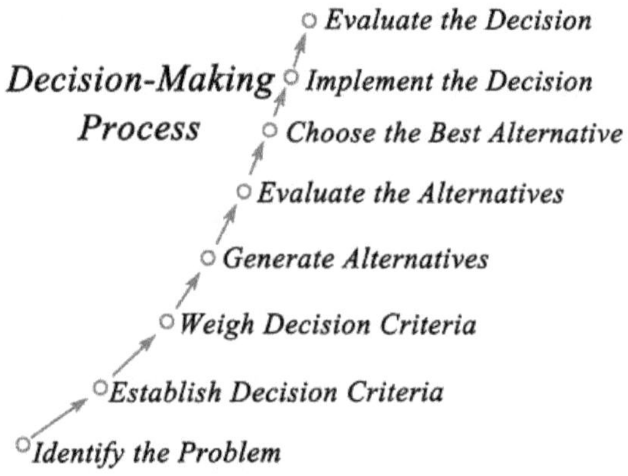

Fig. 2.1: Decision-making process.

Generally speaking, there are two main decision models [Lunenburg (2010)], the **rational** model and the **bounded rational** model. The rational model is a loop process that can be summarized as follows:

- Identifying the problem
- Generating alternatives
- Evaluating alternatives
- Choosing an alternative
- Implementing the decision
- Evaluating decision effectiveness

The step of evaluating decision effectiveness is important as it allows us to update the identified problem with new observations, and start an improved process.

The bounded rational decision-making model can be characterized as follows:

- Decisions are based on incomplete information regarding the problem
- The decision maker cannot consider all the alternatives
- Alternatives that are recognized by the decision maker are partly evaluated
- Optimality cannot be guaranteed and different criteria is required to estimate the quality of alternatives

In this chapter we treat planning and problem solving as sequential decision-making processes. In what follows, we provide several observations on rationality in the sequential decision-making process. We start with a definition of rationality and highlight several challenges in the sequential decision-making process through the lens of rationality. We then suggest several approaches to overcoming these challenges and increasing and refining the rationality in the decision-making process. We then put some of our observations into practice in the following chapters.

2.3 Rationality

Decision actions can be ***rational*** or ***irrational***. We define a decision action as rational if it results in a global optimum, based on logical principles and derived from complete relevant information [Marwala (2015)]. A decision based on irrelevant or incomplete information is irrational, and cannot guarantee guidance towards a global optimum. A rational decision-making process is comprised of rational decision actions, and the entire process is optimized in time and results in a global utility optimum [Grüne-Yanoff (2012); Marwala (2014, 2015)].

2.3.1 *Deterministic Rationality?*

From the above definition, it follows logically that fully rational decisions can only be made in a deterministic, perfect world with complete information. However, real-world scenarios are more complicated than this. It is not always possible to analyze all available and relevant information in order to evaluate all possible options so as to make a responsible decision action. For instance, the decision-making process in uncertainty scenarios with a shortage of information is by default irrational, due to limitation of relevant information needed to evaluate all available decision alternatives.

2.3.2 *(Flexible) Bounded Rationality*

Rational decisions are made by rational decision-making agents with the cognitive capability to analyze all relevant information and to globally optimize the decision-making process [Marwala (2013)]. The concept of ***bounded rationality*** [Simon (1957, 1990, 1991)] explains irrational decision making which is based on incomplete data analysis which leads to incomplete information for decision making. [Marwala (2013)] extended this term to ***flexible bounded rationality***, based on the concept that the advancements in AI and information analysis make the bounds of rationality flexible. Advanced information analysis methods can assist in repairing (partially) the imperfection of information to lead to a (partial) rationalization of a decision process.

2.4 From Overabundance of Information to Artificial Irrationality

Having incomplete information for a decision-action does not only occur in uncertainty scenarios. It also occurs in scenarios with an overabundance of data. An overabundance of data with a limited capacity for processing results in an incomplete data analysis. Decision-making processes that are based on (too) Big-Data or (too) Small-Data result in irrational decisions. When there is too little data, we have uncertainty from missing information and when there is too much data we gain the same uncertainty but due to the difficulty in processing and the collecting the data. The amount of data is good if it fits the boundaries of processing capabilities and time budget to make it useful.

In planning problems with an oversubscription of goals/achievements and a limited budget of time or resources, we choose a sequence of actions that will reach maximum utility within the bounds. In this case, an overabundance of available achievements results in an incomplete analysis and evaluation of alternatives.

2.5 Bounded Determinism

Traditional approaches to deterministic automated action planning, at their core, assume rational-deterministic decision making without calling it rational and without defining the bounds of rationality/determinism. In many decision-making processes and planning problems, as with the classical planning problem, the goals are set without taking time and processing capacity into account. Nevertheless the solution is measured in terms of time and processing capacity. Setting goals without taking the bounds of time and processing capacity into account is an irrational action because the data is infinite in many cases, at least in relation to our processing capacity.

2.5.1 *Resource Bounded Rationality*

We argue that in order to rationalize the decision-making and planning processes, goals should be set and problem-solving approaches should be chosen in a resource-bounded manner. When resources are bounded and budget limitations are clear, a more compact problem definition and more accurate utility function definition can be created within the bounds. We put this observation into action in our discussion on value rational planning in Chapter 7. We present the budget reduction compilation in order to reduce the effective search space. The net utility of an action will allow us to create a more accurate utility evaluation. To exploit the net utility of an action definition to reduce the effective search space, we present in Chapter 7 the value-driven landmark compilations which exploits 'optimal plan properties' and compiles them into the task representation.

2.5.2 *Rationality Within Time Bounds*

Most current problem solving approaches are measured in terms of time. Time as a measure provides information regarding the efficiency but not the effectiveness of the approach. Logically, effectiveness should come before efficiency since if a process does not achieve what it was for, the most efficient solution is to not initiate the process at all. Thus, time should be set as a resource and not as a measure, and the duration of actions should be learned.

2.5.3 *Bounded by Assumptions and Definitions*

Assuming resources are unbounded in real-world problems is the first irrational decision, and as such, starts an irrational planning process. Without changing the logical basis we are solving a bounded problem under unrealistic assumption. ***Assumptions and non-flexible definitions are bounds over skills and reality perception*** and prevent us from scaling-up to real-world problem solving. Once assumptions are made the problem is assumed to be gone and solutions are not looked for. Processing capacities are bounds of rationality for machines and the duration of an action has a cost in the form of time. Action costs in terms of time should be learned. The bound of processing capacity is flexible and can be solved by knowledge of the real world that can be implemented into the problem.

2.5.4 *Rationalization by Utilization*

When we encounter problems with an oversubscription of achievements and limited resources we need to create more accurate utility functions and restrict the problem structure. The more accurate the utility function and the more restricted the problem structure, the more rational the decisions within the bounds become.

2.5.5 *Globally Local Rationality*

Rational decisions are made by rational decision-making agents with the cognitive ability to analyze all relevant information and globally optimize the decision making process [Marwala (2013)]. The ***Rational decision-making process*** is comprised of rational decision actions, and the entire process is optimized in time and results in a global utility optimum [Grüne-Yanoff (2012); Marwala (2014, 2015)].

On the one hand, this implies that we should strive to make decision actions that have positive utility while avoiding negative effects. On the other hand, due to the dependencies between the outcomes of sequential decision actions, it is likely that reaching a global positive utility outcome requires local decision actions with negative effects along the way. In particular, in decisions with multi-attribute effects it is possible that the same decision action achieves mixed positive and negative utility effects. It follows then that the rationality of the decision-making process is end-means oriented.

Rational decision-making processes are comprised of the sequential (interrelated) application of rational decision-actions. ***Rationality is not***

dividable [Marwala (2013)], meaning a process of applying a sequence of depended decision actions cannot be partly rational and partly irrational. Even one irrational action makes the entire decision process irrational. Within the optimization framework a series of optimum steps become sub-optimal if one of the steps is sub-optimal. An imperfection of relevant information for a single decision action, leads to an entire decision process that is irrational with a sub-optimal end in time or utility. Advanced information analysis methods can assist in repairing (partially) the imperfection in information and lead to (partially) the rationalization of the decision process.

By focusing on an optimal set of actions rather than individually optimal actions we are engaging in, what is known in financial terms as, investment in planning. An investment in planning can be described as a series of locally irrational actions that result in negative utility propositions on the way to an optimal end state. These actions are not individually optimal, but are instrumental in reaching an optimal end result, and are only recognized as such in the context of a series of actions, the end state and specific reference points. This concept is captured by the definition of gross positive actions [Muller and Karpas (2018a)]. These are actions that may be locally irrational and cause negative utility outcomes but are effective in guiding the process toward global optimally.

Pollock [Pollock (2006, 2001)] suggested using globally-local problem solving techniques to address real-world complexity since actions cannot be chosen in isolation, because they interfere with other actions. Choosing actions in isolation with a local perspective neglects to have the end of the process in mind. Concerning global and local prospective rationality, sequential decision making processes should be measured at the local level for decision actions, and on the global level for sequences of actions (i.e. process level).

Local irrationality is likely to be globally rational. Accordingly, global irrationality is likely to be constituted of locally rational sub-sequences of decision actions. Concerning the rationality of a process, everything in the process is measured from the perspective of its end, i.e. rationality is end-means oriented. In what follows, we combine these observations and define instrumental and value-rational decision actions.

2.6 Instrumental and Value Rational Decision Actions

The interplay between instrumental and value rational actions allows for the realization of the global decision-making process. Instrumental actions are actions that need to occur in order to make a sequential action process happen. Instrumental actions are the tools that make the decision-making process happen. They do not necessarily bring actual value to the process. Value rational actions bring actual value or impact to the process. In this work, we define actions as value rational if they result in net positive utility. Note, while the effects of an action might be positive, the net utility (and the rationality) of an action can differ depending on the circumstances in which it is applied. We discuss this further in what follows.

2.6.1 *Value Rational Decision Action*

In many real-world problems, an action's impact differs according to the place, time and context in which the action is applied. The same action with the same effects can result in a different outcome in different contexts or states. Simply put, actions represent a set of tools that are applicable in different situations, states and circumstances. The obtained flexibility of actions with a degree of freedom in prerequisite requirements creates ambiguity regarding the real-world impact even in deterministic environments. The rationality of such actions can only be determined in real-time interaction with the environment in many cases.

Definition 2.1 (Rational Decision Action). A decision action is rational if it is applied in a deterministic environment based on complete information regarding the state in which it is applied and if the impact caused by the action is deterministic.

2.6.2 *Incremental Improving Decision-Making Process*

In Chapter 7 we provide an incremental improving procedure [Muller and Karpas (2018a)] which that learns based on a closed loop that incrementally updates the structure of a problem with the learnt "properties of an optimal plan". These properties are represented by value driven landmarks which are actions that must accrue in each optimal sequence of actions, that is an optimal plan or problem solution. At each iteration more informed landmark-actions are produced and compiled into the problem structure which forces a solution to conform to these properties. With the objective of rationalizing and increasing the effectiveness of the decision-making process, we want to increase action informativeness and refine the structure of task representation. The incrementally improving procedure is based on the state with the best utility which has, up to this point, been seen as a reference point as well as the properties of optimal plans that are provided in Chapter 7, which are based on the information gained from actions. Hence, to increase rationality we need to increase the informativeness of decision actions as well improve the number of decision choice alternatives for a reference state to indicate an improvement during the incremental choice evaluation procedure.

2.7 Conclusion

In this chapter, we discussed the value rational decision-making process. We presented the rational and the bounded rational decision models. We discussed the definition of rationality in the decision-making process as well as bounded and the flexible bounded rationality. We showed some of the bounds of rationality. We presented instrumental and value rational decision actions and discussed the aspects of effectiveness and efficiency of actions. In the following chapters, we discuss rationality in the context AI (Chapter 3) and optimization (Chapter 4), and we present several approaches to rationalizing the planning and decision-making process. We discuss how data treatment can increase the informativeness of actions and thus rationalize them (Chapter 5). We also discuss net utility and relative net utility (Chapter 5) and how they can be used to rationalize the decision process in the famous St. Petersburg paradox (Chapter 6). In Chapter 8 we show how the online and the offline techniques for net utility detection increase the informativeness of actions in the planning and decision-making process and hence rationalize the entire process.

Chapter 3

Artificial Intelligence

This chapter on AI is a broad, top-down, and didactic take on the topic. It starts with a historic account of AI so the reader is aware of the context of the development of AI and that the current age of intelligence derives from decades of hard and incremental work, as well as brilliant yet simple ideas. We go on to provide important definitions and ontologies so that the reader can develop a firm understanding of how AI and associated algorithms actually work and realize that they are not mere smart code. The conceived trio of sections: 'types of inference', 'learning paradigms' and 'classes of problems' is designed to help the reader link the reasoning mechanisms to the results they produce in real-world problem solving. Finally, in the 'families of AI algorithms' section, the reader is given a modular perspective on the potency of the tools within these AI families alongside the possibilities of their use.

3.1 Introduction

AI is an umbrella term for the many empowering technologies that now fuel the Fourth Industrial Revolution (4IR). However, AI is not completely new as the historical account provided in this chapter will reveal. AI can be seen and defined from multiple perspectives. For example, it could be seen as the ability of systems to learn, or as the set of approaches to producing learning systems. In this chapter we are framing AI as the tool-set that allows machines to become adaptive. In this way, the new 'intelligent' machines are able to analyze information in a human like manner, and perhaps even go beyond the capacity of humans due to their ever-growing capabilities. So much so that, from a rationality standpoint, machines have the potential to become even more rational than humans. Of course, it is not easy to categorize AI because it is a collective of several sub-areas with multiple possible classification criteria. In addition to being a collective term, one can assume that there are at least two types (or flavors) of AI, namely: Classic or Symbolic AI and Computational Intelligence of Soft Computing (considering Machine Learning inside this clique). Both types, in different ways, help create intelligence capability in machines so that, for example, rational decisions be made swiftly. Obviously, there are several overlaps between these flavors of AI. However, in this chapter, we focus rather on the 'whats' (i.e., big picture of establishing the epistemological highlights of such AI flavors) and on the 'hows' (i.e., explaining the existing inference methods and learning paradigms). We comment on classes of problems that can be solved by AI in a pragmatic manner and provide an overview of the main families of AI algorithms that can be used to tackle these problems. All this is to pave the way for the coming explanations of how the non-natural intelligence (in whatever form or shape) that equips current machines can give rational solutions in an automatic manner.

3.2 A Quick Account of History

Living beings, especially animal species, have proven that adaptation to the environment is the most important ability for sustainable individual success as well as collective success. Even though the mechanisms involved in such an ability are partly inherited, bestowed through evolution, another substantial portion is learned through interactions. Interactions then lead to knowledge that can be gathered from other individuals (both, of similar and of different species) and from the ecosystem itself. Humans are particularly good at acquiring knowledge through interaction, hence their position at the top of the "food-chain".

Obviously, such preponderance of humans being intelligent "beasts" is not by chance. It is a consequence of various traits that evolution granted to us. To name but a few: (1) the ability to stand on two legs (this enabled our ancestors to better spot threats of imminent danger on the African savanna), (2) the rare ability in the animal world to pronounce vowels (this affords us elaborate communication skills so that we can inform allies of threats, opportunities and broadcast group strategies), (3) the gift of possessing a large and highly interconnected brain (this allow us to come up with complex problem strategies even put these in words and into action), and (4) the, literally, quite handy feature of opposing thumbs (that give all primates with possibility of producing sophisticated tools which can be part of strategies to overcome threats).

As humans are, and have always been, grand masters of tool building, in this chapter we are focusing precisely on this ability to conceive of and to make use of such "extensions of our body". Yes, all tools produced by humans somehow enhance the physical abilities of oneself. New IT tools can also be understood as instruments that supplement some of our limitations; as such, they enhance our minds. We very much see human made tools, whatever they are, as "survival enhancement kits". This has been the case throughout our history, even more so when electronic digital computers were invented. This is because these latest tools have become inseparable enhancements to our mental "embodiment", as their help is no longer limited to physical tasks. Hence, just as regular tools a long time ago became artificial hands, arms and legs, computers now help us to carry out virtual tasks.

Since the invention of the first digital computers in the 1940s the desired outcome was always to use these wonders of technology to automate thoughts and therefore to embody reasoning. But, as it is widely known, the limitations of early hardware technology prevented that from happening until the latter quarter of the twentieth century. Digital computers are true wonders of technology. They are tools like no other. They are able to speed-up logical tasks and perform computations in a quasi-simultaneous way that was previously only possible in human minds. Reaching or surpassing Human levels of reasoning has always been the goal, so much so that early computers were called electronic brains. As early as 1950, Alan Turing, the father of Computer Science, wrote a seminal paper arguing that machines could think [Turing (1950)]. Unlike any other tools though, computers can transform themselves into different tools. This without any physical change; almost like magic.

With the revolution created by the development of the microprocessors everything changed. Computers, which used to be expensive, inaccessible, difficult to use and thus only beneficial to a few, suddenly became just the opposite of all that. There were a number of pioneers responsible for this radical transformation. Two in particular excelled in the early 1980s, namely, Steve Jobs (the founder of IT giant Apple) who toiled for computers to become user-friendly and aesthetically beautiful, and Bill Gates (the founder of IT giant Microsoft), who heralded his dream of seeing computers in every home and worked hard so this dream has become a reality. Eventually, such "outrageous" ideas came into being towards the end of the twentieth century. Computers then truly became ubiquitous, accessible and powerful tools. At last, humans could recruit their ultimate ally in the "fight" at the dawn of the information age. Notice that the two culprits for initially preventing computers from being readily absorbed into society, i.e. hardware limitations and high costs, were no longer a problem. Around this time, the commercial internet also catalyzed the dissemination of information, crowning the third industrial revolution.

In parallel to all these developments, scientists were working hard to create a myriad of approaches to endowing computers with adaptability. Thus, the old desire to use the computers to mimic the human minds, to think, and ultimately to behave intelligently was achieved. Computers now could not only think (i.e., learn) but could also be programmed to be rational. Indeed, computers are now indisputably able to perform non-trivial logical operations, and can therefore evoke rationality that even more sound than human rationality. More recently, intelligent systems that can automatically improve their performances are also able to explain what they have learnt. And currently researchers are pursuing ways for these intelligent systems to consider the morality of what they are computing. If they are able to do this well it will deserve an entire other book. All the superb abilities that we have mentioned have drawn unprecedented centrality to those wonder-tools (computers and intelligent algorithms), as they can now become truly artificially intelligent. Indeed, the powerful combination of the latest computers with their huge memories, fast processors, and the prodigious abilities of the latest algorithms are astounding. This, to deal with cumbersome logic, is greatly reinforced by the tremendous added capability of deep learning. All of this yields plenty of opportunities for us, humans of the twenty-first century. We are prolific tool makers, who are now armed with tools that can perform strikingly intelligent deeds to help us in the coming "new fights" on the "new savannas" (in this dawn of the revolution of intelligence).

3.3 Flavors of AI

Algorithms are finite sequences of instructions that are diligently executed by computers. They have accompanied computing machines since the inception of the latter in the form of programs or operating systems (i.e., programs that are devoted to control the machinery). Millions of people have been regularly writing computer programs for over 60 years for the myriad of hardware platforms and dozens of different operating systems using the thousands of programming languages. Surprisingly enough, most of the programs, produced so far, are deterministic. This means that their internal logic already includes the conditions needed to directly solve the problems at hand. Hence, most programs are somehow believed to know exactly how to solve the problems they are confronted with. However, this is not necessarily the case, especially when the problems at hand are large (high input dimension), combinatorial (variables interfere with one another), dynamic (change with time), multi-perspective (evaluations vary from users), multi-modal (admit several solutions), and are of unknown behavior (i.e., the input-output relations are not evident to the programmer).

Luckily enough, computers are still able to help with all the complicated problems around, even the ones that programmers do not have the knowledge to solve. However this is only the case if programs are able to learn, in other words if they use AI. Contrary to what some people might think, computer programs with AI approaches in them are not hard to code. They can be written with ordinary languages, can use regular operating systems, and can be used on standard hardware platforms. The only difference is the fact that instead of containing the embedded sequence of commands (i.e., logic) that solves the problem, programs with AI components are written so that they are capable of finding appropriate solutions. This may seem obvious, but this is the chief difference between a classic computer program and an intelligent one [Smolensky (1987)]. Obviously, there are many ways to produce such intelligence in machines. This section aims to describe two existing ways (or flavors) of putting AI into practice (or into standard computer programs).

3.3.1 *Classic or Symbolic AI*

In Classic or Symbolic AI algorithms, information is processed so that humans can easily perceive the symbols being manipulated and stored, e.g., the rules or cases in Expert Systems and Decisions Trees (both explained later). This paradigm of AI not only dominated the first half of AI history (roughly, 1960s–1980s) but has driven research (not completely successfully) towards obtaining high goals such as creating artificial minds, understanding nature and the meaning of languages, as well as solving mathematical theorems. It was common to find researchers in that paradigm (back then) refer to their camp as Strong-AI, which in summary means producing systems that behave not only intelligently but also knowingly. Of course, neither all researchers who pursued these paths, nor all the classical families of symbolic AI algorithms (see later some examples) are devoted to reaching these high goals. It is suggested that newcomers to the field of Classic AI, understand that it makes use of explicit representation and sometimes provide clearer explanations of the performed computations. Nowadays, with the recent advances both in hardware and innovative algorithms, Symbolic AI is experiencing a marked resurgence, particularly for dealing with growing demands for human level cognition (e.g., to better interface with autonomous cars, robots, and avatars). It is important to highlight that Classic AI is an important 'tool-box' for producing more rational (programs) with less ethically biased mistakes.

3.3.2 *Computational Intelligence or Soft Computing*

In Computational Intelligence (CI) algorithms information is processed using metaphors that mimic nature (i.e., meta-heuristics that are higher-level problem solving mechanisms [Maniezzo *et al.* (2021)] like Neuro-computation and Evolution — see explanations later), Machine Learning [Mitchell (1997)] (i.e., mathematical models created by observation of behavior or statistical data analyzes), or by fuzzy constructs [Zadeh (1965)] (i.e., flexible mathematical models that escape from the Boolean logic; Lofti Zadeh usually referred to them as "Soft-Computing" and "Computing with Words" [Zadeh (2012)]). As always when attempting to categorize big areas of research, the proposed categories may not please everyone. This is especially true because many important approaches can be placed into two categories. E.g., artificial neural Networks can be classified as meta-heuristics as well as Machine Learning techniques. Since the 1990s, the computational intelligence paradigm has grown fast and currently dominates research due to the large number of excellent results it has produced and many fronts it encompasses. It is important to acknowledge the successful application of this kind of AI technology for solving hard problems. Therefore the term Weak-AI as a synonym should not lead one to think this technology if ineffective. Rather, the Weak-AI is a reference to the unpretentious decision to not produce an actual understanding of the computations by the machines themselves when computational intelligence is used (i.e., there is no chief intention to understand whatever is computed). In summary, meta-heuristics, Machine Learning and soft-computing would all deserve individual books as they have created massive breakthroughs and accompanying opportunities of innovative application. For example, the fact that fuzzy systems do not have fixed boundaries on computed classes makes fuzzy-computations much more flexible, which favors human-machine interfaces greatly. Ultimately, Computational Intelligence (CI) avoids abstract top-down models and focuses on data-driven modelling, which is the way nature seems to function, e.g., in swarms. Thus decisions generally emerge as a collective phenomenon of several processing units at work. It is important to highlight that in contrast to Classic AI, Computational Intelligence techniques are not transparent methods (regarding explainability and storage) hence they are less rational, and are prone to more ethically biased mistakes.

3.4 Types of Inference

When we state that computers (machines) can think and are able to learn, implicitly we subscribe to the notion that inferences are not only possible but central to attaining intelligence. But what is inference? Briefly, an inference refers to the conclusions produced by means of operating on knowledge (mental-models) and evidence (objective-data). Why is inference so important for AI? We have already established that AI requires some form of learning, and inferences are exactly the means of achieving that. Therefore, learning mechanisms are inevitably linked to models and data.

In addition to the way learning happens (i.e., model-driven, and data-driven), the granularity of the added values is also important for the approach to take. This means that machines can learn from both highly structured pieces of information and the simplest pieces of data. Additionally, other than highlighting the level of added value, it is not easy to draw boundaries in the information continuum (i.e., data, information, knowledge, and wisdom). A useful way of analyzing this is to consider the utility and net utility of the learnt information (to a specific user/group of users). Another didactic way of perceiving those concepts is to separate them into symbols (that humans can compute more easily) and otherwise (i.e., "sub-symbols", which alone are meaningless for humans). The straightforward notions that arise from this are that symbols can be deconstructed and that sub-symbols can be combined.

So far, we have discussed that inferences are means by which to mechanize learning and that those mechanisms have to be able to operate upon various granularities of information. The take home message is that for a machine to be deemed intelligent, it must utilize at least one inference method and needs information (of any granularity level) so that learning can occur. The natural next question would be how such inference methods could be put to use inside the machine. But before that, let us focus on how inferences actually happens. For a swift explanation of types of inference, let us study a relationship between the general theory of systems and their mathematical functions. That is input (**I**), processing (**P**), and output (**O**), are here suggested to be seen as domain (**x**), function (**f**), and image (**y**), see that in Fig. 3.1. As a computer program can be understood as both the mathematical functions and the evoked behaviors of a system, the relation depicted in Fig. 3.1, is also useful when the various types of inferences are being programmed into machines.

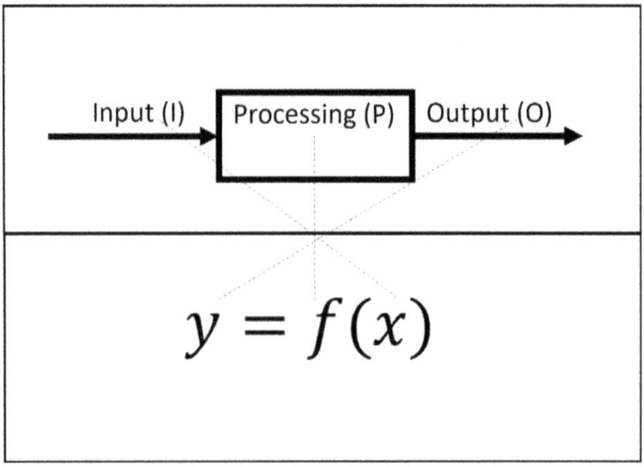

Fig. 3.1: Relations between elements of general system representation and a generic mathematical function.

There are three ways to make an inference, namely deduction, induction, and abduction. But, given the great influence of Aristotle in his syllogisms, deduction is by far most commonly known and used inference type today.

3.4.1 *Deductive Reasoning*

Deductive reasoning is an inference method in which conclusions are drawn entirely from existing premises. This means that, based on combinations of parts of what is known, conclusions can be drawn. It is important to note that deductions do not necessarily produces new knowledge, as they are specializations of general concepts. In fact, the mechanic is only a re-writing of what is already known. An example of a correct deduction (but not necessarily true) is:

Premise-1: `Computers can execute Intelligent Systems.`
Premise-2: `Every Intelligent System is rational.`
Conclusion: `Computers can be rational.`

A conventional computer program (even simple ones that are not necessarily intelligent) can be seen as an instrument for generating deductions. That is, when mapping rules (**f**) operate on the input data (**x**) to produce conclusions (**y**). Figure 3.2 depicts a mathematical function as a metaphor for a deduction, where inputs are subjected to programmed rules to produce the desired outputs.

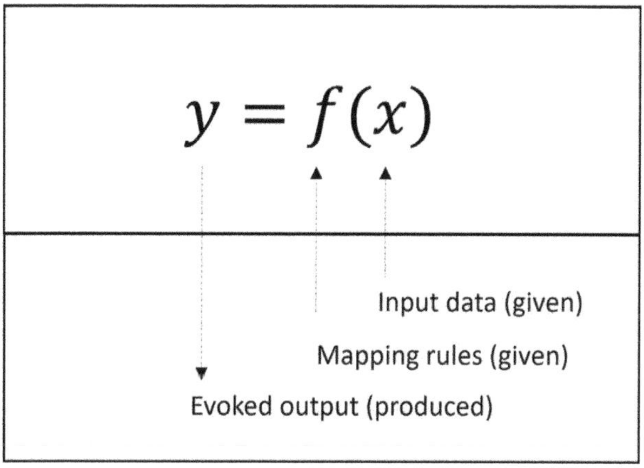

Fig. 3.2: Schematic representation of a deductive process seen as a generic mathematical function.

The manipulation of premises, as happens in deduction, does not actually generate new knowledge. However, deductions are accurate and do not vary over time (if there are no changes in the premises). That is why they are limited in their ability to surprise us and are not very useful when it comes to learning tasks, and these are big limitations. On the other hand, a deduction by itself cannot be biased (e.g., become inconsistent), which is quite reassuring, unless new assumptions lead to this (e.g., contradictory new premises). Techniques that use deductive reasoning can be considered to be expert systems (rule and case based).

3.4.2 *Inductive Reasoning*

Inductive reasoning is an inference method in which conclusions are derived from observations rather than premises. In other words, the conclusions are probably not known beforehand. This is striking because, based on specific sets of information, it is possible to approximate general conclusions. And these generalizations can be seen as new knowledge (which is very interesting and useful utility-wise). An example of induction is:

Observation-1: `System A using data-1 surprised me.`
Observation-2: `System B using data-1 surprised me.`
`...[inductive step]`
Conclusion: `System C using data-1 may surprise me.`

An induction method involves a generalization process based on observations and these allow for the generation of new information. In contrast to deduction, conclusions here may be imprecise. This happens precisely because induction deals with only part of the possible existing observations. Figure 3.3 depicts a mathematical function as a metaphor for an induction, where pairs of input (**x**) and output examples (**y**) are repeatedly presented to the intelligent algorithm, aiming to produce the rules that generalize the solutions (**f**) for the problem (i.e., the processing occurs from the specific to the general).

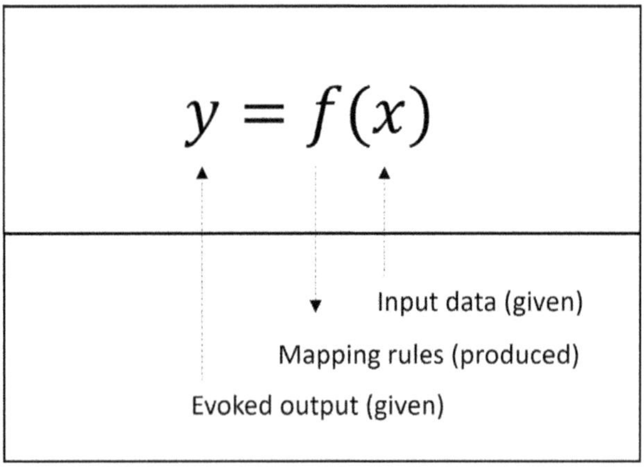

Fig. 3.3: Schematic representation of an inductive process seen as a generic mathematical function.

Despite the likely impression that systems that use inductive reasoning may not be useful due to potential inaccuracy, such systems, when properly constructed, can be very useful in decision problems where the solving steps are not known. Because of this, they are being used increasingly and serve as the basis for intelligent techniques such as Artificial Neural Networks and Evolutionary Computing. Both these techniques use inductive reasoning therefore both can learn and can surprise users. On the other hand, unfortunately, algorithms that use inductive reasoning can become biased when used in isolation (e.g., become inconsistent over time), which is not reassuring at all.

3.4.3 *Abductive Reasoning*

Abductive reasoning, the least known and most peculiar inference method, generates outcomes based on the best estimates of inputs given partial observations of the problem. It can be seen as a combination of induction and deduction. In other words, based on some *a priori* information (rules, for example) and given desired goals, it is possible to try to infer the generating premises (i.e., input data) in a non-unique way. This inference can discover cause and effect relationships, which is certainly new knowledge and very useful in some reasoning processes. An example of an abduction is:

Conclusion-1: `The RGPD was approved by the European Parliament in 2020.`

Premise-1: `Cases of abuse of improper data sharing were observed.`

Plausible explanation-1: `The European Parliament considered that a general regulation would be a good way to find human-perpetrators.`
`...[inductive step]`

Plausible explanation-n: `The European Parliament considered that a general regulation would be a good way to find aliens-perpetrators.`

This means that abductive reasoning, like inductive reasoning, generates new information which may be imprecise. The difference is that instead of a conclusion being the output, one receives a plausible explanation of what might have led to that conclusion. Notwithstanding the inaccuracies, if properly constructed, systems using abduction can be very useful when causal explanations are desired. Figure 3.4 depicts a mathematical function as a metaphor for abduction, where examples of possible-inputs (**x**) are generated as rules (**f**) are inferred and directly applied to desired outcomes (**y**), i.e., plausible causality is obtained by combining induction and deduction.

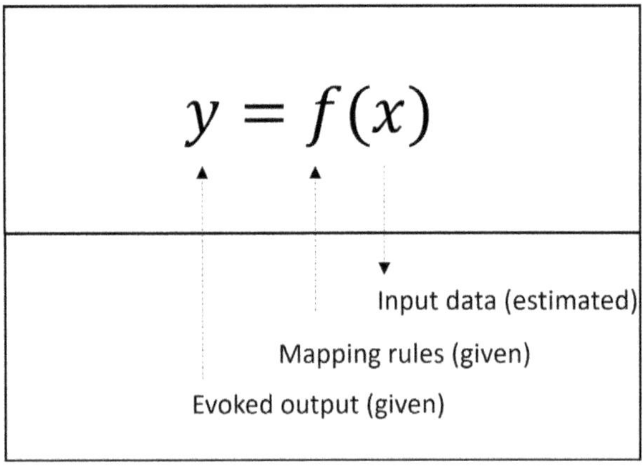

Fig. 3.4: Schematic representation of an abductive process seen as a generic mathematical function.

Combining intelligent techniques such as Artificial Neural Networks (inductive technique) and Expert Systems (deductive technique) can produce good abductions. Unfortunately, abductions accuracy can be skewed over time and therefore must have an additional level of control, ideally having a human in their assessment and control.

Even though deduction is very handy, induction and abduction are perhaps even more interesting because they can add value to the computation. This is because they generate new information to be used in the reasoning process. Precisely because of this, induction and abduction are of special value and are widely used in modern AI systems.

3.5 Learning Paradigms

The computational systems mentioned so far have not included feedback, which can be defined as a cybernetic arch that somehow informs the system of errors observed in the output (e.g., difference between observed and expected output values). This allows systems to correct their outputs towards desired behaviors (or values). In AI systems, this concept is one way

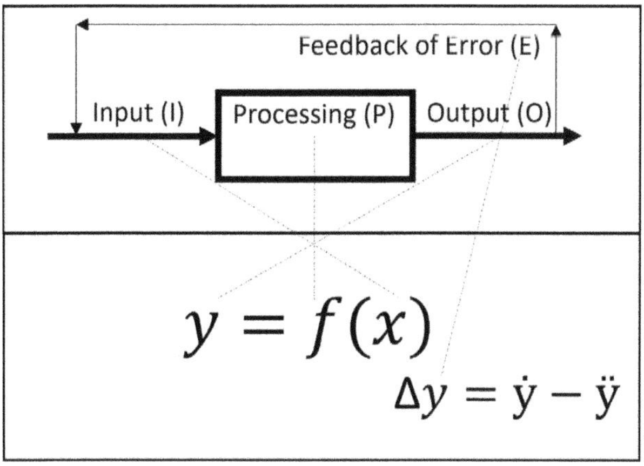

Fig. 3.5: Relations between a general system representation and a generic mathematical function, including feedback of errors.

(of the many) that systems can learn. Figure 3.5, based on Fig. 3.1, shows the difference between desired and evoked results in the output providing feedback to the input (i.e., "the delta of error", $\Delta\mathbf{y}$).

As previously discussed, intelligent systems can learn and they can do so in several ways, each one with advantages and disadvantages. Every intelligent algorithm, unlike their classic counterparts (i.e., non-adaptive systems), needs to be taught. This happens either through rules/knowledge provided by experts, that is the model-driven approach, or alternatively, through examples and patterns, that is the data-driven approach. The former is an explicit training method, whereas the latter is implicit. Thus, in the latter, knowledge needs to be extracted from the data before being incorporated into the system's "core", e.g., via learned rules or cases from data.

The training of model-driven intelligent systems uses existing expertise or structured data that is readily available. The training of data-based intelligent algorithms can take various forms, namely, supervised, semi-supervised, unsupervised and by reinforcement. Basically, what varies is the volume and type of feedback needed so that AI systems can learn effectively (i.e., extracting the gist of the problem from the data). Notice that in either case, variations of the same algorithm can have different types of the training required and, therefore, one cannot assume a fixed or even a unitary relationship (i.e., one to one) between a given family of algorithm and a specific type of training.

3.5.1 *Supervised Training*

Supervised training requires that each observation or data pattern used to train the system (examples of system behaviors) conveys relevant relations between inputs and outputs values. From that, the algorithm will try to find the elements that bind (or map) inputs into outputs. Supervised training is recommended (and only possible) when the signal and magnitude of the correction for a given pattern are known. Of course, this method of training only makes sense when there are sufficient examples of the problem to be solved by the AI algorithm and the data encompasses both independent and dependent variables (i.e., output values that express the corresponding input). The overall logic of supervised training is depicted in Fig. 3.6 and is similar to a teacher-student relationship. When a student makes a mistake, the teacher informs them what the mistake was and what would be expected as the correct answer. The aim of supervised training is to directly avoid future mistakes in similar situations.

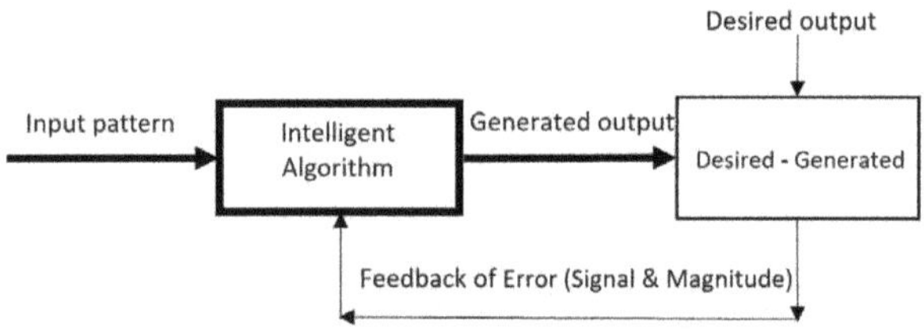

Fig. 3.6: Error correction schema used in supervised training, where the desired output is known in advance so that the signal and magnitude of the correction can be feedback to the input.

3.5.2 *Semi-Supervised Training*

Semi-supervised is similar to supervised training in many ways. The major difference is that not all training patterns have dependent variables (i.e., expected out values) for a given input. Sometimes the desired output information is not complete. So, in that sense the analogy of a teacher could be applied here but perhaps a critic would be more the appropriate analogy. Thus, the learning tasks is a little harder. For example, instead of signal and magnitude being provided, only the signal of the correction is available. This can be shown in Fig. 3.7.

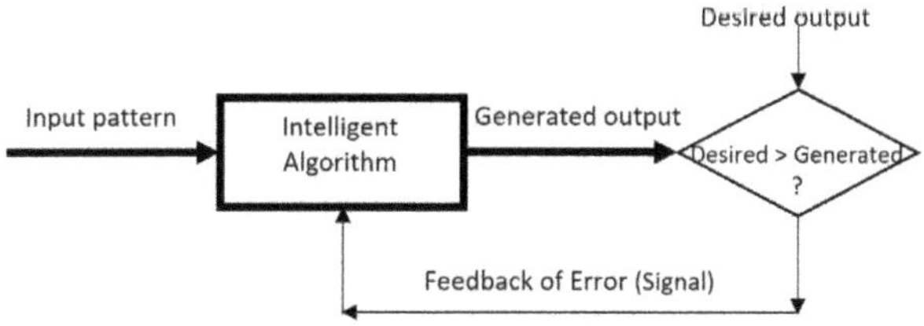

Fig. 3.7: Error correction schema used in semi-supervised training, where the desired output is only partially known in advance. Thus, for example, only the signal (and not the magnitude) of the correction can be feedback to the input.

3.5.3 *Unsupervised Training*

Unsupervised training does not require explicit outputs from the system during training (i.e., it does not require labelled output data). The learning process only uses the objective intrinsic information available within the inputs (including probabilistic information). This, much harder, way of learning (i.e., without any teacher) is appropriate for problems where no objective output is known. Hence the updates the models receive about the problem, produce clusters of data that have to be further analyzed by the users. Normally, unsupervised training is not as objective as supervised/semi-supervised training and should only be considered when other training options are not available. Figure 3.8 shows that no external feedback exists in unsupervised training.

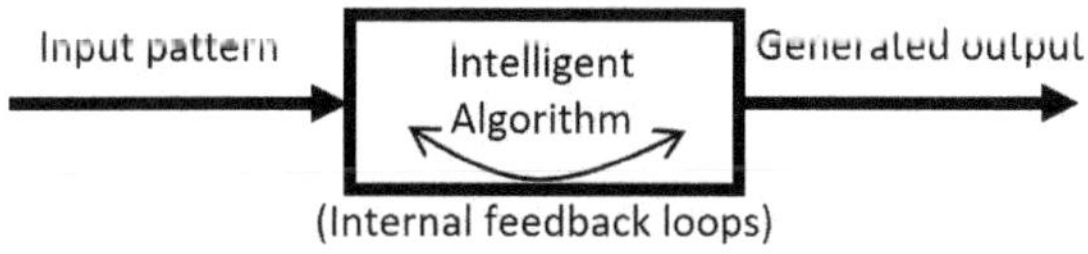

Fig. 3.8: Unsupervised training, where no external feedback exists, which produces training (and interpretation of results) not so objective.

3.5.4 *Reinforcement Learning*

Reinforcement learning, which is primarily based on trial-and-error types of interactions, requires feedback to be substantial and of good quality. An analogy to facilitate understanding is that of a fully-fledged critic who, after identifying an error or success, signals it to the system. Thus, the algorithm only receives a numerical performance score as guidance for the training process. This means there is not much detail in the error correction process. Overall, this is a much slower process than the previously mentioned processes that causes an update in the "reward" that also leads to acceptable mappings of inputs to outputs (i.e. the learning can also converge). Figure 3.9 depicts the general idea behind reinforcement learning.

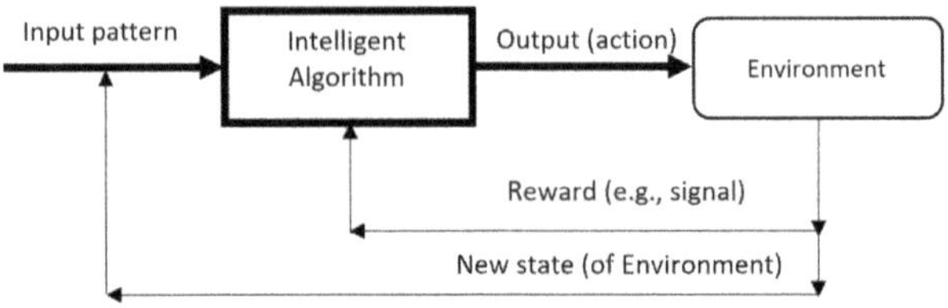

Fig. 3.9: Reinforcement learning overview. The system receives a reward (or penalty) in relations to its perception on the environment state change.

3.6 Classes of Problems

The type of training used is dependent on the class of problem that needs to be solved, the nature of the problem itself (e.g., static or dynamic etc.), the data or knowledge available (e.g., if it is abundant, expensive, accurate etc.), and the resources available (e.g., time, computers, internet connectivity etc.). All of these factors must be considered when planning the training of Intelligent Systems, as they are directly linked to the accuracy/usefulness of the reasoning processes obtained.

The real world has always presented many challenges, especially when it comes to decision making. With the explosion of data availability, paradoxically, decisions are increasingly more difficult to make without powerful support tools. This is precisely because decision makers and computer users have more and more information that needs to be considered in the decision-making process. As the nature of problems can differ so much, from a reasoning perspective, it makes sense to divide such problems into classes. As a matter of fact, an understanding of the specifics of each class of problem is seminal to the selection of the most suitable intelligent computational technique and learning paradigm to use.

Without going into too much detail, we describe some of the main classes of problems (not to be confused with application domains) that can be handled by AI below. We also provide some rationale for using AI to solve these classes of problems.

3.6.1 *Search Problems*

One of the most frequently encountered problems in computing is searching for something in a given domain. If the search space is not large, AI is not needed at all. However, since search spaces can be very large, dynamic, and sometimes deceiving, conventional searches can be expensive (i.e., not efficient) and may not produce good results (i.e., not effective). There also might be complications in the form of: many restrictions being imposed upon the search, many conflicting search objectives, many answers being possible (required) simultaneously, etc. One way to avoid these complication is to use meta-heuristics, which simply put is a short-cut that accepts good solutions instead of solutions that are optimal but expensive. Figure 3.10 shows a simple example on how search strategies can produce quite different results.

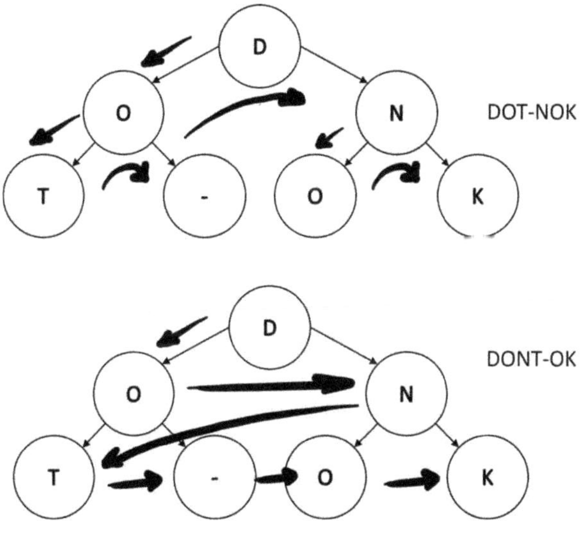

Fig. 3.10: Two different search algorithms on a binary tree. Although all nodes are visited the sequences are different and this may be relevant for finding the desired solution in each problem.

3.6.2 *Classification Problems*

Sometimes patterns need to be classified according to their similarities. For example, classes of decisions that can be very similar in some respects but quite different in others. It is not unusual to encounter an absence of a well-defined prototype for desired classes that can be found using AI techniques. Another reason for using AI in classification problems is that the examples used for training may not be abundant and/or are expensive. Moreover, the context of classification may vary over time, which poses even more difficulties. Furthermore, there may be a high number of classes, training examples may not be balanced (i.e., too many for one class and too few for others), there may be anomalous patterns, etc. Hence, classification algorithms are quite useful for escaping these complication. Figure 3.11 shows an example of linear classification.

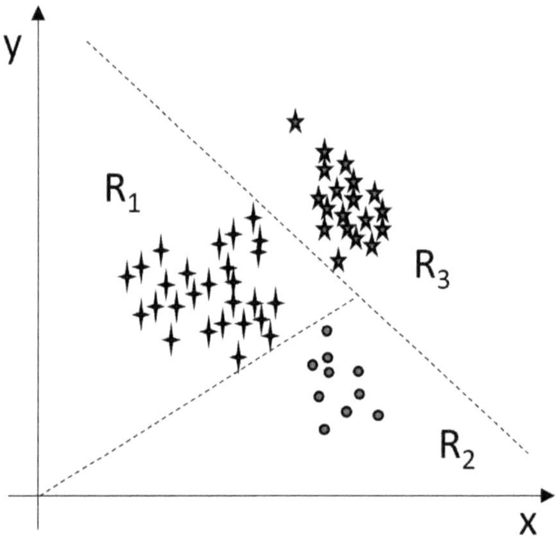

Fig. 3.11: Three different classes are linearly separated in a 2D plan. Notice that three distinct regions are formed which can accommodate further pattern according to the class prototypes.

3.6.3 *Clustering Problems*

Similar to classification problems, clustering is quite a common challenge posed by real-world application. The distinction is that no class labels are available in clustering problems. AI might be used in these problems if the patterns that must be grouped are also very similar (i.e., there is no way to assign group prototypes) and it is not known how many groups are needed for the data to be represented well, in a separated manner. As with classification problems, the context of the grouping can vary over time, possessing even more difficulties. There also may be a high number of clusters as well as anomalous patterns and missing values. There is a close connection between clustering problems and unsupervised training as they share lack of labels (as a problem and as a training method). Figure 3.12 shows an example of clustering.

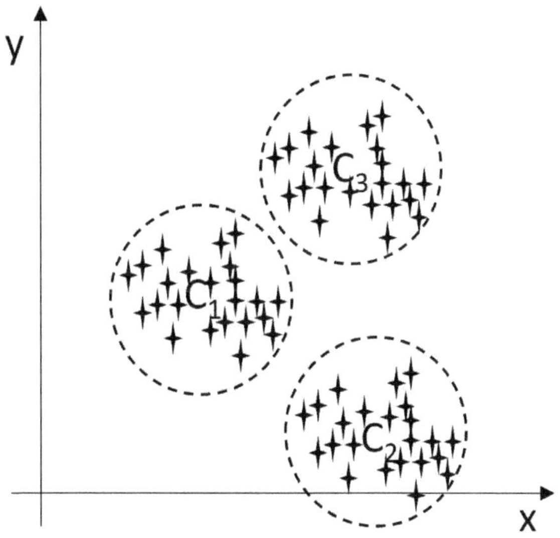

Fig. 3.12: Three different clusters are represented in a 2D plan. Notice that the three distinct clusters, differently of classes, do not possess a prototype of a class but even so still can accommodate further pattern according to their features.

3.6.4 *Prediction Problems*

Knowing the future values or behaviors of systems can be highly valuable. One might use AI on these kinds of problems if there is not much available data or if the available data is limited to traditional extrapolation techniques, especially if the problem domain is complex. Training patterns can also contain characteristics such as trend, seasonality, and cycles, which make training more difficult. Anomalous patterns and missing values also make training cycles longer. Fortunately, inductive methods are able to generalize future instances of the problem, particularly when abundant examples from the past are available, and this is when supervised methods excel. Figure 3.13 shows the general idea of prediction of future values.

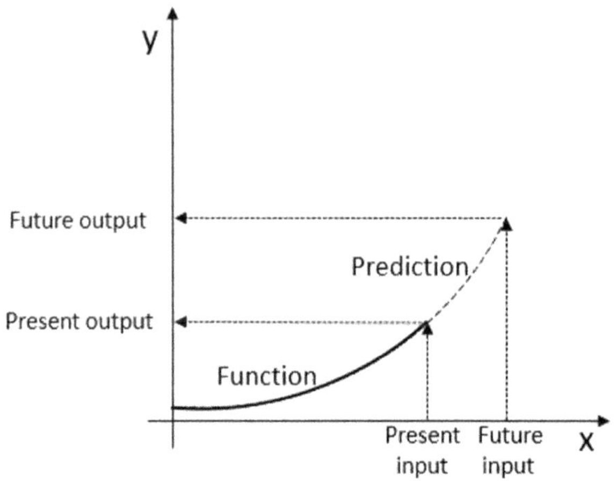

Fig. 3.13: Prediction of future values of a non-linear function in a 2D plan. In here the future is inferred as based on past values.

3.6.5 *Optimization Problems*

Optimization processes are comprised of two components (or functions), the first component governs the process itself (that is sometimes known, but to which parameters are hard to tune). The second component is the utility function which assesses the quality of the optimization. It is often not easy to be carry out these processes (e.g., control of industrial processes, planning deliveries in a large city etc.). Paradoxically, apart from the control task itself, it is rather straightforward to identify when a process is well controlled (i.e., their evoked results). This means two things: (i) the assessment of a utility function for optimization problems is often not difficult, and (ii) the search for parameters (of the control function) is generally what makes the problem difficult (i.e., they are hard to attain). In other words, optimizations can be seen as a search for parameters of control functions (that describe the behavior of the problem). Most of the difficulty in such problems is due to the non-linear interactions among parameters and their interference in the controlled process (that is aimed to be optimized). Furthermore, previous examples of system behavior may be non-existent, the dimensionality of some problems may be prohibitively high, and the dynamics can be highly non-linear. All of these factors impede the use of classical optimization methods, hence these problems are excellent candidates for AI techniques. Figure 3.14 shows the search for a global maximal point.

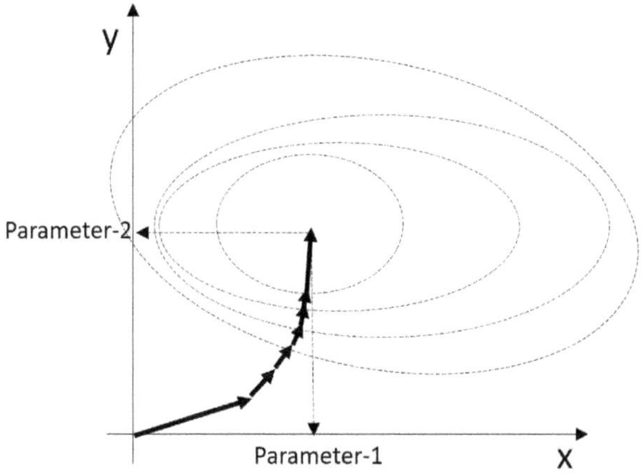

Fig. 3.14: Illustration of an optimization (maximization) task of a non-linear search space in a 2D plan. In here, the **x** and **y** coordinates are the sought parameters of the control function.

3.6.6 *Problems of Causal Inference*

Ascribing causes to effects is perhaps the most complex, sometimes even impossible, task to do. This is because it deals with the inverse problem in Mathematics (where from image/output one tries to infer the domain/input), hence it being called 'ill-posed'. However, these kinds of applications are often found in the real world, so even approximations or short lists of possible solutions are very welcomed. In short, effects/outputs can be generated by different causes/inputs (or combinations of them). The task of investigating the possible causes of an effect quickly becomes a combinatorial problem and the search can be lead to prohibitively expensive computations. Similar to optimization problems, one can use tacit knowledge to develop solutions that often work in practical applications, but building a precise cause-effect relation is generally very tough. The context of these problems may vary over time, which poses even more difficulties. Furthermore, there may be anomalous patterns (which complicates training), and the dimensionality of some problems may be prohibitive for classical search methods. Figure 3.15 shows a probabilistic attempt to ascribe causal relations.

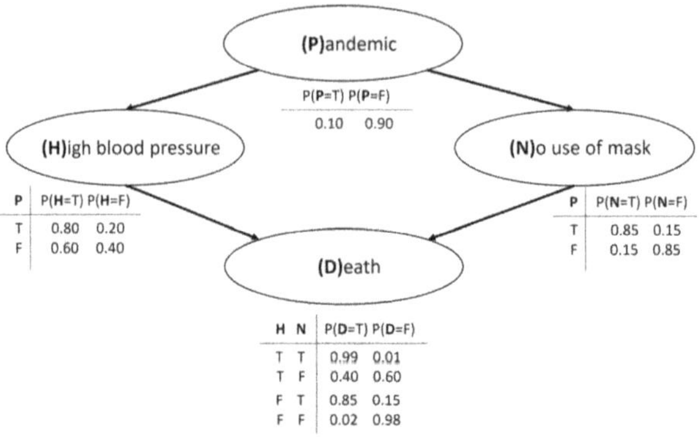

Fig. 3.15: Probabilistic network aiming at ascribing death causality given prior knowledge on two population variables ("High blood pressure" & "No use of mask"), given the possibility of a pandemic.

3.7 Families of AI Algorithms

After decades of development and advances in AI there are thousands of algorithms and libraries available. Each one with its own characteristics and specific purposes. It is, therefore, impossible to describe them individually. So, the most representative current algorithms are presented in groups, i.e., clustered by families. This is because all members of each family tend to share core characteristics. It is expected that the general characteristics shared by members of a family convey what kind of inferences are made, what types of data and training are used and their relationship to rationality.

Alongside the creation of the first digital computers in the 1940s, the first attempts to build artificial neurons by Warren McCulloch and Walter Pitts — MCP Neuron [McCulloch and Pitts (1943)] and to train algorithms for artificial neurons by Donald Hebb [Hebb (1949)] were made. The hardware limitations were a hindrance to wide dissemination and development of these technologies for a long time. It is worth mentioning though, that some early pioneers were not stalled by these limitations. Frank Rosenblatt and Bernard Widrow for example, managed to build actual algorithms that ran in electronic devices, exhibited some adaptability, respectively the Perceptron [Rosenblatt (1957)] and the Adaline [Widrow (1960)]. Despite this, the term "Artificial Intelligence" was only coined in 1956 by pioneers such as John McCarthy, Marvin Minsky, Nathaniel Rochester and Claude E. Shannon who first used the term in an article for the Dartmouth Conference of that year. This gathering is deemed to be the cradle of AI as a discipline and still resounds many decades later [Moor (2006)]. But the ride on the AI quest has not been smooth. In fact, it is often said that AI had two winters, referring to periods of almost no progress, in the 1970s and late 1990s [Wikipedia contributors (2021)].

Of course AI, both as a discipline and a massive toolbox, bounced back in grand style and took the driver's seat of the 4IR — the age of intelligence. This did not happen by chance. A long list of creative and resilient pioneers toiled bravely to bring AI to where is today. The list is enormous so we are only able to mention a few, such as John Holland in the 1970s who championed for Genetic Algorithms [Holland *et al.* (1992)], in the 1980s, David Rumelhart, Geoffrey Hinton and Ronald Williams reinstated the power of Artificial Neural Networks when they proved that Multi-Layer Perceptrons (MLP) could be trained using partial derivatives using Backpropagation of errors ('Back-prop') [Rumelhart *et al.* (1986)]. In the 1990s Marco Dorigo, and James Kennedy and Russell Eberhart pushed Swarm intelligence forward, with their Ant Colony [Dorigo (1992)] and Particle Swarm Optimizations algorithms, respectively [Kennedy and Eberhart (1995)]. These developments were followed by Yoshua Bengio, Geoffrey Hinton and Yann LeCun and their contributions to deep learning [LeCun *et al.* (2015)]. As stated, the list is immense and certainly this account lacks many pioneers. However, it would not be complete without reference to Lofti Zadeh who introduced Fuzzy Sets and Logic and hence a softer way to compute [Zadeh (1965)], Allen Newell and Herbert Simon for their work on problem solving and human cognition [Newell *et al.* (1972)], or John Quinlan and Leo Breiman who worked separately on Decision trees and inductive methods [Quinlan (1988); Breiman *et al.* (1984)].

AI researchers frequently disagree quite a lot about the taxonomy and definitions of families of intelligent algorithms. But in general, just a handful argue against the idea that AI algorithms store their knowledge in either a symbolic or sub-symbolic way. For example: the rules of an Expert System (ES) can be seen as a symbols (which is are constructs a human can understand), whereas the many weights that make up an Artificial Neural Network (ANN) only represent something meaningful to a human when put together (not alone) because neurons only store parts of a symbol). As previously mentioned, knowing this helps us to comprehend the granularity of the stored knowledge, the eventual ethical risks posed by AI, and the implications of rationality evoked by AI algorithms. It is not by chance then that intelligent systems with symbolic representation are easier to audit and thus it is easier for them to produce explanations. This is not so easy in systems that use sub-symbolic representations. Nonetheless, there are other advantages to the sub-symbolic clique. For example, a Genetic Algorithm (GA) is more powerful when it comes to handling large combinatorial problems as compared to a Decision Tree (DT) which has an elegant and structured symbolic representation.

Many other aspects of intelligent algorithms and their families can also be argued and taken into consideration when evaluating their effectiveness, such as: generalization, robustness, flexibility, facility to training (and re-training), storage cost, processing cost, etc. So, whenever designing, constructing or using an intelligent system, one should consider balancing all of these aspects before starting.

Every family of intelligent algorithms has some outstanding general characteristics and it is important to consider their collective pros and cons. In what follows, we provide an overview of the best-known "families" of AI algorithms and consider their inspiration, main features and functioning.

3.7.1 *Expert Systems (ES)*

Expert Systems (ES) are symbolic AI approaches that mimic human level knowledge in order to become an artificial expert for decision making. A human expert provides prior knowledge about a given problem domain, which is then structured into the rules or cases so that human rationale is emulated. Another intelligent system can also serve the purpose of providing rules or cases. ES were one of the first practical AI systems to be developed, introduced around 1965 by Edward Feigenbaum and his team at Stanford. The acquired knowledge is primarily stored as rules [Jackson (1986)] or cases, in Case Based Reasoning [Watson (1997)]. Both can be used to decide on complex scenarios in an elegant and structured manner. Although new rules can be generated inductively, ES tend to be deductive. ES work well when the application domain is not very large and therefore where many rules are not likely to be needed. This is because, in addition to the fact that many rules are not so simple and cheap to obtain, rules tend to conflict with each other, which reduces the effectiveness and reliability of wide use. Furthermore, suitable human experts are not cheap or easy to get hold of. In addition, when more than one expert is utilized, they will likely disagree with each other on some matters, which is a difficulty that is not normally easy to resolve. However, there are many advantages of using expert systems, namely, they are less prone to bias over time (except if new rules directly incorporate bias), they can explain the results of their computations, they allow for standardization of processing (very useful in large corporations that have various locations), and they maintain good consistency over time. The latter is dependent on the rule creation polity, as the rules are not codified in the algorithm (but within a knowledge base) and overall, they are relatively easy to maintain. Take note however, that the inference engine can produce unwanted behavior if new/ill-posed rules are synthesized. Figure 3.16 presents the main modules and information flow of a standard ES. Despite the long history of ES, they are still very popular and useful today in various domains of application. Finally, as with all symbolic systems, ES are quite "rational".

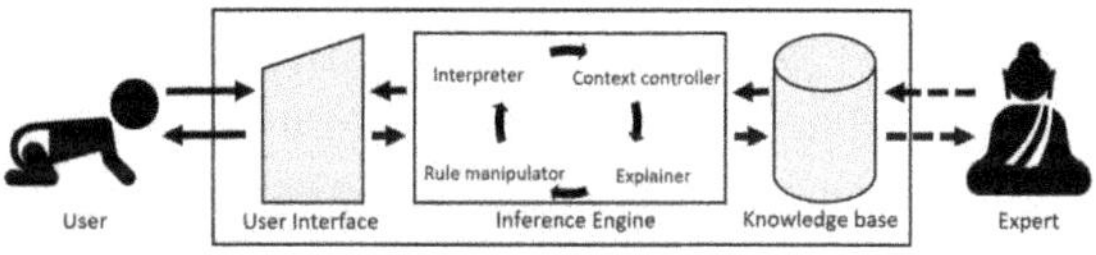

Fig. 3.16: Schematic view of the information flow and main modules of a general Expert System.

3.7.2 *Decision Tree (DT)*

A decision tree (DT) is a symbolic AI approach that hierarchically structures the logic of carrying out a decision. In other words, initial questions should discriminate (i.e., better separate) the possible answer. Although the inception of regression trees dates back to the 1960s, their practical use only grew in the 1980s when Leo Breiman and colleagues proposed the CART models (Classification And Regression Trees) [Breiman *et al.* (1984)]. Following this, John Ross Quinlan proposed trees that could accommodate multiple answers [Quinlan (1988)] (i.e., non-binary trees), namely ID3 (i.e., Iterative Dichotomiser 3) [Quinlan (1986)] and C4.5 [Quinlan (1992)]. ID3 uses an impurity measure to help build the trees (that can grow quite unbalanced), whereas C4.5 allows for pruning and several other advancements. A DT emulates the decision-making ability of humans fairly-well. And unlike ES, the central principle in DTs is the acquisition of rules through the use of available data about the problem (i.e., not from experts). The tree-like structure represents the logic that has been about the decision problem. The learning is usually inductive and the training is frequently supervised. The use of a DT has many advantages: there are several approaches to dealing with categorical data (rather than just numbers, which is handy), several ways to balance the tree (to avoid too many questions and simplify the decision process) and even the possibility of training several trees at the same time known as Random Forests (i.e., several trees to account with partition of large decision spaces) [Ho (1995); Breiman (2001)]. A DT can work with small as well as large application domains but is very sensitive to new data. That is, new data can force radical restructuring of the tree(s) and therefore processing can be easily skewed. Like ES, the DT model was introduced a long time ago but is still very popular and useful today in various domains of application. And the new versions of the DT offers several advantages when it comes to tackling large problems. One of the benefits of DTs is the fact that they can explain the results of their computations straightforwardly. Hence, they allow for the standardization of processing in large decision set ups, as long as the application domain is not very dynamic (since new data may impose reconstruction on trees). DTs are quite "rational" (as with all symbolic systems). Figure 3.17 depicts a practical problem of how to dress given the weather.

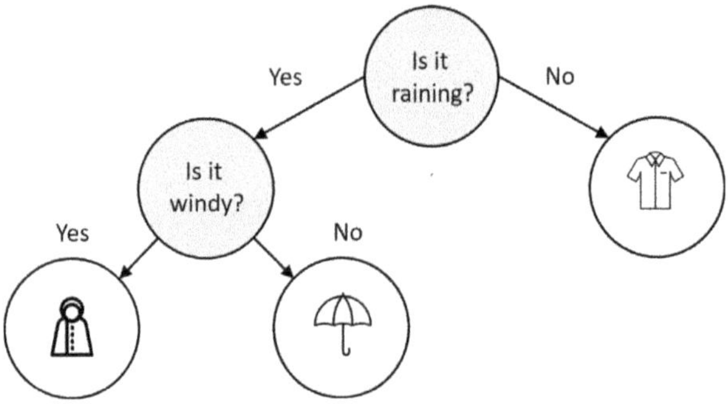

Fig. 3.17: Schematic view of the hierarchical structure of a symbolic Decision Tree, where questions lead to a decision on how to cope with the weather.

3.7.3 *Artificial Neural Networks (ANN)*

Artificial Neural Networks (ANN) are a very large family of Machine Learning algorithms that take slight inspiration from the nervous system of animals. Common to all ANNs is the neuron, which is actually nothing more than a small non-linear processor, and synapses that store experiences, which could be seen as a weights in a weighted average. They are organized in diverse architectures, for example: layers, topological maps, recurrently organized (i.e., outputs linked to inputs) etc. ANNs found huge early success in the form of multi-layer perceptron (MLP) with back-propagation [Rumelhart *et al.* (1986)] which is a powerful tool for classification, time series prediction, regression etc. Other Artificial Neural Networks include Self-Organizing Maps (SOM) and Kohonen Maps which are used for clustering and data visualization [Kohonen (1982)]. More recently Adversarial Networks [Goodfellow *et al.* (2014)] and Deep Neural Networks [LeCun *et al.* (2015)] have become immensely popular because of their impressive abilities to extract most of the information from the available data. Training of these can be performed in many ways, and the type of neurons may also vary a greatly (which may be of different natures and with many parameterizations). Learning comes down to updating the synaptic weights which is effectively is where the intelligence of this technology resides. As inductive techniques, ANNs produce new knowledge (i.e., they can be biased, depending on the training dataset) and are powerful function approximators, classifiers, groupers, in addition to being easily hybridized with other technologies. One of the biggest problems with ANNs is their low transparency. In other words, as they are sub-symbolic techniques, they are generally do not easily convey explanations on their rationality. Figure 3.18 depicts a general structure of a feed-forward, multi-layered architecture, with several hidden layers (an MLP looks like this).

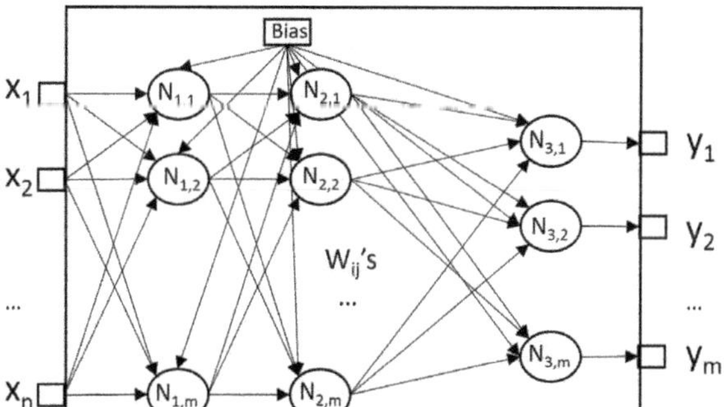

Fig. 3.18: Schematic view of a multi-layered neural network, featuring neurons (processing units), synaptic weights (where knowledge is stored), input layer (X_n, where problem variables are presented), output layer (Y_m, where classification/regression results are presented) and bias connections. Notice that the number of hidden layers can grow and is large in deep neural networks.

3.7.4 *Evolutionary Computation (CEVO)*

Evolutionary Computation (CEVO) is another large family of Machine Learning/meta-heuristic algorithms based on Darwin's theory of the evolution of species [Darwin (1859)]. Common to all evolutionary algorithms (e.g., Genetic Algorithms which are described in the next chapter, Genetic Programming, Evolutionary Strategies, Social Algorithms, Co-evolution etc.) is the metaphorical use of genes, chromosomes, and population, which represent respectively, aspects of the problem to be solved, possible solution and the set of solutions considered for the problem [De Jong (2006)]. In CEVO a parallel search occurs for combinations of aspects (or parameters) of the problem that can then perform an efficient and effective search for good solutions. This is without the combinatorial explosion of inputs, which creates great difficulty for classical (brute-force) algorithms. There are several different approaches to using CEVO, e.g., optimization in continuous spaces, optimization in discrete spaces (and even symbolic — not necessarily of numbers), and hybrid approaches. CEVO can also be hybridized with other AI algorithm families. For example, CEVO can use the parameters obtained from ANNs. As the evolutionary process does not have human supervision there can be bias. This can be minimized by the imposition of restrictions or recruiting human supervision ("Human-in-the-loop"). CEVO is relatively transparent when it comes to its explanatory process through the time stamp in their genes representing variables of the chosen solution. Figure 3.19 shows the main operations within an evolutionary algorithm.

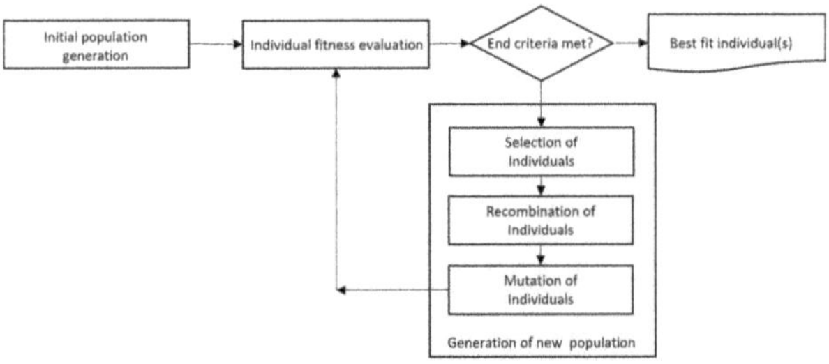

Fig. 3.19: Schematic operation flow of a generic evolutionary algorithm (e.g., Genetic Algorithms), featuring the main operations usually present in this family, namely, initialization of the population, selection of individual solutions (for, both, combination and be kept in the population), the often-used evolutionary operations (e.g., recombination and mutation), and the fitness evaluation for attaining the best solutions.

3.7.5 *Swarm Intelligence (SI)*

Swarm intelligence (SI) is a relatively recent family of Machine Learning algorithms based on the gregarious behavior of some animals (e.g., insects, fish, etc.). Common to all Swarm algorithms (e.g., Particle Swarm Optimization (PSO), FSS — Fish School Search, ACO — Ant Colony Optimization, etc.) is the use of the metaphor of particles working collaboratively within their community [Maniezzo *et al.* (2021)]. The PSO is described more thoroughly in the next chapter. It usually involves two actions being performed in parallel: the individual tries to maximize its task and the group, after receiving individual information, tries to act as a single organism. In this way, the individual and social aspects being carried out in parallel result in a great acceleration in the search for good results. As with CEVO, SI algorithms are good examples of meta-heuristics for complex problem solving. Like CEVO, SI has several different approaches, e.g., optimization in continuous space, optimization in discrete (and even symbolic — not necessarily with numbers) spaces, and hybrid approaches. What stands out with regards to using SI is its ability to handle really complex problems (e.g., hundreds of decision variables and dozens of conflicting goals). SI can also be hybridized with other families of AI algorithms, for example, SI can be used to obtain parameters for analytics systems (e.g. global supply chains). As the optimization process within SI algorithms does not have human supervision, there may be bias. This can be controlled by imposing restrictions, penalties on the utility function, or with human supervision ("Human-in-the-loop"). With regards to rationality, SI is not very transparent when it comes to its explanatory process, despite having high power to search for solutions in complex domains of objectives. Figure 3.20 provides an example of how population based methods such as Swarm intelligence behave through time.

3.8 Conclusion

In summary, current AI paradigms are powerful, diversified, and effective for tackling even the most cumbersome real-world problems. There are many other paradigms and families not discussed here, e.g., statistical (like Bayesian Networks), symbolic (like NLP — Natural Language Processing), and the many variations of fuzzy constructs. Fuzzy logic, although not necessarily intelligent, can be hybridized with other algorithms, greatly improving the flexibility of the interface with humans, and improving the

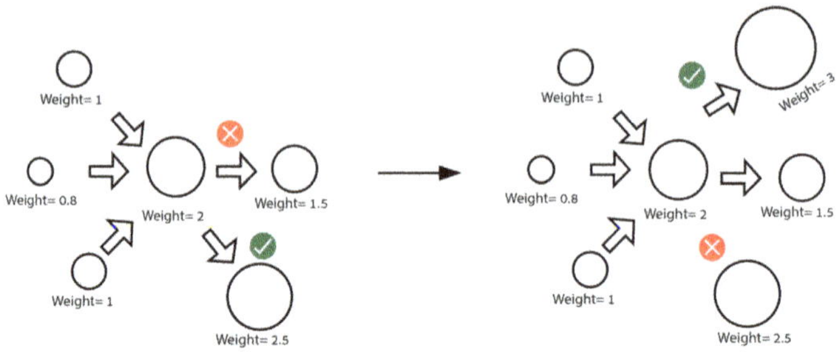

Fig. 3.20: Schematic status-shot of swarm in its dynamic and organic behavior. In this example, a FSS (Fish School Search) [Neto and de Lacerda (2014)] features how sub-swarms are formed due to the change in size of leader (due to individual success) and competition among next leader candidates. In this approach, the evoked possible solutions are given by the largest fish and the radius of sub-swarms may also indicate convergence/end of processing.

overall performance of the produced algorithms. Hybridization represents a member of interesting possibility as it blends the highlight of AI and CI algorithms. Readers who are can get much more details about this topic in books such as: AI: "Machine Learning" by Tom Mitchell [Mitchell (1997)] and "AI: A Modern Approach" by Russell and Norvig [Russell and Norvig (2020)]; and, on CI: "Computational Intelligence: Concepts to Implementations" by Eberhart and Shi [Eberhart and Shi (2011)], and "Computational Intelligence: An Introduction" by Andries Engelbrecht [Engelbrecht (2007)].

Chapter 4

Optimization

This chapter explores different optimization methods and how rational each method is. The optimization methods we explore are as follows: Broyden-Fletcher-Goldfarb-Shanno (BFGS), conjugate gradient, Genetic Algorithm, particle swarm optimization and simulated annealing. The Nelder-Mead simplex method, BFGS, and conjugate gradient are local methods and are more precise when used for local optimization problems. In contrast, the Nelder-Mead simplex method, Genetic Algorithms, particle swarm optimization and simulated annealing are global but less precise methods even when used for global problems. A hybrid of global and local methods is proposed to increase the extent of rationality, by incorporating global exploration with local exploitation. The hybrid method is more rational than the local and global methods used individually.

4.1 Introduction

This chapter explores the mathematical technique of optimization. Suppose you want to travel from Tel Aviv to Johannesburg. One way of doing this is to fly directly from Tel Aviv to Johannesburg. Another alternative is to fly from Tel Aviv to Dubai and from Dubai to Johannesburg. It is possible to connect Tel Aviv to any airport and then make connections to Johannesburg. Suppose we add another objective which is to travel from Tel Aviv to Johannesburg in the shortest time possible. In this case, the procedure of identifying the route with the shortest time is called optimization [Marwala and Leke (2019)]. Optimization in this case means identifying the route that minimizes the travel time. All the possible routes are called feasible solutions. Identifying the route with the longest travel time is known as the maximization of travel time. Nature provides us with many lessons on optimization. For example, a colony of ants normally identifies the shortest route between their nest and a food source in the natural world. When birds fly, they flap their wings in such a way that they minimize the amount of energy they use. The shape of a whale is such that it minimizes its drag force and thereby minimizes the energy needed to swim. All these are optimization problems that were perfected using the evolutionary processes. In Physics, there is a concept known as the stationary-action principle or the principle of least action. It states that natural systems behave in such a way that they minimize energy usage.

4.2 Optimization

Optimization is the process of identifying the least or the most of an object, process, or quantity. If it seeks to identify the least it is known as a minimization problem. If it seeks to identify the most it is known as a maximization problem. The design variables are those variables that need to be identified to achieve the goal of Maximization or Minimization. The mathematical representation of the goal to be realized through optimization is known as the objective function. Sometimes, there are constraints in an optimization problem. For example, suppose one needs to move from the 5th Ave & W 55th St to 59-08 70th St, Flushing, New York, USA [Marwala and Leke (2019)]. The most optimal route would require going over buildings, and therefore the buildings are constraints. A depiction of the optimization method is in Fig. 4.1 [Marwala and Leke (2019)]. The y-axis is the objective, while the x-axis is the design variable. The optimum point is the lowest point on the graph.

At times there are multiple optimum solutions, as illustrated in Fig. 4.2. At least one of them will be the globally optimum point. It is when there are multiple optimum points that the problem becomes difficult to solve. Figure 4.1 is a convex problem because the minimum point is the global minimum point [Bertsekas *et al.* (2003)]. Figure 4.2 is not convex because the minimum point is not necessarily the global minimum point [Marwala and Leke (2019)].

The concept of rationality has been intricately linked to the concept of optimization [Marwala (2014, 2015)]. One definition of a rational agent is an agent that maximizes its expected utility. The maximization of this expected utility is achieved using optimization methods, some of which are described below. The first method we describe is the Nelder-Mead simplex method [Coope and Price (2002); Avriel (2003)].

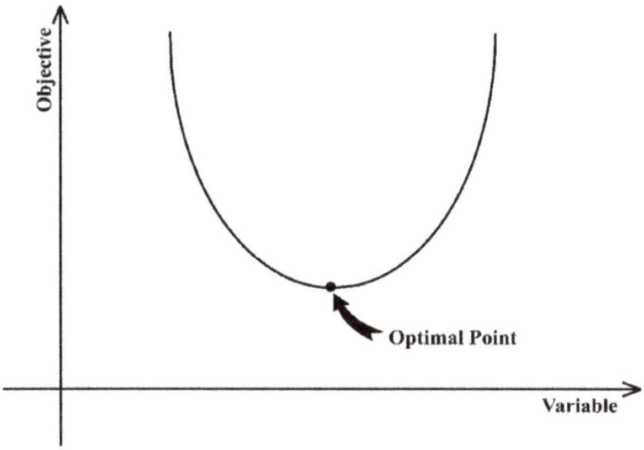

Fig. 4.1: Optimization with a single optimum point.

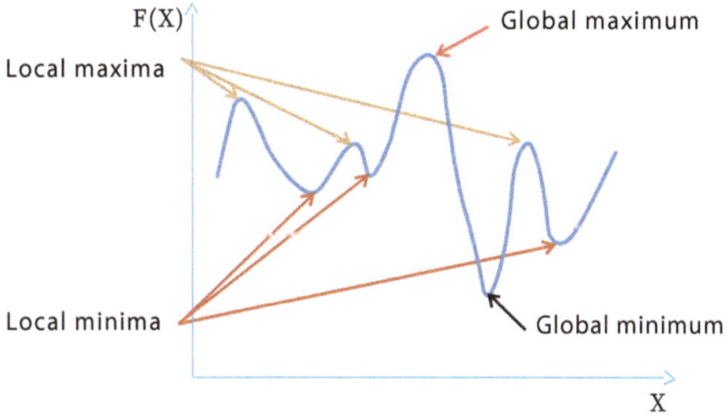

Fig. 4.2: Optimization with multiple optimum points.

4.3 Nelder-Mead Simplex Method

The Nelder-Mead (NM) simplex method is a direct optimization technique that creates a simplex with $N+1$ vertices (x_i) in an N-dimensional space. A simplex of an exact dimension (a) is set around x_0 using this rule [Coope and Price (2002); Ransome (2006); Marwala (2010); Marwala and Leke (2019)]:

$$x_i = x_0 + \frac{a}{n\sqrt{2}}(\sqrt{n+1}+n-1)e_i + \sum\nolimits_{k=1\neq i}^{n} \left[\frac{a}{n\sqrt{2}}(\sqrt{n+1}-1)\right] e_k, i = 1, n \tag{4.1}$$

here e is the unit base vector. We transform the simplex vertices coordinates using the reflection, expansion and contraction operators as follows [Ransome (2006); Marwala (2010); Marwala and Leke (2019)]:

- For a given iteration in the optimization procedure, we substitute the vertex with the worst fitness measure as defined by Eq. (4.1) by a new vertex.
- We establish the new vertex coordinates by reflecting the old vertex's information regarding the outstanding vertices. We illustrate an easy reflection of a two-dimensional simplex in Fig. 4.3 [Ransome (2006); Marwala (2010)].
- If the fitness measure of the current vertex is lower than the initial removed vertex's fitness, the dimensions of the simplex are minimized. If not, they are enlarged.
- This process is repeated until the functional evaluation values of the vertices become similar, which is measured using the following equation:

$$\sqrt{\sum_{i=1}^{n+1} \frac{(f_i - \bar{f})^2}{n}} < \tau, \tag{4.2}$$

where τ is a small positive scalar and is calculated using:

$$\bar{f} = \frac{1}{n+1} \sum_{i=1}^{n+1} f_i. \tag{4.3}$$

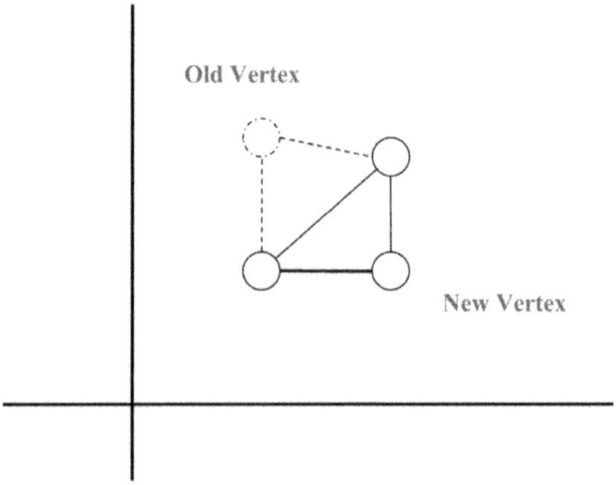

Fig. 4.3: Reflection of a two-dimensional simplex.

The NM simplex method has the following advantages [Bürmen *et al.* (2006); Marwala (2010); Marwala and Leke (2019)]:

- It demonstrates significant progress from the beginning and gives good results rapidly.
- It uses a single or double functional evaluation per iteration, except in shrink transformation.
- It achieves an excellent decrease in the function value using minimal function evaluations.
- It is easy to use and understand.

The NM simplex has the following disadvantages [Marwala (2010); Marwala and Leke (2019)]:

- There is no convergence theory.
- It exhibits numerical failures even for smooth functions.
- It converges slowly.
- It converges prematurely.

Due to these disadvantages, the NM method is not ideal to build a rational machine.

4.4 Broyden-Fletcher-Goldfarb-Shanno (BFGS) Algorithm

The Quasi-Newton optimization method is a robust and quadratically convergent optimization technique that uses the gradient of the objective function. This technique is a derivative of the Newton-Raphson technique [Ypma (1995)]. The difference being that the inverse of the second derivative is updated by using a one-dimensional or multi-dimensional Hessian estimation method. The Newton-Raphson algorithm is represented as follows [Ypma (1995); Ransome (2006); Marwala (2010); Marwala and Leke (2019)]:

$$x_{n+1} = x_n - \eta \frac{f'(x_n)}{f''(x_n)}. \tag{4.4}$$

Here $f(x_n)$ is the objective function, the Jacobian (first derivative), and the Hessian (second derivative). A single-dimensional function, $f''(x_n)$ can be updated by using the following equation [Ransome (2006); Marwala (2010); Marwala and Leke (2019)]:

$$f''(x_{n+1}) = \frac{s_n}{q_n}, \tag{4.5}$$

where

$$s_n = x_{n+1} - x_n, \tag{4.6}$$

$$q_n = f'(x_{n+1}) - f''(x_n). \tag{4.7}$$

The most commonly used multi-dimensional technique to approximate the Hessian is the Broyden-Fletcher-Goldfarb-Shanno (BFGS) procedure where the inverse Hessian H_{n+1} is given by [Broyden (1970); Fletcher (1970); Goldfarb (1970); Shanno (1970)]:

$$H_{n+1} = H_n + \frac{q_n q_n^T}{q_n^T s_n} - \frac{H_n^T s_n^T s_n H_n}{s_n^T H_n s_n}. \tag{4.8}$$

We approximate the Hessian from the expected x_0 and Hessian matrix, H_0, by using Algorithm 4.1 [Ransome (2006); Marwala (2010); Marwala and Leke (2019)]:

Algorithm 4.1 Estimation of the Hessian

(1) Compute a step s_n through $s_n = -H_n^{-1}\nabla f(x_n)$.
(2) Perform a line search to calculate the optimal step-size λ_n in the direction from the initial step, and then update $x_{n+1} = x_n + \lambda_n s_n$.
(3) Compute $q_n = \nabla f(x_(n+1)) - \nabla f(x_n)$.
(4) Approximate $H_{n+1} = H_n + \frac{q_n q_n^T}{q_n^T s_n} - \frac{H_n^T s_n^T s_n H_n}{s_n^T H_n s_n}$.
(5) Repeat until convergence.

4.5 Conjugate Gradient (CG) Method

The conjugate method is a non-linear optimization process. One type of *CG* method is the scaled conjugate gradient technique [Hestenes and Stiefel (1952); Møller (1993); Marwala (2010); Marwala and Leke (2019)]. This technique works as follows: the design variable vector x, which offers the minimum error, is reached by taking successive steps through the feasible space as demonstrated in the gradient descent equation until convergence is reached. Convergence is obtained when a set stopping criterion is achieved. The gradient descent equation is [Bishop *et al.* (1995); Marwala (2010); Marwala and Leke (2019)]:

$$x_{n+1} = x_n - \eta \frac{\partial E}{\partial x}(x). \tag{4.9}$$

Here, η is the learning rate, and E is the objective function. Different algorithms choose their learning rates differently. The gradient descent method is the basis for the conjugate gradient method [Hestenes and Stiefel (1952); Marwala and Leke (2019)]. In the gradient descent procedure, we define the step size as $-\eta \frac{\partial E}{\partial x}(x)$, where η is the learning rate, and we calculate the gradient of the error.

If the learning rate is sufficiently low, the error value decreases at each step until a minimum error value between the model prediction and training target data is obtained. In the conjugate gradient technique, we minimize the quadratic function of the error, in each iteration, over an increasingly expanding linear vector space that includes the global minimum of the error [Luenberger and Ye (2008); Fletcher (2000); Marwala (2010); Marwala and Leke (2019)]. In the conjugate gradient technique, Algorithm 4.2 is implemented [Hestenes and Stiefel (1952); Marwala (2009); Marwala and Leke (2019)].

Algorithm 4.2 Conjugate Gradient Method

(1) Choose the initial weight vector $\{x\}_0$.
(2) Compute the gradient vector $\frac{\partial E}{\partial x}(x_0)$.
(3) In each step, n, use the line search to find $\eta(n)$ that minimizes $E(\eta)$ expressing the objective function which is articulated in terms of η for fixed values of n and $\frac{\partial E}{\partial x}(x_n)$.
(4) Evaluate that the Euclidean norm of the vector $-\frac{\partial E}{\partial x}(x_n)$ is sufficiently less than that of $-\frac{\partial E}{\partial x}(x_0)$.
(5) Update the design variable vector using Eq. (4.9).
(6) For x_{n+1}, compute the updated gradient: $\frac{\partial E}{\partial x}(x_{n+1})$.
(7) Use Polak-Ribiére method to calculate:
$\beta(n+1) = \frac{\nabla E(x_{n+1})^T(\nabla E(x_{n+1}) - \nabla E(x_n))}{\nabla E(x_n)^T \nabla E(x_n)}$
(8) Update the direction vector:
$\frac{\partial E}{\partial x}(x_{n+2}) = \frac{\partial E}{\partial x}(x_{n+1}) - \beta(n+1)\frac{\partial E}{\partial x}(x_n)$
(9) Set $n = n+1$ and return to step 3.
(10) Stop when the following condition is satisfied:
$\frac{\partial E}{\partial x}(x_{n+2}) = \epsilon \frac{\partial E}{\partial x}(x_{n+1})$ where ϵ is a small number.

The convergence of the conjugate gradient method, when compared to the steepest descent method, is illustrated in Fig. 4.4 [Marwala and Leke (2019)].

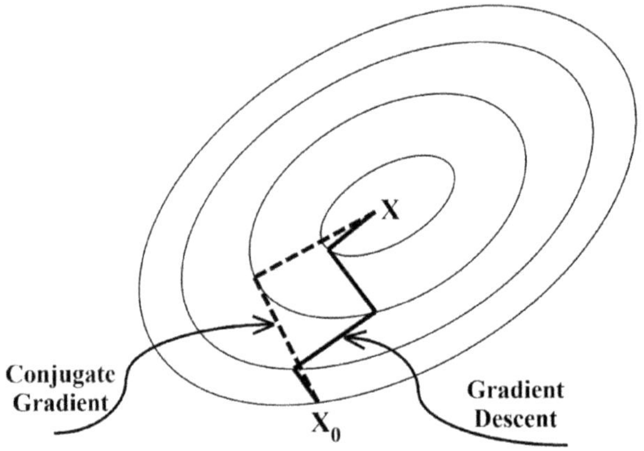

Fig. 4.4: Conjugate gradient method versus the steepest descent method.

While the conjugate gradient method is a good local optimization method in many ways, it is not good for solving non-convex global optimization problems. Therefore, with regards to building a rational machine, the conjugate gradient method is only able to maximize the attainment of maximum utility for convex problems.

4.6 Genetic Algorithm

The Genetic Algorithm (GA) optimization method has a higher probability of converging to a globally optimal solution than a gradient-based method. It is a population-based, probabilistic technique that operates to find a solution to a problem from a population of possible solutions [Marwala (2009); Marwala and Leke (2019)]. It is applied to estimate optimal solutions for complex problems by applying concepts from evolutionary biology to computer science [Michalewicz (1992); Vose (1999); Tettey and Marwala (2006); Marwala (2010); Marwala and Leke (2019)]. It is inspired by Darwin's theory of evolution, where members of a population compete to survive and reproduce, and the weaker ones are gradually eliminated from the population. We assign each individual a fitness value according to how well it meets the problem's objective function. Evolutionary-fit individual solutions are created during a cycle of generations, wherein selection and re-combination operations occur in a similar manner to the way that gene transfer applies to individuals. This continues until a termination condition is achieved, after which the strongest individual thus far is considered the optimal solution.

Genetic Algorithms have been applied in engineering by Marwala [Marwala (2002, 2007)] and Marwala and Chakraverty [Marwala and Chakraverty (2006)], in health [Crossingham and Marwala (2008)], conflict modelling [Tettey and Marwala (2006)], missing data estimation [Abdella and Marwala (2005)], robotics [Xing and Marwala (2018a)], and crowd-funding [Xing and Marwala (2018b)].

GA considers learning to be a matter of competition in a population of evolving problem solutions. A fitness function assesses each solution to determine whether it will contribute to the next generation of solutions. *GA* generates a new population of candidate solutions through operations akin to gene transfer in sexual reproduction [Goldberg and Holland (1988)]. The three most important facets of using Genetic Algorithms are defining the objective function, implementing genetic representation; and implementing the genetic operators. The Genetic Algorithm is implemented using the steps in Algorithm 4.3.

Algorithm 4.3 Genetic Algorithm

(1) Choose the initial population.
(2) Estimate the fitness of each chromosome in the population.
(3) Repeat
  (a) Select chromosomes with higher fitness to reproduce.
  (b) Produce a new population using crossover and mutation to produce offspring.
  (c) Estimate the fitness of each offspring.
  (d) Replace the low fitness section of the population with offspring.
(4) Repeat until termination.

4.6.1 *Initialization*

As described by Marwala [Marwala (2010)], initialization starts with a large number of possible individual solutions that are randomly generated to form an initial population. This initial population is sampled so that it covers a good representation of the solution space. The size of the population depends on the nature of the problem and is determined by the number of variables being targeted. For example, if there are four variables to be estimated, the population should be larger than when there are only two variable to be estimated.

4.6.2 *Crossover*

As described by Marwala [Marwala (2010)], the crossover operator combines genetic information in the population by slitting pairs of chromosomes at random locations along their length and exchanging them over the cut sections [Holland (1975); Rawlins (1991)]. This has the potential to join successful operators together. Crossover is an algorithmic operator used to alter the programming of a potential solution to the updating problem from one generation to the other.

The probability of crossover is higher than the probability of mutation. One example is a simple crossover technique [Goldberg (1989); Marwala (2010)].

As Marwala asserts [Marwala (2010)] in a simple crossover, one crossover point is chosen, a binary string from the start of a chromosome to the crossover location is copied from one parent, and the rest is copied from the second parent. For instance, if two chromosomes in binary space $a = 11001001$ and $b = 11011101$ go through a one-point crossover at the midpoint, the resultant offspring is $c = 11001101$. In an arithmetic crossover, a mathematical operation is performed to make an offspring. For example, an AND operator can be performed on $a = 11001011$ and $b = 11011111$ to form an offspring 11001011.

4.6.3 *Mutation*

In mutation, the operator chooses a binary digit of the chromosomes at random and reverses it. This has the potential to introduce new information to the population. This prevents the Genetic Algorithm simulation from becoming stuck in a local optimum solution. Mutation occurs with a certain probability. In many natural systems, the mutation probability is low (i.e., less than 1%). One such type of mutation is a binary mutation [Goldberg (1989); Marwala (2010)]. A number expressed in binary form is selected when binary mutation is used, and the one-bit value is inverted. For instance, chromosome 10001011 may become chromosome 10000011.

4.6.4 *Selection*

A selection process is performed on the current population to choose a proportion of the current population to produce a new population for every generation. This selection process is performed using a fitness-based procedure, where fitter solutions are assigned a relatively high selection probability. Some selection techniques rank the fitness of each solution and select the best solutions. Others rank a randomly selected sample of the population to achieve computational efficiency.

Many selection functions are stochastic in nature and therefore are designed such that a selection procedure is performed on a small proportion of less fit solutions. This assures that there is a level of diversity in the population of and, therefore, prevents poor and incorrect convergence. There are numerous selection approaches, including roulette-wheel selection [Goldberg (1989)].

Roulette-wheel selection works by applying a genetic operator applied to choose potentially beneficial solutions in a Genetic Algorithm optimization process. Each possible solution is assigned a fitness function which is used to map the probability of selection of each individual solution. Suppose the fitness f_i is of individual i in the population, then the probability that this individual is selected is [Marwala (2010)]:

$$p_i = \frac{f_i}{\sum_{j=1}^{N} f_j}. \tag{4.10}$$

Here, N is the total population size.

This process ensures that candidate solutions with higher fitness values have a lower probability of being eliminated those with lower fitness values. Solutions with low fitness have a low probability of survival in the selection procedure. The advantage of this is that, even though a solution may have a low fitness value, it may still have some components that may be beneficial in the future.

The procedures described here result in a population of solutions that is fitter than the previous generation of solutions.

4.6.5 *Termination*

Crossover, mutation and reproduction are repeated until a termination condition has been attained, either because a desired solution that satisfies the goal has been identified, a specified number of generations has been attained, the solution's fitness function has converged or any combination thereof.

The procedure described above can be expressed in pseudo-code, as shown in Algorithm 4.3 [Goldberg (1989); Marwala (2010)] (Goldberg, 1989; Marwala, 2010). Table 4.1 shows the operations, types and parameters in implementing the Genetic Algorithm [Marwala (2010); Marwala and Leke

Table 4.1: Operations, types and parameters of Genetic Algorithm.

Operation	**Types**	**Parameters to Select**
Genetic Representation	Binary, Floating Point	Bit Size
Initialization	Population, Random Seed	Population Size, Distribution of the Random Seed
Crossover	Arithmetic, Simple, One-point, Two-point, Uniform	Probability of Crossover
Mutation	Non-Uniform, Binary	Probability of Mutation
Fitness Function Evaluation	Problem Specific	
Selection	Roulette Wheel, Tournament Selection	
Reproduction	Two parents, Three Parents Reproduction	

(2019)]. This table indicates that in Genetic Algorithm implementation, many choices need to be made which makes this procedure highly subjective with implications on the subjectivity of rationality achieved.

4.7 Particle Swarm Optimization

This section presents the Particle Swarm Optimization (PSO) method [Kennedy and Eberhart (1995); Marwala (2010)]. The PSO is a population-based approach that is inspired by a mathematical description of the swarming of birds [Shi and Eberhart (1998); Kennedy (1997); Kennedy and Eberhart (2001)]. The drivers of Particle Swarm Optimization are individual and group intelligence. Using group intelligence, individual birds follow the group and using individual intelligence they decide on their next move. This interplay between individual and group intelligence is what makes the PSO method such a powerful method. The advantages of the Particle Swarm Optimization method are [Kennedy and Eberhart (2001)]:

- it handles the scaling of the design variables well;

- it is easy to execute;
- it is easily implementable using parallel processing;
- it does not require the calculation of the objective function derivatives;
- it contains a small number of adjustable parameters; and
- it is a practical algorithm for identifying a globally optimum solution.

The disadvantage of Particle Swarm Optimization is that it is not good at searching for a local solution, and so might converge prematurely and therefore is not ideal for creating a rational machine.

The *PSO* method is a stochastic, population-based evolutionary algorithm that is used for optimization. It is based on psycho-social values inspired by the intelligence observed in the swarming of birds. These observations offer understanding into social behavior and have contributed to social, economic and technological development. Society allows an individual to sustain cognitive robustness through influence and learning. Individuals learn to tackle problems by communicating and interacting with other individuals, thereby, developing generally similar techniques for tackling problems. Swarm intelligence is driven by two features: group and individual knowledge. Each member of a swarm acts by finding a balance between its individual knowledge and the group knowledge.

In order to solve optimization problems using the *PSO*, a fitness function is created to describe a measure of the desired outcome. In Machine Learning, the fitness function is the error value between the prediction of the neural network and the observed data. A social network representing a population of possible solutions randomly generated in order to reach an optimum solution. The individuals within this social network are assigned neighbors to interact with. These individuals are called particles, hence the name Particle Swarm Optimization. Thereafter, a process is initiated to update these particles. This process is conducted by evaluating the fitness of each particle. Each particle can recall the position where it had its best results as measured by the fitness function. The particle's best solution is known as the local best and each particle makes this information accessible to their neighbors and in turn observes their neighbor's success. These successes guide the process of moving in the search space and the population ultimately converges by the end of the simulation on an optimum solution.

Particle Swarm Optimization is implemented by finding a balance between searching for a good solution and exploiting the success of other particles. If the exploration for a solution is too restricted, the simulation will converge to the first solution encountered, which may be a local optimum position. If the successes of others are not exploited the simulation will not converge.

PSO has the following advantages: it is computationally efficient, simple to implement, has few adjustable parameters when compared to other competing evolutionary programming methods such as Genetic Algorithm and can adapt to search locally and globally.

When applying PSO, the procedure is set with a population of randomly generated solutions, each abstracted as particles. Each particle is assigned a random velocity and is iteratively moved through the particle space. At each step, the particle is attracted towards a region of the best fitness function by the location of the best fitness achieved in the population so far.

On implementing the standard PSO, each particle is represented by two vectors [Kennedy and Eberhart (1995); Marwala (2010)]:

- $p_i(k)$, which is the position of particle i at Step k; and
- $v_i(k)$, which is the velocity of particle i at Step k.

The initial randomly generated positions and velocities of particles are subsequently updated using the position of the best solution that a particle has encountered during the simulation, which is called $pbest_i$ and the best particle in the swarm, which is called $gbest(k)$. The updated velocity of a particle i can be calculated using the following equation [Kennedy and Eberhart (1995); Engelbrecht (2007); Marwala (2010)]:

$$v_i(k+1) = \gamma v_i(k) + c_1 r_1 (pbest_i - p_i(k)) + c_2 r_2 (gbest(k) - p_i(k)), \quad (4.11)$$

where γ is the inertia of the particle, c_1 and c_2 are the 'trust' parameters, and r_1 and r_2 are random numbers between 0 and 1. In Eq. (4.11), the first term is the current motion, the second term is the particle memory influence and the third term is the swarm influence. The subsequent position of a particle i can be calculated using the equation below [Kennedy and Eberhart (1995); Engelbrecht (2007); Marwala (2010)]:

$$p_i(k+1) = p_i(k) + v_i(k+1). \quad (4.12)$$

The particle's inertia controls the influence of the previous velocity of the particle on the current velocity of the particle. These parameters control the exploratory properties of the simulation with a high value of inertia encouraging global exploration and a low value of the inertia encouraging local exploration.

The parameters c_1 and c_2 are trust parameters. The trust parameter c_1 indicates how much confidence the current particle has in itself while the trust parameter c_2 indicates how much confidence the current particle has in the successes of the population. The parameters r_1 and r_2 are random numbers between 0 and 1 that regulate the degree to which the simulation should search the space.

The position of the particle is updated, based on the social behavior of the particle's population and it adapts to the environment by systematically returning to the most feasible region that has been identified. This process is stochastic, and it can be summarized in Algorithm 4.4 [Kennedy and Eberhart (1995); Engelbrecht (2007); Marwala (2010)].

Algorithm 4.4 Particle swarm optimization

(1) Initialize a population of particles' positions and velocities. The positions of the particles should be randomly distributed in the solution space.
(2) Estimate the velocity for each particle in the swarm.
(3) Update the position of each particle.
(4) Repeat steps 2 and 3 until convergence.

4.8 Simulated Annealing (SA)

Simulated annealing was inspired by natural annealing, where objects are cooled down slowly until they reach a point of equilibrium. Simulated annealing has been effective in the optimization of many complex systems. The advantages of simulated annealing for optimization are [Kirkpatrick *et al.* (1983); Marwala (2010); Marwala and Leke (2019)]: it can deal with any arbitrary systems and objective functions with any size of design variables, it converges to a global optimum solution when the number of iterations approaches infinity, it is easy to code, even for difficult problems, and it has sound statistical grounding; and it frequently gives a solution that is adequately optimal to be of substantial use in practice. Simulated annealing also has the following disadvantages [Marwala (2010); Marwala and Leke (2019)]: It is expensive to estimate the objective function, simulated annealing is a slow process because Simulated annealing is a Monte

Carlo simulation technique; simulated annealing is not as efficient as other approaches, such as the conjugate gradient approaches, for non-smooth objective functions [Marwala (2010)]. However, for many problems, the features of the objective function are unknown beforehand, and consequently, for a certain class of problems, it is not possible to know whether one should use simulated annealing or the conjugate gradient method. The implementation of simulated annealing depends on the nature of the problem in consideration and it takes advantage of extra information about the system. It cannot identify an optimal solution easily, unlike the conjugate gradient technique, where a second derivative of the objective function can be used to control whether an optimal solution has been reached. It is also difficult to choose which temperature cooling schedule to use.

As stated previously, simulated annealing was inspired by the physical annealing process. In annealing, an object such as a metal is heated until it is molten at which point its temperature is slowly decreased such that the metal, at any given instance, is approximately in thermodynamic equilibrium. As the object's temperature is decreased, the system becomes more ordered and converges to a *frozen* state at $T = 0$. However, suppose the cooling process is not performed well or the initial temperature of the object is not adequately high. In this case, the system may become quenched, forming defects or freezing in meta-stable states. This is because the system is stuck in a local minimum energy state.

The process that is followed to simulate the annealing process was proposed by Metropolis *et al.* in 1953, and involves choosing an initial temperature and holding that temperature constant, perturbing the initial formation and calculating the error at the new state [Metropolis *et al.* (1953)]. If the new error value is less than the old one, then the new state is accepted with a high probability; otherwise, this state is accepted with a low probability. This makes it a Monte Carlo method.

Simulated annealing substitutes an existing solution with a "close" random solution with a probability that depends on the difference between the matching objective function values and the temperature. The temperature reduces throughout the process, so there is less random change in the solution as temperature begins approaching zero. Simulated annealing keeps moving towards the best solution. This means that it can move to a solution with a lower fitness than it has achieved. The advantage of Simulated annealing is that the solution is a global optimum solution rather than a local optimum solution. This is the key advantage that simulated annealing has over other approaches. The disadvantage is that it is computationally expensive. Simulated annealing identifies the global optimum if quantified, but it can take a long time to achieve this. Boltzmann's equation gives the probability of accepting the reversal:

$$P(\Delta E) = \frac{1}{Z} \exp\left(-\frac{\Delta E}{T}\right). \tag{4.13}$$

Here, ΔE is the difference in error between the old and new states. T is the system's temperature; Z is a normalization factor that ensures that integrating the probability function to infinity gives a value of 1. The rate at which the temperature drops depends on the selected cooling schedule. When using simulated annealing, the first task that needs to be performed is the selection of parameters.

4.8.1 *Simulated Annealing Parameters*

On using simulated annealing, a number of parameters and choices must be specified and these are [Marwala (2010)]:

- The state-space which are the design variables;
- The objective function;
- Random number generator to sample a solution;
- The acceptance probability function; and
- The annealing temperature schedule.

The selection of parameters is crucial as it has a major impact on how effective the simulated annealing procedure is at identifying an optimal solution. However, there is no optimal way of choosing these parameters that is ideal for all problems, and no systematic technique for optimally choosing the design variables. Accordingly, the selection of parameters is subjective, and the technique of trial and error is generally applied.

4.8.2 *Transition Probabilities*

When simulated annealing is used, a random walk process is embarked upon for any given temperature. This random walk process entails transiting from one temperature to another with the transition probability of moving from one state to another. This probability is dependant on the present temperature, the order of candidate moves, and the acceptance probability function. A Markov Chain Monte Carlo ($MCMC$) method is used to make a transition from one state to another. The $MCMC$ creates a chain of possible solutions and accepts or rejects them using the Metropolis algorithm [Marwala (2010)].

4.8.3 *Monte Carlo Method*

The Monte Carlo technique is a computational system that uses recurrent random sampling to estimate a result. The Monte Carlo technique relies on recurrent calculation, and random or pseudo-random numbers which require computers. The Monte Carlo technique is typically used when it is not possible or feasible to calculate an exact solution using a deterministic algorithm.

4.8.4 *Markov Chain Monte Carlo (MCMC)*

The Markov Chain Monte Carlo ($MCMC$) technique simulates a chain of states through a random walk process using the Markov process and a Monte Carlo simulation [Marwala (2010)]. To understand the $MCMC$ method, we consider a system whose evolution is described by a stochastic process consisting of random variables $\{x_1, x_2, x_3, \ldots, x_i\}$. If a random variable x_i is in state x at the discrete time i, then the number of all possible states that all random variables can possibly occupy is the state space. If the probability that the system is in state x_{i+1} at time $i+1$ depends completely on the fact that it was in state x_i at time i, then the random variables $\{x_1, x_2, x_3, \ldots, x_i\}$ form a Markov chain. In the Markov Chain Monte Carlo technique, the transition between states is achieved by adding a random noise (ϵ) to the current state as follows:

$$x_{i+1} = x_i + \epsilon. \tag{4.14}$$

4.8.5 *Acceptance Probability Function: Metropolis Algorithm*

When the current state is reached, it is either accepted or rejected using the Metropolis algorithm. This algorithm, which was invented by Metropolis *et al.* (1953), has been widely used in statistical mechanics. In the Metropolis algorithm, on sampling a stochastic process $\{x_1, x_2, x_3, \ldots, x_i\}$ with random variables, random changes to x are introduced and they are either accepted or rejected using the following criterion [Metropolis *et al.* (1953)]:

$$\begin{aligned} &\text{If } E_{new} < E_{old} \\ &\qquad \text{accept } state(S_{new}) \\ &\text{Else} \\ &\qquad \text{accept } state(S_{new}) \text{ with probability } \exp\{-(E_{new} - E_{old})\}. \end{aligned} \tag{4.15}$$

4.8.6 *Cooling Schedule*

The *cooling scheduling* is a process through which the temperature T is reduced during Simulated annealing [Atiqullah (2004); Marwala (2010)]. Physical Simulated annealing dictates that the cooling rate should be adequately slow so that the probability distribution of the current state can be close to thermodynamic equilibrium at all times during the simulation. The time it takes to restore equilibrium in the simulation (also known as the *relaxation time*) after a temperature change depends on the topology of the objective function, the current temperature and the candidate generator. The type of simulated annealing, called *thermodynamic simulated annealing*, attempts to sidestep this problem by eliminating the cooling schedule and adjusting the temperature at each iteration of the simulation, based on the energy difference between the two states, in accordance with the laws of thermodynamics. The framework of simulated annealing is shown in Algorithm 4.5.

Algorithm 4.5 Simulated Annealing

(1) Define SA parameters.
(2) $i = 1$.
(3) Set T.
(4) $x_{i+1} = x_i + \epsilon$.
(5) If $f(x_{i+1}) < f(x_i)$:
  (a) If *yes* $x_i = x_{i+1}$ and then proceed.
  (b) If *no*
    i. If $P(T) > random$ then $x_i = x_{i+1}$.
    ii. Else proceed.
(6) $i = i + 1$.
(7) If $i > i_{max}$:
  (a) If *no* reduce the temperature using a cooling schedule and go to Step 3.
  (b) If *yes* End.

Simulated annealing is a global method but is also able to sample locally provided that the number of samples approaches infinity. Another way of achieving this is to combine global and local optimization methods which is the subject of the next section.

4.9 Hybrid Global-Local Optimization Technique

A technique of combining local and global optimization method, has proven successful in the optimization of complex systems. The general framework for achieving this is shown in Algorithm 4.6.

Algorithm 4.6 Hybrid Global-Local Optimization Technique

(1) Choose a global optimization method (e.g. GA or PSO).
(2) Optimize using this global optimization method.
(3) Use the solution of the global optimization method as an initial solution to the local optimization method.
(4) Execute the local optimization method (e.g. conjugate gradient method).
(5) Stop when convergence is achieved.

Pan *et al.* [Pan *et al.* (2000)] combined conjugate gradient methods to build a hybrid optimization method. An example of the hybridization of classical methods with Genetic Algorithm is the work of Mitras and Hassan [Mitras and Hassan (2013)], who hybridized GA with the steepest descent method and conjugate gradient method. Qteish and Hamdan [Qteish and Hamdan (2010)] hybridized the PSO with the conjugate gradient method as did Warsito *et al.* [Warsito *et al.* (2019)]. Guarracino and Velis [Guarracino and Velis (2007)] hybridized simulated annealing and gradient-based algorithms to estimate unsaturated soil parameters while Martín-Clemente *et al.* [Martin-Clemente *et al.* (2001)] hybridized the conjugate gradient method with simulated annealing for the blind separation of sources. With regards to the rationality of these methods, Simulated annealing is generally accurate because it is both global and local and hybridizing it with conjugate gradient refines its convergence.

4.10 Conclusion

This chapter described different optimization techniques and the extent of their rationality. The optimization approaches studied are: the Broyden-Fletcher-Goldfarb-Shanno ($BFGS$) method, the conjugate Gradient Method, Genetic Algorithms, Particle Swarm Optimization and Simulated annealing methods. The Nelder-Mead simplex approach, $BFGS$, and the conjugate gradient method are local methods but as more precise than other methods. In contrast, the Nelder-Mead simplex method, Genetic Algorithms, Particle Swarm Optimization and Simulated annealing are global methods but are less precise (less rational). A hybrid of global and local methods is proposed to increase the extent of rationality.

Chapter 5

Cost-Value and Utility Dimensions and Dynamics

This chapter presents the cost-value and utility dimensions and dynamics. We discuss basic economic terms, such as: value, utility, costs, and their hidden dimensions. We discuss how economic values are changed through the application of decisions and actions. We show negative and positive changes in costs, values, and utility and discuss the net utility and the relativity of achievements. We present value rational actions and the value rational judgment function. We introduce the concept of landmarks in sequential decision-making and planning and show how these landmarks could represent economic values and dynamics in the decision-making process. We discuss the value of knowledge and show the interplay between data, information, knowledge, and wisdom as summarized in the DIKW hierarchy. Finally, we discuss how data is used in action and emphasize some negative aspects of so-called Big Data.

5.1 Introduction

In this chapter, we present the dynamics and exchanges in values and costs caused by actions and decisions, that lead to changes in these values and costs over time. Constantly changing environments and societal needs are represented in the constantly changing views of what society believes to be important. An aggregation of "what is important in life" to society is represented by the economic term ***market demand***. Not all market demands are available due to limited production capacity and supply constraints. The term ***market supply*** represents the availability of goods and services within the market. The intersection between supply and demand defines the ***market price*** of goods and "what is important in life". The consumption of supplies and the supply of demands is achieved through the decisions and actions of suppliers and the consumers. The market is the dimension in which suppliers and consumers collaborate to create a (dynamic) balance between what people want and what they can get. This collaboration in the market also provides insights into what is missing and what can be done to create a future balance of supply and demand. Products that are not consumed provide insight into what is "no longer important in life" and should be supplied differently or not supplied at all.

The dynamic collaboration in the market between the supplier and the consumer is a process of acquiring the knowledge needed to make useful decisions and to carry out useful actions in the future so as to avoid wasting resources on actions that are not useful. Market dynamics represent the constantly changing decisions and actions made by the society.

The economic system was developed over the years to evaluate what is important and how much it should cost, flexibly and dynamically, in order to represent relatively up-to-date evaluations of the supply and demand of goods aggregated to their market price. However, algorithms and machines act on principles and less flexible decision making policies that have likely been encoded by a single or group of developers. AI decision-making systems create biases with powerful computation towards goals that may not represent the balance between the supply of goods and the demand of society.

The advancements in the development of automated and AI decision making systems have exported the responsibility for the dynamics of values, and hence the evaluation of what is important for humans, to machines, aiming to create greater wealth and lower production cost for the things that humans value.

5.2 Values and Trust

5.2.1 *Value*

Value is a static, world-state related term that quantifies things such as: goods, resources, and knowledge. The Aggregated beliefs of society in a specific object gives value to the object, e.g., money. ***Ethical*** values are the aggregated conceptions of an interrelated society regarding principles and norms to promise its existence and learn from its experience. ***Future value*** is the potential value of an object or the wealth expected from exploiting a resource. Values are not absolute for a few reasons. First, a society is constructed of individuals and the aggregated value of individuals is relatively unfair from a global perspective as each individual is weighted differently in the aggregation. For example, the value of money and the derived pricing of goods is a function of both their existence and availability. Because individuals possess different amounts of money, they are represented differently in the aggregated belief regarding its value. From a goods perspective, the non-balanced distribution of goods affects the value and cost of goods based on its availability.

5.2.2 *Utility*

While the price of a specific product is absolute, each individual evaluates it differently, based on their perspective and relative to their resources. The theory of labor states that people determine the relative value of a product by the amount of labor required to produce it. The literature on economics and labor theory describes the concept of subjective evaluation with the term ***utility***.

In this work, we define utility as the usefulness of an action or the process of creating value. Types of utility creation are:

- A useful action or process that will make a net positive impact on the total value and is defined as ***net positive utility value action/process***.
- Non-useful actions that will make a non or negative impact on the total value and is defined as ***net negative utility value action/process***. Assuming that each action or process is at least time consuming, i.e., wastes the resource of time, it creates negative utility in terms of time.

We distinguish between two ***types of utility;***

(1) ***Individual***, the subjective value of a production process.
(2) ***Social***, the aggregated value of a production process.

The first type of utility will simply be called utility in accordance with the traditional usage of the term. The literature mainly defines utility as the outcome of an action.

The term ***marginal utility*** refers to increased benefit or satisfaction a consumer derives from one unit of a product. Marginal utility is good enough to evaluate the local progress of a process, on the level of a single action and to observe the usefulness of local change per measured unit. While this is enough to model some economic aspects, it does not model the real-world complexity of the change and value dynamics. Real-world economics involves more complex scenarios that cannot be measured marginally or locally.

5.2.3 *Trust*

An ***investment*** can take many forms and involves multi-dimensional value dynamics such as: time, place, emotional effort, investigation effort, etc. Investments are, by their nature, made with a ***future perspective***, i.e., you make a significant effort with limited resources today for a greater gain tomorrow. Therefore, investment is inherently risky, due to uncertainty regarding the future. This implies only partly rational decision planning and making is possible, and that plans should be made responsibly in order to reduce irrationality and reduce risk. Due to the time and uncertainty dynamics of investments, a trusted system and society becomes a significant factor in society/system survival and prosperity. Without a system of trust, long-term projects cannot be undertaken.

The nature of ***competition*** is that you gain value at the expense of someone else. When competition is balanced and ethical we see progress in total terms. However, when competition is unbalanced, it is only a matter of time until the system collapses. The goals we set out and our perception of achievements define what we value, what we desire and how we plan to achieve it. Goals and values provide a useful glimpse into the future and give a good indication of what individuals want and might be (sometimes unconsciously).

From a societal perspective, the aggregation of the values and goals of individuals gives us a good estimation of where we are all going to be. This concept is known as the ***aggregated heuristic***. Since societies and the environments in which they exist are constantly changing, the goals, values and the aggregated heuristics are also constantly changing.

In what follows, we show several dimensions of values and analyze inter-dimensional gaps.

5.3 Hidden Dimensions of Values and Costs

Recent studies have shown interest in a non-monetary evaluation of the value of goods and activities [Poladian *et al.* (2003); Garrison *et al.* (2016)]. This can represent a more complex but more realistic idea of values. The dimensions of values and costs as defined by a society or organization

Table 5.1: Dimensions of values and costs.

	Dimensions of Values	Dimensions of Costs
Ethical	principles and norms that are agreed on by a society to assure its long term existence; Heuristics for a long term existence	reputation, trade of values, war, betrayals, crime
Financial	currency, coins	currency, coins
Knowledge	KHiA "know-how-in-action," potential for creation, productivity	unrealized potential, obtained and shared (e.g., social good), obtained but not enrolled to a value (e.g., stolen, lost)
Labor	the potential of value creation (not only financial, can be enrolled to any value)	usually evaluated with money but includes many human-related issues like motivations and effort, time and more
Emotional	enrolled into motivation and hence to the creation of any value that can be created by labor	implies a decrease in motivation, low productivity
Symbolic	articles, desire, places, traditions, associated with memories and beliefs (related to past, present and future values)	loss of hope, unstable connection to society, individualism
Time	can be invested as a cost of a new production process, acceleration of the production process, travel, surfing, opportunity to have the benefit of a product, creativity, social bonding	all that could happen but did not, unmaintained values, can be enrolled into the decrease of each of the values as mentioned above
Renewable Resources	solar power, geothermal power, wind power, water, air (the total range of living organisms providing man with food, fibers, etc. [Weiss (1973)])	solar power, geothermal power, wind power, water, air (the total range of living organisms providing man with food, fibers, etc. [Weiss (1973)])
Non-Renewable Resources	minerals and metals from the earth (organic carbon material, some types of groundwater, gold, silver, iron)	minerals and metals from the earth (organic carbon material, some types of groundwater, gold, silver, iron)
...	...	...

cannot be fully measured in traditional monetary terms. The non-monetary dimensions of value are separated and measured on different scales. The dynamic between these dimensions creates a value from other values, for example, the value of knowledge can be evaluated by taking the costs of all the values mentioned in Table 5.1 into account. Unlike the traditional financial value and cost evaluation which evaluates costs and values in the same monetary terms, the cost of knowledge can only be partially estimated in monetary terms and its potential can be estimated using all the values mentioned in the table, maybe even into non-renewable resources. When a discussion on the ethics, fairness and survival of a system takes place, the exchange of values must be measured using all the cost dimensions. The dimensions of values and costs must be separated and cannot be treated with different terms or subjectively as with the utility term which is discussed in the next section.

Application of actions and decisions create dynamics and exchange of values and costs. Some actions and decisions may consume values from several dimensions and have multi-dimensional costs. They can also create values in several dimensions. Figure 5.1 illustrates a specific value that is paid for in several dimensions of cost. In this example, the value of knowledge (e.g., academic degree) is paid in several dimensions of cost: time, emotional, and financial. Figure 5.2 illustrates an object/article that possess values in several dimensions. These values are created by paying a cost in several dimensions. This example examines the costs and values of possessing this book. The cost of the possession of this book is in the financial dimension. This cost is paid at the time of purchase. The usage of this book comes with the investment of time in reading the book. This is another cost in the dimension of time. The values of the book are; knowledge, symbolic, financial/economic (if used to achieve the purpose).

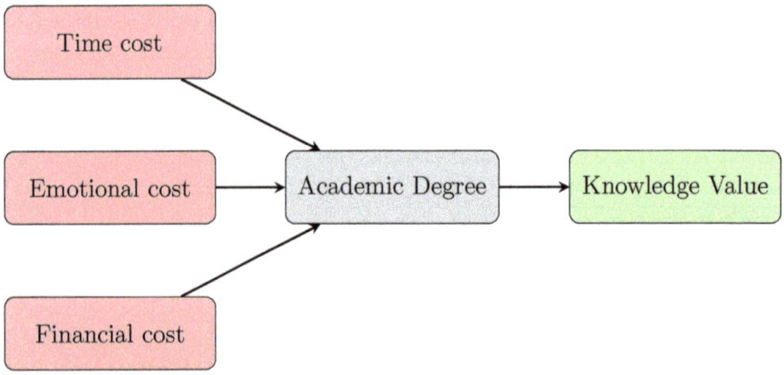

Fig. 5.1: An example that shows a specific value that is paid for in several dimensions of cost. The value of knowledge (e.g., academic degree) is paid in several dimensions of cost: emotional, time, and financial.

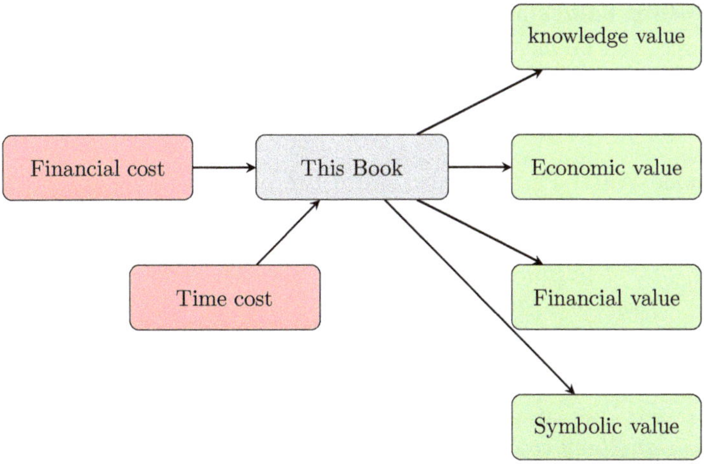

Fig. 5.2: An example that shows values in several dimensions that are created by paying the costs several dimensions. For example, to create value of this book, there are costs in two dimensions; in the financial dimension from purchasing the book and the cost in the time dimension invested in reading the book. The values are all the values of the book; knowledge, symbolic, financial/economic (if used to achieve the purpose).

5.4 Time Dimensions of Values and Costs

The dimensions of values differ from the dimensions of costs and thus are related to different time dimensions. Costs are values that must exist at the moment that they are paid, unlike values which are treatable. A cost is a value with present or past time properties, while values have past, present and future time properties.

Past values are known as sunk-costs. They are a memory that can be represented well in knowledge, and point in time perspective, for the benefit of a process that consumed these values as costs for the maintenance of the process. Accurate representations of ***sunk values*** at the moment that they existed, captures a more accurate picture of process productivity when time allows us to calculate the value of the output of the consuming process that they maintained.

Present values, are resources that may be renewable, not renewable or diminishing if use is not adequately planned for. When present values are invested they become costs. Present values that have not paid been are values with potential and are called resources.

Future values are the potential of sets of resources. The potential of resources can be measured by a ***planning process***.

5.5 The Diamond-Water Paradox

Diamond-Water Paradox, also called the paradox of value (and utility) is presented by [Smith (1976)] as follows:

> *The things which have the greatest value in use have frequently little or no value in exchange; and, on the contrary, those who have the greatest value in exchange have frequently little or no value in use. Nothing is more useful than water: but it will purchase rarely anything; Rarely anything can be exchanged for it. A diamond, on the contrary, has rarely any value in use; but a very great quantity of other goods may frequently be exchanged for it.*

Utility is the subjective evaluation by an individual of the wealth that they gain from a specific value. The labor theory of value [Farber *et al.* (2002)] solves this paradox by explaining that the cost of what one wants and the relative difficulty of fulfilling the want, can be different as Table 5.2 shows. Note, autonomous, AI and information systems produce some utility types that are listed in Table 5.2. For example, the development of the internet combined with the development of the mobile phone has created different types of utilities. A mobile phones with an internet connection utilizes information, knowledge, service and other values by making them available at the right place and time. At the same time, the same phone is the reason that working days continue after working hours which prevents the utilization of many different values, and this represents a ***duality of availability***.

5.6 Value Bias and Lost Utility

The dimensions of values and different types of utility, as well as the subjectivity and value of bounded rationality creates gaps in the perception of exchange and creation of values. Gaps create risks, errors and opportunities that depend on the observer and the subject of the gap. Having a beneficial ethical policy that the society expects individuals to follow is one way bridge these gaps. Bridging gaps and avoiding arbitrage by individuals creates value-driven progress.

Table 5.2: Types of utilities and examples for creating positive and negative utility.

Utility Creation		**Examples**	
Types	**Definition**	**net positive utility ↑**	**net negative utility ↓**
Form	created by design/reshape/ reformulate/assemble of goods or services	software upgrade, marketing reshapes information	error in upgraded software, waste
Place	created by making goods and services more accessible **where** needed (deliverable)	markets, stores, selling water at a mountain peak	missing stocks in a store, a bank that cannot give a loan
Time	created by making goods and service easier to obtain **when** needed	fast-food, opening hours of stores	absence of emergency medical services
Task, Knowledge, Service	created by providing professional and personal service, assistance, guidance, etc.	bankers, layers, academic advisor, ministers, reviews, doctors, etc.	supplying bad service, false and non-promoting tips, bureaucracy
Possession	created by a transfer of ownership	car	debt
Information	Set of facts in a context, created by communication, experiments, etc.	marketing, teaching, answering questions, navigation directions, etc.	false information, flood of data, inflation of words/data, oversubscription of names to ideas

An expression of the value-biased policy of individuals, from the perspective of society, is the exploitation of gaps by individuals to make a self-concentrated arbitrage. Arbitrage is an easy profit with no costs or risks for the individual. However, arbitrage does involve costs, but they are paid in a different dimension. Rational value perception and awareness of the risks posed by gaps created by the society and its individuals is critical for both survival and the creation/preservation of values. A cost-optimal policy, without a full value aware judgment function, is by default gaps/ traps oriented because free is always going to be the most optimal position when optimizing the cost. The exploitation of gaps can be the result of a lack of awareness or ignorance. Active exploitation of gaps is the output of a thinking process enrolled into a conscious, value-irrational decision. To take a step towards solving the irrational economic error of the exploitation of gaps, we provide the following terms and definitions to create awareness and provide a tool to avoid crimes of lack of awareness.

5.6.1 *Negative Costs Value of Actions*

Individuals or society can adopt a ***negative-cost arbitrage*** policy. Current possession values are values developed by a creation process in the past and thus they are a product of investment (i.e. pre-paid actions). The costs possession values were pre-paid in the past by the owner of the values. Possession values are present values and constitute resources to be used in the present and the future that are obtained by the processes of creation. Resources that are used as part of the production process can be defined as value-potential when we taking a future perspective, i.e. the expected future state of resource. Resources are defined as costs when we take a present perspective or sunk costs when we take a past perspective. Thus observers view resources differently, depending on the position of the observer in time and the time-perspective that they take on the resource. Combining the time perspective of costs with the perspective of an individual on the value of the property of other individuals (or the community) creates, among other things, an opportunity for value-crimes. On the other hand, an altruistic opportunity is defined as good advice, i.e. sharing information for the purpose of creating value in which the advisor has captured time-perspective on a particular resource.

A **rational negative cost** is the output of a rational decision for a chosen cause. We call this charity, donation or investment. An individual takes rational negative cost decisions based on their resources, i.e. sharing values in their possession without the expectation of values in exchange. A rational negative cost decision is the output of a local (individual) action for a global (society) greater good.

An **irrational negative cost** is the output of a cost-irrational decision for a local or self-centered cause. We call this stealing, robbery, slavery, exploitation or inter-dimension value gaps. An individual takes an irrational negative cost decision based on someone else's resources, i.e. sharing values that are ***not*** in their own possession ***with*** the expectation of these values being an easy or zero effort way to make a profit. An irrational negative cost decision is the output of a local (individual) action for a local (individual) greater good at the expense of global (societal) values.

When we state that we are cost-optimal in action, we should expand this and state at what expense. In the next section, we discuss several aspects that address this question.

Another peculiar example of irrational negative cost decision is also what happens in the blockbuster Korean series *Round 6* or *Squid Game.*[1] What makes it so interesting is the fact that the individual (or group) takes an irrational negative cost decision based on someone else's resources (in the movies, the lives of the players with their consent). The players gamble with their lives, which is the ultimate resource that a living being possesses. If this book would have been in Sociology or Anthropology, a very long discussion would be mandatory now, aiming at finding the reasons that such irrationality happens throughout history. As a matter of fact, another extension from the perspective of Psychology, could ponder on the "whys".

5.6.2 *Negative Utility Value Actions*

Rational negative utility occurs in scenarios of investments where a sequence of action incurs some necessary negative effects on the way to a global benefit. Non-rational negative utility of actions occurs when unnecessary negative effects are incurred, which do not serve the process of achieving a global benefit. The cost of actions, as defined in the SAS+ formalism (Section 7.3), for planning can be seen conceptually as negative utility of actions. For the purpose of clarity, in this work we refer to net negative change in state variables when an action is applied as a negative utility of actions.

5.7 Value-Bias in Time Perspective

5.7.1 *The Forgotten Aspects of Problem Solving*

Most approaches in the literature for planning, in particular the goal-oriented approaches, only partially address the real-world complexity of planning. In real-world scenarios, almost every plan has additional phases. When an agent achieves their goals, sometimes they can stay at the location that they planned on but most of the time they must relocate. Consider the well-known example of the logistic domain problem, which has been addressed in many fields. The problem is illustrated by packages needing to be delivered to various locations by various transportation methods such as track and airplane. The goal is usually defined as finding the most efficient

[1] *Round 6* (a.k.a. *Squid Game*) which is a very popular South Korean series produced by Netflix in 2021, where selected destitute people are offered to be part of a lethal game, split in cruel installments. The two striking features of the game are: (i) the "chips" used in the game are the lives of the players and, (ii) the participants are all voluntary.

(cost optimal) trajectories by which to deliver packages to pre-defined locations. Using this definition, the problem is solved when the driver of the truck and the pilot get to the target location. The return phase of planning is not addressed, which leaves the final phase of the problem unsolved. If such a plan reaches the industry, it causes damage to many values, both human and financial, due to a limited perception of reality.

Suppose the goals are of high priority, so-called hard goals, and must be reached at any cost. A responsible solution in such scenarios should plan the goal state and choose a plan that reaches the goal state in a way that will be suitable for retreat or for performing subsequent activities. If a goal can be reached from multiple trajectories, it is responsible not to assume that agents from different paths are equivalent in relation to risks and values.

In complex systems with a diversity of values, goals, and restrictions, assuming a ***binary judgment function*** of achievements while using a domain-independent approach constitutes a paradox with many impacts on the end-user as a result of the suggested solution. The efficiency that is measured using this definition of achievement is an illusion of a success that is the result of simplifying complexity.

5.8 Value Alignment: The Relativity of Achievements and Success

We suggest rethinking the usage of ***binary judgment functions*** of achievements for the sake of safety and effectiveness. Real-world problems are dynamic, and preferences depend on circumstances, while a perception of achievements as hard goals implies an absolute preferences of values. Relative estimation methods are more flexible and realistic, particularly when a domain-independent approach for problem solving is discussed. The relativity of achievements and resource allowance must be considered more closely to scale up to real-world problem solving and domain-independent approaches.

Problems that involve limited resources and have a diversity of achievements are problems of choosing the most desirable achievement within the constraints of a budget from available choices while being aware of the fact that not all choices are allowed. Achievements in such problems are relative by definition. Relative estimation approaches are the bridge between the sparsity of problem-solving approaches and research fields. Net-benefit planning [Van Den Briel *et al.* (2004a); Nigenda and Kambhampati (2005);

Baier *et al.* (2009); Bonet and Geffner (2008); Benton *et al.* (2009a); Coles and Coles (2011); Keyder and Geffner (2009)] is a relative estimation of the achievements concerning the costs that are invested in the process to achieve goals.

The use of landmarks (which is discussed in the following sections) in the process of decision planning allows us to work in phases like cost preserving, investment, damage reducing value preserving; it is the natural bridge for the synergistic combination and cooperation of approaches and agents toward mutual targets. A well-planned decision and good and trust-worthy communication are the key to the creation of win-win and values-aware solutions for individuals and the systems in which they act.

5.8.1 *Collaborate to Learn Each Other's Reality*

Dynamics and exchanges in values and costs are the result of actions and decisions that change the values and costs over time, the constantly changing environment and the constantly changing beliefs of society as to what is important in life. An aggregation of "what is important in life" for a society is represented in the economic term ***market demand***. Not everything that is demanded by the market is available due to limited production capacity and supply constraints. What is available in the market is represented by the term ***market supply***. The intersections between the demands of society and the supply good define the ***market price*** of goods and "what is important in life". The consumption of supplies and the supply of demands is achieved by the decisions and actions of the supplier and the consumer. The market is the dimension in which the supplier and the consumer collaborate to meet each other's reality other and find a (dynamic) balance between what people want and what they can get. The collaboration in the market also provides an insight into what is missing and what can be done to create future a balance between supply and demand. Provided the market price is adequate, products that are not consumed provide an insight into what is "no longer important in life" and should be supplied differently or not supplied at all.

The dynamic collaboration in the market between the supplier and the consumer is a process of learning the knowledge need to make useful decisions and take useful actions in the future and to avoid wasting resource actions that are not useful. Market dynamics represent the constantly changing decisions and actions of the society.

The economic system was built over the years to evaluate what is important to people and how much these things cost, flexibly and dynamically so as to represent relatively up-to-date evaluations of the supply and demand of goods aggregated to their market price. At the same time, algorithms and machines act on principles and less flexible decision making policies that have likely been encoded by a single or group of developers. AI decision making systems create bias with powerful computation toward goals that do not represent a balance between the demand and the supply of the society.

The advances in the development of automated and AI decision-making systems exported the responsibility for the dynamics of values and hence evaluation of what is important for humans to machines aiming to create better wealth, values and lower production cost of the things that humans value.

5.8.2 *Planned Risks Hedging*

An accurate, rational planning process provides a rational estimation of resource definitions and allocations as a ***budget*** for a creative process. Furthermore, a value-rational planning process provides a value-rational estimation of the outcome of the process. An accurate estimation of the costs and net utility of the process allows an estimation of the benefit of making a process happen, and provides a tool for choosing the better, or more value-rational process from a set of alternatives.

Investment in an accurate estimation of the values and costs of an economic process is essential to ***hedging risks*** as costs are paid by individuals and organizations with limited resources and they are not shareable since they are paid in the present or in advance and must exist or take the form of credit. At any time in an ongoing process, costs can be paid and thus become sunk-costs (at least the cost of time). On the other hand, some of the values that are created in a process are shareable if they are produced productively enough, and represent a good investment, i.e., cover the costs to create benefits. For instance, inventions and knowledge are shared with society by default in many cases and can serve in the creation of many other values by other individuals or organizations.

The creation of ***accurate knowledge*** regarding the costs that have to be invested in a specific process can ***refine the uncertainty*** of the benefit and damage that the process can create (i.e. ***risks***). Tools for refining the uncertainty of the values and costs of projects, encourage individuals to create effective projects and innovations and improve the economy of a society. A non-monetary accurate estimation, for instance the *emotional labor*, of a project can reveal labor related risks e.g. difficulties in recruiting, high salary requirements, and employee abandonment. A non-accurate estimation of a project's emotional labor results in out of budget, unexpected costs and may lead to project failure and the *unrealized potential of sunk costs*, i.e. waste of resources. This is even more critical when it comes to long-term investments which are essential to guaranteeing the effectiveness of many creation processes and projects and can lead to bankruptcy if not planned for responsibly.

In recent work [Muller and Karpas (2018a,b)] defined the properties of a process of improvement. This can be defined as the properties of a productive process being treated as a ***planned effective and efficient investment*** and represented within a "window of opportunity" of investment realization. The concept of planning investment is represented by a set of interrelated properties in the exchange of values by actions with multivariate effects and preconditions. An action's net utility is measured by gross and net utility value creation and is allowed to constrain a process in order to execute it effectively and efficiently. The improvement process's effectiveness is a necessary condition for its execution. If a process is not useful there is no point in execution. Efficiency is measured using the budget preservation of an active process.

5.9 Value-Rational Judgment Function

Actions have preconditions and effects. We define an action as applicable in a given state if all of its preconditions are met in that state. The implementation of a decision by turning it into an action is only possible if all the preconditions for the action are met. Once an applicable action has been applied, it affects the decision maker and the state, or the environment in which it has been applied. An action's effects may lead to an exchange of values and costs that are not necessarily in the same dimension. There are many dimensions of values and costs, and they are measured on different scales and are not necessarily comparable. Consider the decision of whether to apply a lockdown during the COVID-19 pandemic. There is a conflict of values inherent in this decision. These values being the community's safety and financial values. Since the exchanged values are not always comparable, a conflict of values might raise questions regarding action's overall and net utility. Are the decision and action beneficial or harmful overall? Is the exchange of values in different dimensions appropriate? When actions with a multi-dimensional exchange of values are being considered, a judgment function is required to design decision-making and understand the benefit of the action and the net benefit that it might lead to. An example of such a judgment function is ethics.

5.9.1 *Ethics Heuristics*

Ethical principles and norms can be understood as common sense (desirably wisdom) gained overtime, the aggregation of perspectives' superpositions on the exchange of values and costs of different human behavior policies — weaknesses and strengths as well as the bounded perception of value, cost and time represented as ethical norms and principles. Ethical norms and values are responsible for the social behavior involved in the exchange of values and costs and the gaps in their perceptions. It is, in practice, aggregated advice from the past that is based on the experience and lessons from many value-rational situations. Furthermore, the majority of society and economic and organizational systems act according to an ethical code that makes unethical policy contrary to society and visible the perspective of time. An unethical policy is a trap and an error in the perception of the value of time. It reminds us, for example, that time can be seen as more valuable than money since crimes are unethical and people that commit criminal activities for easy profit can find themselves in jail. Governors in the service of the people that enjoy a high status through making an easy profit or exploiting people can lose all the credit that they have gained in a long career of multi-dimensional cost investment at once. Ethics is the time perspective of multi-dimensional value-cost dynamics.

5.10 Planning Value Rational Actions

Rationality in problem solving, planning, and sequential decision making requires us to be effective and efficient in choosing a solution. An end-means, goal-oriented problem-solving approach can achieve effectiveness. A process-oriented problem-solving approach can help to achieve efficiency. Treating a planning task as both a process-oriented and goal-oriented problem raises the question of the appropriate optimality criteria such that they restrict both the process and its end. This section provides a deeper look at the term optimality in a sequential decision-making problem and the intuitive basis of our approach to defining the minimal optimality criteria.

Even though a deeper consideration on the morality of all decisions could be pursued, deontological[2] means consequentialism, meaning assessing the consequences of all steps of the process and teleological[3] plans could simply be mapped here as adequate selections of the decision landmarks.

One of the main drawbacks of the classical decision theory is that actions are evaluated in isolation, and selected one at a time [Pollock (2001, 2006)]. In real-world problems, actions can interfere with one another. The result is that an action being individually optimal does not guarantee optimality overall. Pollock suggested that in decision theoretic planning, the concept of optimality is not well defined for real-world complexity and actions cannot be chosen in isolation, because they interfere with other actions. Choosing actions in isolation is locally oriented but not globally oriented as it does not have end of the process in mind. Based on our definition of rationality, it is an irrational way of acting for two reasons. The first is due to the incompleteness of information for decision making and the second is that rationality is end-process oriented.

With our focus on an optimal set of actions rather than individually optimal actions we adopt the financial term investment in planning AI. An investment in planning takes the form of locally irrational actions that collect negative utility propositions on the way to an optimal end state. These actions are not individually optimal, but are instrumental in reaching the greater cause, and are recognized as such in the context of a group of actions, end states and some reference points. We capture this concept with the definition of gross positive actions, that may be locally irrational but their goal effectiveness guides the process.

In what follows, we will present the concept of landmarks that bridge the goal- and process-oriented approaches to problem-solving that allow us to make a more informed and value rational plans of sequences of actions.

5.10.1 *Landmarks — A Rational Glimpse into the Future*

Landmarks (also called milestones) are facts about the world or things that should be accomplished on the way to a larger goal. They are a bridge between the goal- and process-oriented approaches which explains their recent success in Planning AI research. Based on their logical underpinnings, the guidance obtained by action landmark implementation can be explained

[2]By deontological we mean assessing whether an action is moral in and of itself regardless of the consequences.

[3]By teleological we mean that the end result justifies the means.

as breaking the search-process into local-goal-directed sub-processes. Local optimization is much more suitable for tackling the complexity of real-world problems. What makes the landmarks a bridge between goal- and process-oriented approaches is that the fact that the logical basis of action landmark discovery is end-process (goal) oriented.

Fact/Data landmarks are suppositions that must be true at some point in every solution plan for a given planning task [Hoffmann *et al.* (2004)]. A data *s-landmark* is an assignment to a variable that is true at some point in *every* plan for reaching a certain world-state s.

Action landmarks are actions a that have to be applied as part every plan. Disjunctive action landmarks are a set of actions that every plan must contain at least one of [Karpas and Domshlak (2009); Helmert and Domshlak (2009); Bonet and Helmert (2010); Pommerening and Helmert (2013)].

Landmarks are an output of the structural analysis of a given problem and hold the information of regarding the steps that must be taken in a plan toward a future goal. By their nature, landmarks allow for the splitting of a plan (sequence of actions). Between every two landmarks we have a sub-sequence of actions. By exploiting landmarks, we can define phases. Each phase is a sequence of actions that make up a partial plan. A globally-local planning perspective can assist in rationalizing the global plan by rationalizing partial local plans, i.e., making activities (or plans) adaptable to local, and sometimes unplanned reality. In what follows, we build a strategy for flexible global planning with local adoptable phases. For each phase we can choose a different approach, for example; cost preserving, (cost) investment, damage reducing, value preserving, and more. Landmarks are a natural bridge for the synergistic combination and cooperation of approaches that move toward a mutual target. Landmarks are the only rational information we have regarding the process that has to be undertaken in order to solve a problem. Resource allocation and estimations should be done using the information gained from landmarks. The more refined and accurate the landmarks are, the more accurate the knowledge we have about the future is. The extraction of a refined and informative set of landmarks gives us a rational glimpse into the future that tells us a partial but true story about what will happen if we persist and achieve our targets. It is also a check-point and opportunity to take a global perspective on the process in progress, as well as an opportunity to check the rationality of persisting toward goals (goals that are defined irrationally in the past at that point). It is also an opportunity for the re-allocation of resources. We should avoid unnecessary actions in case the budget is not sufficient to allow for the wasting of resources as well the effects waste can have on the environment. The first question that should be asked is "can we do it effectively?". The answer to that question should be rechecked at different points along the plan.

5.10.2 *Planning (Economic) Value Landmarks*

Value driven landmarks are an interrelated set of actions that are confined to properties of a plan that improve the utility of the state s at hand [Muller and Karpas (2018a)]. Treating achievements as landmarks and the evaluation of these achievements in the context of the values that they represent, allows for a so-called improvement approach to decision making in complex systems with over-subscribed goals or information. Empirical evaluations have shown that planning and acting the goal of self-improvement outperforms state-of-the-art goal-oriented approaches, namely collecting approaches. At a high level, an optimal plan consists of two parts: a prefix which achieves some valuable fact, and a suffix which maintains that valuable achievement and improves the utility of the other variables. The prefix can be thought of as "investing" or being "effective", while the suffix can be thought of as "reaping the benefits". Since these landmarks are built to improve relatively instead achieve a goal or value absolutely, they are independent of the polarity of the utility value and apply to scenarios of decreasing damage as well as gaining a benefit. The relative estimation concept of value-driven-landmarks as an alternative perception of goals allows for addressing numerical and negative utilities.

Cost derived landmarks. We define a new set of landmarks here that contain the information of the time or location that an agent has to pay for external services. For example, paying for fuel or toll roads. This information is derived from resources and constraints and is not handled yet by planning AI in the context of landmarks for reachability. Cost derived landmarks are deduced from the cost of value-driven landmarks. The first necessary condition for an activity is that it leads to a substitutable superior, or improved value (effectively), which is represented by value-driven landmarks. Next, costs derived from effective value landmarks represent what and how many resources are required to carry out the plan efficiently. By analyzing the budget and resources needed for a task that requires planning, a planner can recognize and remove actions of pure loss if they are critical to keeping a process alive.

A process of refining and extracting lengthier landmarks promises the better performance of AI agents. Landmarks are the only things that are rational when an agent plans their future actions.

5.11 Value and the Utility of Knowledge

It is not always clear how knowledge should be evaluated in terms of value. The nature of knowledge is such that, most times, it can only be evaluated in the perspective of time, after the realization of its potential. The cost of creating useful knowledge is paid with all the components listed in Table 5.1. The costs of creating knowledge are likely to be paid by individuals while the value that is derived from knowledge realization is generally and becomes the possession of society. Sharing knowledge with larger society allows for evolution, wealth and progress. However, it should be said many of the achievements in science and the history of ideas only derived their value after the creator of the idea passed away. This is the risk we take in the process of creating knowledge, the costs are paid in advance during the process, and the process ends with a potential, rather than immediate value for those who paid the costs.

The other side of the unrealized value potential of knowledge involves crimes, e.g. stealing knowledge and plagiarism. Costs are paid in one dimension and value is created in another dimension. This may appear as an anomaly where a singular discovered observation appears with no signs of costs behind it. From the other side, the dimension of the origin of knowledge, it can be seen as an anomaly expressed by a multi-valued investment with no reward as rationally expected. Plagiarism is a real crime that has to be measured from the perspectives of several dimensions. With the Information Revolution and the increased speed of information transfer that came along with the development of the Internet, this problem becomes a serious issue that requires multidisciplinary attention. If individuals within a society cannot trust each other or society at large when, long-term investments that are oriented towards positive social, such as research, these kinds of investments will be replaced by, short-term, cost-optimal investments with values that are measured from the perspective of the individual.

Another area that highlights the value of knowledge is the entrepreneurship process where a group of individuals takes a risk and make a long-term investments to give life to an idea. When an idea is revealed to the market, the realization of its potential creates value that is shared with society. From the perspective of the entrepreneur, their idea holds the most value at the moment it goes to market and then (without additional innovative steps) it begins a process of value-fading, this is the value and the price of sharing. This phenomenon is embodied in the concept of "time to market" and creates competition which is effective when it is balanced and dangerous when it takes a form of a race. The dangerous aspects of "time to market" in the context of the "race for technological advantage" are well presented by Cave and Ó hÉigeartaigh in their paper "An AI Race for Strategic Advantage: Rhetoric and Risks" [Cave and Ó hÉigeartaigh (2018)].

5.11.1 *Investment in Knowledge*

The creation of useful and effective knowledge requires investment and involves risk, for instance, the risk of failure. Such investments should be encouraged. An individual in a trusted society can take the risk of long term research if the society supports him and hedges the risk taken by the individual. As with economic investment, a natural hedging of the risk of research can be built on values such as the value of effective knowledge and the value of failure. If society can create value out of failure, it will lead to a more significant benefit for academic goals along with additional benefits along several dimensions. Long term investments have proven to be an excellent strategy for creating an effective value. When applying, long term investment strategies, we suggest combining observations from AI problem solving with planning and searching from large-scale domain approaches. Searches in large-scale domains and research are very closely related, not only by name but also by the concept and dynamics of making a quick guess on the path within and to uncertainty. Inspired by these similarities, another hypothesis is proposed to estimate values — the relationship of trust in the community to publishing failures as a key to collaborative and effective research progress.

5.11.2 *(Re) Search*

The branch-and-bound pruning algorithm put forward the idea that being effective in complex oversubscription planning systems [Benton *et al.* (2009a); Bonet *et al.* (1997); Domshlak and Mirkis (2015); Muller and Karpas (2018a)] requires making value from failing by using mistakes to speed up the planning progress with the pruning method that is applied to branches that cannot promise a better node than the branch of interest. Since searching and research are similar in many ways, there is a place to investigate this branch more closely and to exploit what we know about why it does not work.

5.11.2.1 *Retrospective Phase*

Traditionally, approaches to problem-solving evaluation have been based on a "snapshot of the finish line" in terms of the total effort or an aggregated binary evaluation of success i.e. statistics over solved problems. By measuring the total terms from the perspective of the finish line of solving a problem we miss the entire story of ***how*** and ***why*** a specific problem is solved. When we measure complex and time-consuming solutions we can get much more information from the process of problem solving itself, the behavior of the algorithm in different situations of complexity and the real-time interaction of the algorithm with the local problem structure, the dynamics of the exchange of values in the process, etc. Understanding ***why*** one problem is able solved while another is not able to be on a process level, rather than just reporting it as a fact, is what makes progress toward rational-intelligence. A trained rational-intelligence agent will hopefully have some properties of the value rational judgment function or at least reduce the value-bias that is created by encoded artificial irrationality. Each experiment can provide a retrospective on the proposed approach by examining what questions we ask in the process of problem solving. A "snapshot of the finish line" provides data, in that it creates information, but it is not enough to create knowledge. Intelligence in action is knowing ***what***, ***how***, ***why*** and in ***what circumstances*** things are happening in a complex process. Attention to the engineering of the measurements of our research and problem solving through the lens of rational decision planning investigation seems to be a promising guide toward a better understanding of, and progress in, the research process.

5.12 From Data to Action

5.12.1 *DIKW Hierarchy*

In the time of Big Data, it is worth finding a perspective on what exactly that means. The relationship between information and knowledge is modelled in the DIKW hierarchy (data–information–knowledge–wisdom) as illustrated in Fig. 5.3. Some researchers agree that the origins of DIKW can be found in T.S. Eliot's poem "The Rock" [Eliot (1934)]. Years later, the DIKW hierarchy gained attention in the literature on research

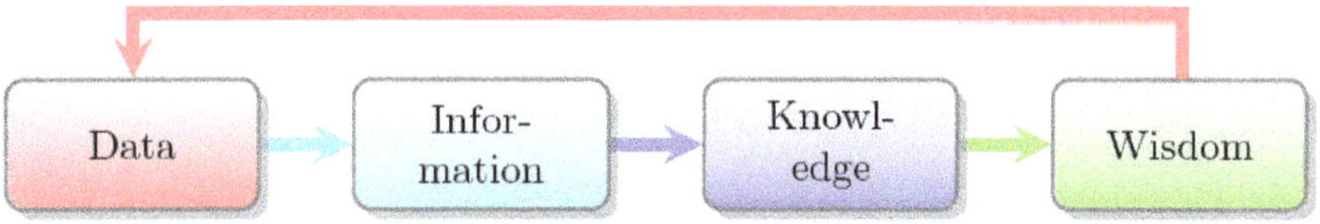

Fig. 5.3: DIKW hierarchy.

[Zeleny (1987); Cooley (1980); Ackoff (1989)]. An in-depth survey by Jennifer Rowley [Rowley (2007)] shows several observations and extensions to the basic model. Ackoff [Ackoff (1989)] made an example of the theory in practice by providing a refined, one-page paper explanation of the relationship between the DIKW hierarchy components and an analysis of the effectiveness and efficiency aspects in the process of obtaining knowledge and wisdom from data. The key concepts of the DIKW hierarchy are as follows:

- **Data** is a set of symbols that represent the properties of objects and events.
- **Information** is processed data directed towards increasing its usefulness (utility), or compactly described data.
- **Knowledge** is the instructions on *how to* use information.
  - Understanding is an explanation of *why*.
  - Intelligence is the ability to learn, and hence, to increase efficiency. This does not necessarily imply ineffectiveness. Information, knowledge, and understanding constitute Intelligence.
- **Wisdom** is the ability to increase effectiveness, in other words, a means by which to assess and improve efficiency and efficacy. Ultimately, an automatic way to add higher orders of value, which requires judgment.

In an imperfect world, we should be aware of the extent to which we allow missing information and its relevance to become part of the decision making process and the process of *turning knowledge into action*. The judgment function which evaluates effectiveness purely, leads to making unconscious mistakes or committing crimes by *turning information into action*.

5.12.2 *From Data to Action*

In the literature on organizational management, KHiA "know-how-in-action" [Swart (2011); Strati (2007); Cunliffe (2008); Empson (2001)] is a model for *turning knowledge into action.* Effective action depends on an effective judgment function and must be based on knowledge. The effectiveness of actions varies depending on the context which depends on the specific people, the place and the time in which they are applied. Knowledge is a static resource, which creates value within a context and through actions, at a specific place and time [Swart (2011); Spender (1996)].

Knowledge without context is data. Unused Knowledge in action does not create value. Knowledge/information/data that is used by the wrong people or in the wrong context may be detrimental to values, i.e. decrease the value. Some of the damaged values can be reconstructed (e.g., renewable resources) while some damaged values are not able to be reconstructed (e.g., non-renewable resources). Automated AI and Human decision action makers exploit and create value from actions. To preserve a balanced in the exchange of values from a local and a global perspective, an awareness of the dynamics and exchange of values should be part of any system or individual that plans to survive.

5.12.3 *Chinese Reading Room (CRR)*

Another interesting (and puzzling) aspect of decision making is the fact that one may not be fully aware of what is being carried out. That is, a task/goal can be pursued in an automated/careless fashion such as it lacks the due reflection. A good example of that is the Chinese Reading Room (CRR[4]) argument, as proposed by the American philosopher John Searle [Searle (1980)]. Despite the context not being the same, as Searle

[4]CRR is a thought experiment in which within a closed room communications are performed only through two outlets with the outside world. Inside there are dictionaries that translate all English words into Chinese and an actor (that could be a human or a Turing-test proof computer, it does not matter) whose sole deed is to perform translation tasks. So, if anyone that would like to have a translation from English to Chinese (it could be the opposite as well), will have the right result quickly ready on the second outlet, for all demands posed on the first. The interesting point is that to all outsiders, the room has somebody that can speak the foreign language. But it is not difficult to imagine that the actor could merely be performing character recognition (without necessarily having a clue on the semantics associated to the tasks). The authors add: it is also possible that the actor in the room may very well be misled about the proficiency possessed in the foreign language.

used it for arguing of mindful/mindful-less actions, in here we use it for claiming that absence of aspects/elements of a decision may lead to less rationality in the process. And similarly, to the context that Searle used the argument, the perspective is relevant for such judgment (that is, of less rationality). This emerges because the level of information of the person performing the task is different from another one observing the same task. Here the striking difference is that the unbalance can be both ways. For example, the decision maker may/may not be oblivious of certain relevant information, which could not be the same for the observer, and vice-versa. Overall, one can never be sure if a decision is completely rational in a simplistic manner. Although simple, the implication is strong: absolute rationality is impossible (also) to attain in an individual perspective. As a corollary of that conclusion, neither creation of value and even teaching of something are dependent on full rationality (as tasks can be carried out perfectly in the absence of mindful actors).

5.12.4 *The (Big) Data Paradox: Artificial Irrationality*

The buzzword "big data" often used in the context of the progress of technology. Companies and people collect data warehouses, as the more data the merrier. Data grows faster than the processes capable of making it useful, i.e., turning it into information, knowledge and effective actions. This leads to the oversubscription of data to limited processing capabilities. The abundance of information with a limited processing capability results in the incompleteness of effective information for a rational decision [Marwala (2013)].

Decision-making processes that are based on (too) Big-Data or (too) Small-Data results in bounded or limited rational decisions. When the data is too small, we have uncertainty caused by missing information and when it is too big we gain the same uncertainty but from the difficulty in processing and the collection of the data. The amount of data is good if it fits into the boundaries of the processing capabilities and time budget to make it useful. Human creators must be aware of the paradox of Big-Data when they create and release algorithms that are immortal, bounded rational, decision makers and obsessive data collectors into the economic market. Overabundance in practice turns AI from Artificial Intelligence into ***Artificial Irrationality***, that in many cases over confidently apply efficient, value-based actions in a value-bias human economy.

Consider the "paradox of choice", its causal relationship to analysis paralysis, and the opportunity cost that is discussed in detail in the book *The Paradox of Choice: Why more is less* by the psychologist, Prof. Barry Schwartz [Schwartz (2004)]. The book shows that rather than being a solution to human needs, the abundance of choices has, paradoxically, become a problem, despite the underlying assumption in the markets that more choice leads to better satisfaction of needs. For example, a customer considering buying new jeans now has hundreds of options to choose from. The opportunity gain from choosing a very good pair of jeans implies that you will not buy any of the hundreds of others. In the past, when a customer had to choose a pair of jeans from several available options, they could be sure that had they found the best fit (out of what was available) and hence were personally satisfied. But when the choice is now between hundreds of jeans, it becomes a less feasible and more complex problem for optimization. This now frequent problem is, in many cases, beyond the human processing capacity. To choose, customers have to rely on simple heuristics such as buying trendy jeans or buying all the options. To a lesser extent, computer based searches can experience the same problem, called the curse of dimensionality. In the context of AI and the Big Data problem, too much data may lead to artificial irrationality. Despite the possible speed of AI heuristic searches, the incapacity to process "Big" data creates in machines the paradox of choice derived from the inability to make rational decisions. However, although AI is also bounded, we argue that it can substantially stretch the bounds of rationality given the plethora of different techniques available for complex heuristic searches, e.g., Evolutionary Computation and Swarm Intelligence.

5.13 Conclusion

This chapter presents the cost-value and utility dimensions and dynamics. We discussed the economic terms: value, utility, costs, and their hidden dimensions. We discussed how economic values are changed by applying decisions and actions. We showed negative and positive cost, value, and utility changes and discussed net utility and the relativity of achievements. We presented the concept of value rational actions and the value rational judgment function. We introduced the idea of landmarks in sequential decision-making and planning and showed how they could represent economic values and dynamics in the decision-making process. We discussed the value of knowledge and showed the interplay between data, information, knowledge, and wisdom as summarized in the DIKW hierarchy. Finally, we discussed how data is used in action and emphasized some negative aspects of so-called Big Data.

In what follows, we define a value rational decision process and the role of net utility in rational decision-making. In the next chapter, we provide a solution to the famous St. Petersburg paradox based on the concepts of net utility and value rationality. We also adopt our findings on value rationality and the net utility of action for the OSP problem in the Planning AI field.

Chapter 6

Relative Net Utility and the St. Petersburg Paradox

The famous St. Petersburg Paradox shows that the theory of expected value does not capture the real-world economics of decision-making problems. Over the years, many economic theories have been developed that attempt to resolve the paradox and explain gaps in the economic value theory in the evaluation of economic decisions, the subjective utility of the expected outcomes, and risk aversion as observed in the game of the St. Petersburg Paradox. In this chapter, we use the concept of the relative net utility to resolve the St. Petersburg Paradox. Because the concept of net utility is able to explain both behavioral economics and the St. Petersburg Paradox, it can be deemed to be a universal approach to handling utility. This chapter demonstrates how the information content of the notion of net utility value allows us to capture a broader context of the impact of a decision's possible achievements. It discusses the conditions that the utility function must conform to in order to avoid the paradox. Combining these necessary conditions allows us to define the theorem of indifference in the evaluation of economic decisions and to present the role of relative net utility and net utility polarity in a value rational decision-making process.

6.1 Introduction

The St. Petersburg Paradox is a well-known problem in probability and decision theory. The St. Petersburg Paradox shows that the theory of expected value does not adequately capture the real-world economics of decision-making problems. The problem was formulated by Nicolas Bernoulli in 1713 and was introduced by his cousin, Daniel Bernoulli [Bernoulli (1738/1954)], to the Imperial Academy of Sciences in St. Petersburg as follows:

> *Peter tosses a coin and continues to do so until it lands on "heads" when it comes to the ground. He agrees to give Paul one ducat if he gets "heads" on the very first throw, two ducats if he gets it on the second, four if on the third, eight if on the fourth, and so on. With each additional throw, the number of ducats he must pay is doubled. Suppose we seek to determine the value of Paul's expectation.*

In the paper, "Exposition of a New Theory on the Measurement of Risk", [Bernoulli (1738/1954)] suggests a solution to the paradox that is based on the subjectivity of the utility of the expected outcome of the game. The St. Petersburg Paradox is referred to by [Samuelson (1977)] as "a dramatic and even over-dramatic case", and it illustrates that the real-world economics of decision-making problems are not captured by the theory of expected value. Throughout the economic literature, the St. Petersburg Paradox has been a key factor in the development of utility function theories, among many other ideas that were born from attempts at its resolution. Over the years, the question of a general utility function that captures arbitrary payoff functions has gained attention in a wide range of scientific and industrial fields and has been addressed by many experts. In his analysis of the financial and economic aspects of the St. Petersburg Paradox, [Libor (2011)] states that by using the analysis and applications of this paradox we could have avoided some catastrophic financial situations. Analyzing high-tech stocks [Székely and Richards (2004)] came to the same conclusion regarding the run-up in stock prices in the late 1990s and the subsequent declines in 2000.

Over the years, most of the solutions and attempts to explain the paradox have dealt with definitions of the subjective utility function and manipulations of the utility function to fit into real world, observed behavior ([Bernoulli (1738); Weber (1834); Fechner (1860); Von Neumann and Morgenstern (1947); Von Neumann *et al.* (2007)]). Bounded utility functions, bounded time or a bounded number of coin flip assumptions remain the most favored explanations of the paradox to date ([Menger (1934); Samuelson (1977); Menger (1979); Arrow (1970); Aumann (1977); Seidl (2013)]).

In this chapter, we take several perspectives on the paradox, including the cost-benefit and time perspectives. We start with an analysis of the paradox and then go on to present the solution attempts and the theories of expected utility that were developed from the resolution attempts. We define the concept of net utility and define a break-even point to be used as a reference point for net utility inference. We continue with a definition of investment (or game) position and discuss the net utility of changing the investment position and show how using the break-even as a reference point along with the concept of net utility allows us to capture the utility of alternative positions in the game. We then define a dynamic reference point and present an incremental net utility evaluation procedure to evaluate the alternative game positions. This allows us to present several new properties in the structure of the problem defined in the St. Petersburg Paradox and to establish the equilibrium position that maximizes the utility while preserving the invested resources. We formulate the Theorem of Indifference concerning the expected utility payoff. This allows us to discuss the opportunity cost and the time factor involved in investment (and St. Petersburg Paradox game). By incorporating time as a factor, the objective in the evaluation of the game becomes maximizing the expected net utility while minimizing the time invested in creating that net utility. We treat time as a resource and extend our observations to a general set of resources, establishing resources based criteria for break-even points where there is indifference concerning the expected value of the game.

Finally, we present the universal theory of net utility and show the role of net utility in a rational decision-making process and how the value of net utility allows for a more informed decision-making process. We present two conditions that the utility function must conform to in order to avoid the St. Petersburg Paradox. The first condition is the boundedness of the utility function. The second condition concerns the polarity of net utility, i.e., the net change of the utility value that is achieved due to the decision-making process. The polarity of the net utility of a decision-making process must be positive, relative to the starting point of the process. The relation point is the break-even position and the most basic break-even position in any investment is the decision not to buy in, i.e., doing nothing. Combining these necessary conditions allows us to define the theorem of indifference and to present the role of relative net utility in a value rational decision-making process. The term *value rational* refers to a decision-making process with net positive polarity, that is, a total net positive utility change. We conclude with the applications of our observation from the St. Petersburg Paradox and net utility in AI and Economic systems and point out some future research directions.

6.2 St. Petersburg Paradox

We begin by presenting a table summarizing the details of the game in Table 6.1. In Table 6.1 each row shows the number of coin tosses that occur until Paul gets "heads" and the game ends. The first column in Table 6.1 represents the number, k, of coin tosses. The second column represents the probability of getting "heads" on k coin toss. The third column represents the reward derived from getting "heads" on k toss. The fourth column represents the expected payoff from getting "heads" on k toss, which is calculated by multiplying the probability of getting "heads" on k toss by the respective value of the obtained reward.

Table 6.1: Illustration of the St. Petersburg Paradox game in terms of number of tosses (k), the probability of getting "heads" on toss k, the respective prize, and the respective expected payoff value.

k (num of throws)	$P(k) = \frac{1}{2^k}$	Prize	Expected Payoff
1	$\frac{1}{2}$	1	$\frac{1}{2}$
2	$\frac{1}{4}$	2	$\frac{1}{2}$
3	$\frac{1}{8}$	4	$\frac{1}{2}$
4	$\frac{1}{16}$	8	$\frac{1}{2}$
5	$\frac{1}{32}$	16	$\frac{1}{2}$
6	$\frac{1}{64}$	32	$\frac{1}{2}$
7	$\frac{1}{128}$	64	$\frac{1}{2}$
...	...	...	...

The mathematical value of a fair price for playing the game is the accumulation of expected payoffs,

$$\frac{1}{2} + \frac{1}{2} + \frac{1}{2} + \frac{1}{2} .... = \infty.$$

This implies that a player should be willing to pay any price to participate in the game. However, most agents will only pay a small amount of money to participate in the game, contradicting the prediction of the expected value theory. This is the paradox. While most of the literature talks about the paradox of the infinite value of the game, there is an additional paradox which has been ignored. The minimum win if one chooses to participate in this game is 1 ducat even though utility theory expects a win of a half a ducat. This is because the definition of expected utility is a first-order approximation of the real utility. This can be viewed as the first-order components of a Taylor expansion of the real utility.

The failure of the expected value theory to predict the real economic value of the game has attracted many researchers over the years and served an important role in the development of economic theories. A survey of the history of ideas, both theoretical and empirical, to explain and solve the paradox was conducted by [Samuelson (1977); Neugebauer *et al.* (2010); Seidl (2013); Cox *et al.* (2019)]. The explanations of this well established challenge to the expected utility theory, concentrated on diminishing marginal utility function, treating small probabilities as zero, the boundedness of utility functions, time boundedness or a bounded number of coin flips.

The concept of utility function was first introduced by [Bernoulli (1738/1954)] to represent the subjective value of winnings and is also referred to as the moral value or the moral hope by Gabriel Cremer in Bernoulli's paper. Gabriel Cremer and Daniel Bernoulli attempted to explain the paradox by decreasing the marginal utility and suggested using a concave transformation to solve the paradox. Cremer suggested using the square root of the original utility function and Bernoulli suggested using a natural logarithm to solve the paradox. The subjectivity assumption was experimentally confirmed [Weber (1834); Fechner (1860)] and formalized in the Expected Utility model [Von Neumann and Morgenstern (1947); Von Neumann *et al.* (2007)]. However, some experimental works have shown that the concepts of marginal utility and treating of small probabilities as zero cannot explain the paradox but do support Bernoulli's observations of risk-aversion tendency in decision-making [Cox *et al.* (2011); Neugebauer *et al.* (2010); Cox *et al.* (2019)]. Bounded utility functions or a bounded number of coin flips remain the most favored explanations of the paradox to date.

[Menger (1934)] work on the St. Petersburg Paradox showed that the marginal diminishing utility transformation is not sufficient since the rewards can increase faster than the rate at which the utility diminishes. This observation led to the conclusion that boundedness of the utility function or coin flips is a necessary condition to prevent the occurrence of a

St. Petersburg Paradox [Menger (1934, 1979); Arrow (1970); Aumann (1977); Seidl (2013)]. The time boundedness assumption [Brito (1975); Aumann (1977); Cowen and High (1988)] suggests that limited time will bind the utility function. Even infinite rewards will create finite utility with the natural bound of individual life. In this chapter, in the context of boundedness in the St. Petersburg paradox, we discuss the basic bounds of the budget and time of the player and provide a framework for tracing and setting bounds on the net utility change between alternative game scenarios, i.e., the boundedness of the incremental change in net utility rather than the boundedness of the utility function outcomes.

Non-Expected Utility theories were developed due to the paradox discovered in the expected utility theory. These include: the dual theory of choice under risk [Yaari (1987)], prospect theory [Kahneman and Tversky (1979)] and the cumulative prospect theory [Tversky and Kahneman (1992)]. These theories do not address the St. Petersburg Paradox, however, they do provide several important observations that can be used to solve the paradox.

The concept of a reference point and relative utility is observed in prospect theory. Prospect theory assumes the existence of a reference point for the perception of decision outcomes as losses or gains. Recent work by [Werner and Zank (2019)] provides a survey on models with reference points and suggests a model for revealing the reference point in prospect theory. In the next section, we use prospect theory's observations on the reference point and relative utility to build a framework for revealing dynamic reference points for net utility change of game positions in the St. Petersburg Paradox, which we exploit in order to choose a policy and evaluate the game. The theoretic contribution to this chapter suggests an explanation for the experimental observations in the expected utility theory and behavioral economics on reference points and relative utility as well as risk-aversion and diminishing marginal utility.

6.2.1 *Petersburg Game Decision-Making Process Diagram*

Representations of the game as in Table 6.1 is common in most discussions about St. Petersburg Paradox, although they are missing a few important details regarding the decision-making process of participating in the game and the evaluation of possible scenarios in the game. In what follows, we take a deeper look at the decision-making process in the St. Petersburg Paradox game and provide a diagram to illustrate it.

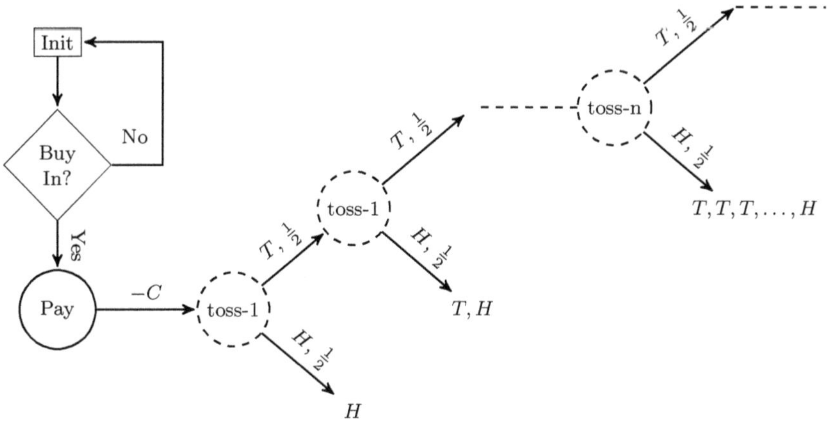

	$t = 0$	$t = 1$	$t = n$
	toss $- 1$	*toss* $- 2$	*toss* $- n$

$B = b$	$b - c$	$b - c + 1$	$b - c + 2^{n-1}$
Init Pos.	*Buy In*	*toss* $- 2$	*toss* $- n$

$E = 0$	$\frac{1}{2}$	$\frac{1}{2}$	$\frac{1}{2}$
Init Pos.	*Buy In*	*toss* $- 2$	*toss* $- n$

$E(B) = b$	$b - c + \frac{1}{2}$	$b - c + \frac{1}{2}$	$b - c + \frac{1}{2}$
Init Pos.	*Buy In*	*toss* $- 2$	*toss* $- n$

Fig. 6.1: An illustration of a single game as described in the St. Petersburg Paradox. The game is illustrated by a decision-event diagram on a scale of time, budget, expected value and expected total budget associated with achievable positions in the game.

Figure 6.1 illustrates an event-decision diagram of a single St. Petersburg Paradox game as suggested to Paul by Peter. The diagram represents the game scenarios and the decision process that Paul has to undertake in the game. Generally speaking, the process constitutes the various states in the game, one decision, and one deterministic action followed by a sequence of stochastic events. The process starts from an initial state as illustrated by a rectangle that represents the position before the start of the game. A decision state is illustrated by a rhombus and represents Paul's decision of whether or not to participate in the game. An action state is illustrated by a circle and represents the action of Paul's payment to Peter in the event that he decides to participate in the game. A sequence of stochastic events, illustrated by dashed circles, represent the sequence of tosses until the coin lands on "heads".

The game as illustrated in Fig. 6.1 can be analyzed from different time, value and budget perspectives. In what follows, we will cover some of the main perspectives used to analyze the game in order to estimate the expected value of the game.

We will now take a closer look at the different game scenarios in the St. Petersburg Paradox which are represented by the diagram in Fig. 6.1. Paul's budget at the initial state of the game is $B = b$ ducats. Peter suggests that Paul participate in the game which leaves Paul with two choices: If Paul declines Peter's offer, he stays in his initial position with the initial budget of b ducats. If he accepts Peter's offer, he has to pay c ducats to participate in the game. Once Paul decides to buy into the game, the decision phase is completed. The action of paying for the game is then applied and the reward is determined according to the outcome of a sequence of stochastic events. By stochastic events, we refer to the sequence of coin tosses that takes place until the coin lands on "heads".

Given the terms of the game, Paul can calculate the expected **break-even point** for the amount of money c that was paid to participate in the game, within his budget restrictions $c < B$, that he is willing and able to pay to participate. Based on the fact that only one of the presented scenarios can occur in any one game, Paul chooses his expected position based different prospective scenarios, i.e., his payoff expectation for a break-even or an improved position from participation in the game. As illustrated in this example, the expected value of each possible sequence of tosses that ends with "heads" is $\frac{1}{2}$ which can be calculated by multiplying the scenario probability by the related prize as illustrated in Table 6.1. Hence, for each sequence of tosses that ends with "heads", the expected break-even value is $\frac{1}{2}$. This is without taking the cost of time into account. Taking the time invested in the game into account (which can be represented as a monetary value through lost alternatives of investments also referred to as the opportunity cost), we can formulate a decreasing utility function. The rate of the decrease is dependent on the alternative investments. Paul is aware of his evaluation methods for alternative investments (or opportunities).

6.3 Net Utility and St. Petersburg Paradox

6.3.1 *Evaluation With Respect to the Break-Even Point*

To put it simply, the break-even point is the point at which the costs we pay for participating in the game are equal to the benefits that are derived from participating in the game. The first and the most basic break-even point in the game is the initial state which is achieved by the decision to not participate in the game at all.

6.3.2 *The Decision-Choice of Not Participating in the Game*

The decision to do nothing, depicted in decision nodes "Buy In" in the game diagram in Fig. 6.1, is always implicitly available. To evaluate the alternatives and the expected outcomes of the game, we set the decision-choice of doing nothing, i.e. not participating in the game, as the first and the most basic reference point.

The reference point of "doing nothing" allows us to define the break-even point of the game. When we take the costs of participating in the game and the budget of the participant into account, the reference point of "doing nothing" is the break-even point. We define the break-even point as follows.

Definition 6.1. Given a sequence of events $e_0, e_1, e_2 \ldots e_k$ a cost function $c(e_i)$ and a value function $u(e_i)$ for each $i \leq k$ the break even point of the game BEP occurs when $\sum_{i=1}^{k} u(e_i) = \sum_{i=1}^{k} c(e_i)$.

We define the break-even point as the utility achieved in the last event (heads on a coin toss) of a sequence of events. The cost, however, is paid at the initial point of the sequence of events with the decision to participate in the game. The expected payoff depends on both "tails" and "heads". The number of "tails" determines the payoff whereas "heads" is a critical indicator of when the game is stopped and the payoff is effected.

Table 6.2 extends Table 6.1 with the details of the initial position at the initial state, which is depicted in nodes "init" in the game diagram in Fig. 6.1. The additional row "Init/Fold" in Table 6.2 represents the pre-decision state where there is no reward and no costs are paid to participate in the game. It also represents the decision "Fold", that is the decision not to participate in the game, in which case the reward, as well as the expected payoff, are 0.

Table 6.2: Illustration of the St. Petersburg Paradox game as in Table 6.1 with the initial position description added, colored in gray, which describes the "init" state and the decision of not participating the game.

k (num of throws)	$P(k) = \frac{1}{2^k}$	Prize	Expected Payoff
Init/Fold	–	0	0
1	$\frac{1}{2}$	1	$\frac{1}{2}$
2	$\frac{1}{4}$	2	$\frac{1}{2}$
3	$\frac{1}{8}$	4	$\frac{1}{2}$
4	$\frac{1}{16}$	8	$\frac{1}{2}$
5	$\frac{1}{32}$	16	$\frac{1}{2}$
6	$\frac{1}{64}$	32	$\frac{1}{2}$
7	$\frac{1}{128}$	64	$\frac{1}{2}$
...	...	...	...

6.3.3 *Net Utility of Changing Position*

In what follows, we present an incremental evaluation approach to finding the optimal position in the St. Petersburg Paradox game.

Using the Oxford dictionary definition [Dictionary (2008)] we define a Game Position as follows:

Definition 6.2. A Game Position is:

- A person's point of view or attitude towards the game payoff.
- The extent to which an investor, dealer, or speculator has made a commitment in the market by buying or selling securities.

Definition 6.3. Given the set of game positions $p_0, p_1 ... p_k ...$, the utility of game position p_k in the St. Petersburg Paradox, $u(p_k)$ is the expected payoff of a game with k coin flips.

Our initial reference point is the break-even point of the initial state with a value of 0 (no costs or benefit produced in the game). Using our initial reference point, we can evaluate Paul's other applicable positions in the game with respect to the initial break-even point.

We define the net utility of game position with respect to a reference point as follows.

Definition 6.4. Given a set of game positions $p_0, p_1...p_k...$, the net utility of game position p_k with respect to a reference position p_i is the net change in the expected payoff, i.e., $u(p_k) - u(p_i)$.

Assuming the initial position of $u(p_0) = 0$, we have a special case in which the utility of game position p_k is also the net change in the expected payoff from the initial position where $i = 0$ and equals, $u(p_k)$. However, in most real-world scenarios, we cannot assume a zero utility for the state in which we consider an investment or gambling decision. Hence, we cannot assume that considering the utility of an arbitrary game position will reflect the real impact of obtaining it. In what follows, we show how the informativeness of net utility allows us to capture a broader context of the impact of a decision's possible achievements.

Table 6.3: Illustration of the St. Petersburg Paradox game with the initial position details (colored in gray row) and a "Net Utility" with respect to initial position (colored in gray column).

k (num of throws)	$P(k) = \frac{1}{2^k}$	Prize	Expected Payoff	Net Utility
Fold	–	–	0	0
1	$\frac{1}{2}$	1	$\frac{1}{2}$	$\frac{1}{2}$
2	$\frac{1}{4}$	2	$\frac{1}{2}$	$\frac{1}{2}$
3	$\frac{1}{8}$	4	$\frac{1}{2}$	$\frac{1}{2}$
4	$\frac{1}{16}$	8	$\frac{1}{2}$	$\frac{1}{2}$
5	$\frac{1}{32}$	16	$\frac{1}{2}$	$\frac{1}{2}$
6	$\frac{1}{64}$	32	$\frac{1}{2}$	$\frac{1}{2}$
7	$\frac{1}{128}$	64	$\frac{1}{2}$	$\frac{1}{2}$
...	...	...	...	...

Table 6.3 expands on Table 6.2 with the details of the net utility of changing position with respect to the initial state. As Table 6.3 shows, in terms of the net utility with respect to our initial position, there is indifference with regard to each position with $k > 0$.

6.3.4 *Dynamic Reference Point for Net Utility of Changing Position*

Using our initial reference point, we can evaluate Paul's other applicable positions in the game and update the reference point dynamically when a reference point with better utility is found.

Table 6.4: Illustration of the St. Petersburg Paradox game with the initial position details (colored in gray row) and a "Relative (dynamic) Net Utility" with respect to best position found so far (colored in gray column). Highlighted in yellow is the first (and last) beneficial changing position decision.

k (num of throws)	$P(k) = \frac{1}{2^k}$	Prize	Expected Payoff	Net Utility	Relative Net Utility
Fold	–	–	0	0	0
1	$\frac{1}{2}$	1	$\frac{1}{2}$	$\frac{1}{2}$	$\mathbf{\frac{1}{2}}$
2	$\frac{1}{4}$	2	$\frac{1}{2}$	$\frac{1}{2}$	0
3	$\frac{1}{8}$	4	$\frac{1}{2}$	$\frac{1}{2}$	0
4	$\frac{1}{16}$	8	$\frac{1}{2}$	$\frac{1}{2}$	0
5	$\frac{1}{32}$	16	$\frac{1}{2}$	$\frac{1}{2}$	0
6	$\frac{1}{64}$	32	$\frac{1}{2}$	$\frac{1}{2}$	0
7	$\frac{1}{128}$	64	$\frac{1}{2}$	$\frac{1}{2}$	0
...	...	...	...	...	...

Table 6.4 expands on Table 6.3 with the details of the net utility of changing position with respect to the best position found so far. Figure 6.2 depicts a pseudo-code of an incremental net utility evaluation with a dynamic reference point which puts our observations on the net utility change in the St. Petersburg Paradox into practice.

In the next section, we present the Theorem of Indifference as well as the resource preserving, tie-breaking decision criteria that allows us to define the termination criteria for the incremental net utility evaluation procedure.

```
Incremental-Net-Utility-Evaluation
 RefPos := 0        // Initialize Reference Position
 CurrPos := 0       // Initialize Current Position
 NUC := 0           // Initialize Net Utility Change
 NUC* := 0          // Initialize Best Net Utility Change so far
 loop:
   CurrPos = CurrPos + 1
   NUC = EU(CurrPos) - EU(RefPos)    // Calculate Expected Net Utility Change
   if NUC > NUC*:
     NUC* = NUC
     RefPos = CurrPos
   if Termination-criteria:
     return NUC*, RefPos
```

Fig. 6.2: Incremental net utility evaluation with dynamic reference point update.

The Theorem of Indifference will allow us to find the point of equilibrium. The net utility change and the resource preserving, tie-breaking decision criteria will allow us to define an *efficient* evaluation termination point within the equilibrium zone.

6.4 Theorem of Indifference and Resource Preserving Tie-Breaking Decision Criteria

In the St. Petersburg game, we pursue an optimal position from which to improve the net utility. Table 6.4 shows that the increase in the number of coin flips (the incremental change in game position) after the initial coin flip, results in no change in the expected utility, with respect to the reference point. Although the Payoff be increasing with each coin flip, the probability of achieving the payoff is decreasing at a rate that preserves the same expected utility for each game position. This results in the increase of risk in the game, respective to the number of coin flips (i.e. the respective game positions) without the justification of improved expected utility. We now explore how we can find a game position that achieves equilibrium in the game, meaning a position that preserves resources without damaging the potential expected utility. Note that in what follows, we optimize the evaluation process used for choosing Paul's game position and in doing so we find the resource preserving position among positions that are equally attractive in terms of the expected utility.[1]

[1]This can be seen as a process of planning a solution, i.e. planning a decision in the case of the St. Petersburg Paradox.

The evaluation process used for choosing a position in the game, described in Fig. 6.2, consists of the evaluation actions of incremental change and evaluation of game positions. Treating the evaluation process as a sequential action application allows us to adopt action planning methods. Theorem 6.1 was suggested by [Muller and Karpas (2018a)] to solve problems of sequential action planning in which the objective is choosing a sequence of actions to maximize agent utility under budget restrictions. It allows us to optimize a sequence of actions that leads to an effective net positive change in utility by truncating actions that exploit resources (such as time) and do not lead to a net positive utility value change. This will then allow us to define efficient termination criteria for the incremental net utility evaluation procedure (Fig. 6.2). Put simply, the Theorem states that; for each sequence of actions π, there is a sub-sequence π' that; (i) ends with a net positive utility value action (the net utility of the action of changing game position in the St. Petersburg Paradox), (ii) that is at most as costly as π, and (iii) and is at least as valuable as π.

Theorem 6.1 (Theorem of Indifference). *Given a game Π with an additive utility function u, for any policy π for Π such that $u(s[\![\pi]\!]) > u(s_0)$, there is a prefix π' of π such that:*

(1) $u(s_0[\![\pi]\!]) \leq u(s_0[\![\pi']\!])$, and
(2) for the last action a_{last} along π', we have $u(a_{last}) > 0$.

Proof. The proof is by induction on the plan length n. For $n = 1$, we have $\pi = \langle a_1 \rangle$, and since $u(s[\![\pi]\!]) > u(s_0)$, the action a_1 has a positive net utility value. Hence, $\pi' = \pi$ satisfies the claims. Assuming that the claim holds for $n \geq 1$, we now prove it for $n + 1$.

Considering a plan $\pi = \langle a_1, \ldots, a_{n+1} \rangle$, for $i \in [n + 1]$, let π_i denote the prefix of π consisting of its first i actions. If the last action a_{n+1} along π has a positive net utility value, then we are done with $\pi' = \pi$. Otherwise, if a_{n+1} has either negative or zero net utility value, then $u(s[\![\pi]\!]) > u(s_0)$ in particular implies $u(s[\![\pi_n]\!]) > u(s_0)$. If π' is a prefix of π_n that satisfies the lemma by our assumption of induction, then π' also satisfies the lemma with respect to π since $u(\pi') \geq u(s[\![\pi_n]\!]) \geq u(s[\![\pi]\!])$. □

6.4.1 *Tie-Breaking Decision Criteria*

Although the expected utility is the same for all alternatives when it comes to choosing positions in the game, it would be wrong to state that a rational player would play infinite games. In terms of the expected value, there is no benefit to changing position in the game, i.e., the net utility obtained from changing position from one toss, is zero. At the same time, the implicit costs can be enormous in terms of time. These costs in terms of time mean that changing position from one toss to any other position is not optimal. In summary, using logical principles, a rational choice among equal opportunities would optimize the cost of time invested in each opportunity.

6.4.2 *Utility Tie-Breaking With Time Factor*

As Table 6.3 shows, there is no difference in the dimension of benefit among the alternatives that Paul can choose from. In such a case, Paul can choose a random position or find a tie-breaking criterion that is measured in different dimensions, for instance, the dimension of time. Given two alternatives of optional St. Petersburg games, game A and B, with equal expected utility, $u(A) = u(B)$, a rational player would choose the game that optimizes the factor of time.

We assume that each toss has a time duration and we annotate the duration of a single toss with ϵ. Given a St. Petersburg game A that constitutes of k tosses, with $k > 0$, the duration of game A is $k\epsilon$. In a St. Petersburg game B that consists of i tosses where $i < k$, the duration of game B is $i\epsilon$ and $i\epsilon < k\epsilon$. Suppose that in terms of utility there is no difference between games A and B, i.e., $u(A) = u(B)$. In terms of time, it is obvious that game B is preferable. Since in terms of the cost of time, game B is preferable to game B, a rational player that both maximizes the utility and optimizes time would choose game B, which is time preserving.

We now extend the tie breaking point to a set of game alternatives. Let a set

$$STP = X_1, X_2, X_3 \dots X_k$$

be a set of St. Petersburg games with respective expected utilities of

$$u(X_1), u(X_2), u(X_3) \dots u(X_k)$$

and respective time duration

$$t(X_1), t(X_2), t(X_3) \dots t(X_k).$$

Let the expected utility of each two games in the set be equal, i.e. for each $X_i, X_j \in STP$ holds $u(X_i) = u(X_j)$. Suppose

$$t(X_1) < t(X_2) < t(X_3) \dots < t(X_k)$$

a rational player would pursue game X_1, which optimizes the time required to achieve the expected utility. In other words, among games that are equally attractive in terms of their expected utility, a rational player would pursue the time-preserving alternative which is the least number of tosses.

6.4.3 *From Time to Resource-Based Utility Tie-Breaking Point*

A tie-breaking point that is based on the factor of time, can be easily extended to a general case of resource-consuming actions or games. We treat time as a resource when we define the tie-breaking point and pursue the scenario that preserves this resource from scenarios with equal net utility change. The logic of preserving time is the same for preserving any other resource.

6.5 The Net Utility in (Bounded) Rational Decision-Making Process

In this section, we define and discuss the conditions that are necessary for a value rational decision-making process. The term *value rational*, refers to a decision-making process with a net positive utility polarity, that is, a total net positive utility change. We start with a review of the rational and bounded rational decision-making processes. We then present two conditions that the utility function must conform in order to avoid the St. Petersburg Paradox. The first condition is the boundedness of the utility function. The second condition concerns the net utility polarity, i.e., the net change of the utility value that is achieved as a result of the outcome of the decision-making process. The net utility polarity of a decision-making process must be positive relative to the starting position. The reference point is the break-even position, where the most basic break-even position in any investment is the decision not to "buy in", i.e., doing nothing. Combining these necessary conditions allows us to define the theorem of indifference (6.1) and to present the role of the relative net utility in a rational or sequential rational decision-making process.

6.5.1 *Value Rational and Bounded Rational Decision-Making Process*

Problem solving, planning, and decision-making processes constitute ordered decision choices and decision actions [Kriger and Barnes (1992);

Marwala (2015)]. Instantaneous decision-choices are the atomic units that a decision's action is compose of. An optimized decision results in a global maximization of utility [DeGroot (2005); Berger (2013)]. ***Decision actions*** can be ***rational*** or ***irrational***. Based on the work of [Marwala (2015)], we define a decision action as rational if it results in a globally optimum outcome and is based on logical principles and derived from complete and relevant information. A decision based on irrelevant or incomplete information is irrational, and cannot lead to a global optimum solution. A rational decision-making process comprises of rational decision actions, and the entire process is optimized in time and results in a global utility optimum [Grüne-Yanoff (2012); Marwala (2014, 2015)]. The quantification of the extent of this irrationality is what is called bounded rationality.

The concept of ***bounded rationality*** [Simon (1957, 1990, 1991)] explains irrational decision-making based on incomplete data analysis which leads to incomplete information for making a decision. The concept of ***Flexible-bounded rationality*** is based on the fact that advancements in AI and machine data analysis make the bounds of rationality flexible ([Marwala (2013)]).

The rational decision-making process constitutes a sequential (interrelated) application of rational decision actions. ***Rationality is not dividable*** [Marwala (2013)], a process of applying a sequence of depended decision actions cannot be partly rational and partly irrational. Even one irrational action makes the entire decision-making process irrational and compromises the attainment of a globally optimal solution. The imperfection of information in a single decision action leads to the entire decision-making process being irrational with a sub-optimal end, in time or utility. Advanced information analysis methods can assist in repairing (partially) the imperfection of information to lead to a (partial) rationalization of a decision-making process.

We now present two conditions that the utility function must conform to in order to allow for a value rational decision-making process.

6.5.2 *The Boundedness of the Utility Function*

[Bassett Jr. (1987); Samuelson (1977)] provide detailed historical reviews on the boundedness of utility conditions. The first researcher to observe the necessity of a bounded utility function to avoid the paradox was [Menger (1934)]. Menger's observations were later extended and proven by [Arrow (1970)]. The paradox was extensively investigated in the work of [Menger

(1934)],[2] which among other things devised the Menger theorem, which can be described as follows:

Theorem 6.2. *A path has a finite price with the use of utility function $f(x)$ for any sequence of possible payoffs $\langle a_1, \ldots, a_n \ldots \rangle$ when and only when function $f(x)$ is limited.*

[Arrow (1970)] proves the utility boundedness theorem.

Theorem 6.3 (Utility Boundedness Theorem). *Any utility function that satisfies the conditions of the Expected Utility Theorem must be bounded from above and below.*

The Expected Utility Theorem [Arrow (1970); Samuelson (1977); Bassett Jr. (1987)] provides a condition for preference among two actions.

Theorem 6.4 (Expected Utility Theorem). *It is possible to define a real-valued utility function over actions [or decisions with their implied respective possible outcomes, each with specifiable probabilities], with the following properties:*

(1) $a_1 > -a_2$ *[i.e., action 1 definitely preferred to action 2] if and only if* $u(a_1) > u(a_2)$
(2) $u(a) = E[u(a[\![s]\!])]$ *[i.e., equals the expected value of utilities of* **outcomes** *implied by action a].*

Assuming state s_1 to be the original state, the expected utility of action a is the expected utility value of the target state s_2, i.e., the utility of the state that is achieved after the application of an action a. In simple terms, a_1 is preferable to a_2 if the expected value of utilities of outcomes of the application of a_1 in state s, $E[u(a_1[\![s]\!])]$, are greater than the application of a_2 in state s, $E[u(a_2[\![s]\!])]$.

Note that the expected utility theorem takes the utility of the target state, $u(s_2)$ into account, but not the utility of the original state $u(s_1)$. The theorem captures a process of strictly positive net utility action (or decision) application. That is, each action applied necessarily improves the state in which it is applied. However, most real-world decision-making processes, and in particular, sequential decision-making processes, involve the application of actions or sequences of actions of negative utility polarity.

[2] The paper was translated into English in [Menger (1979)].

Such actions may worsen/decrease the utility of the state in which it is applied.[3] In such cases, the theorem provides a recommendation of preferring actions over other actions, although they both might be negative in total net terms.

Let us consider the following example to stress this point. Consider an original state s_1 with two actions a_1 and a_2 applicable in state s_1;

(1) $u(a_1) = E[u(a_1[\![s_1]\!])] = E[u(s_2)] = 100$
(2) $u(a_2) = E[u(a_2[\![s_1]\!])] = E[u(s_3)] = 150$

The expected value of utility outcomes of applying action a_2 are greater than those of applying a_1. Using the theorem of expected utility, we will choose to apply action a_2 to achieve a greater utility outcome. It should be noted, to that end, that a piece of available information that is essential for the decision-making process is neglected. The utility of the original state is not incorporated into the preference system that is implied by the theorem of expected utility.

Now let us consider the utility of the original state s_1 and incorporate it into our preferences system. We are interested in the net utility polarity in our example and consider several different utility values for the original state s_1 as follows:

(1) $u(s_1) = 75$
  (a) $E[u(a_1[\![s_1]\!])] = 100 > u(s_1)$
  (b) $E[u(a_2[\![s_1]\!])] = 150 > u(s_1)$
(2) $u(s_1) = 100$
  (a) $E[u(a_1[\![s_1]\!])] = 100 = u(s_1)$
  (b) $E[u(a_2[\![s_1]\!])] = 150 > u(s_1)$
(3) $u(s_1) = 125$
  (a) $E[u(a_1[\![s_1]\!])] = 100 < u(s_1)$
  (b) $E[u(a_2[\![s_1]\!])] = 150 > u(s_1)$
(4) $u(s_1) = 150$
  (a) $E[u(a_1[\![s_1]\!])] = 100 < u(s_1)$
  (b) $E[u(a_2[\![s_1]\!])] = 150 = u(s_1)$

[3]The discussion is about negative utility, not the costs of actions that can be seen as investments.

(5) $u(s_1) = 175$

(a) $E[u(a_1[\![s_1]\!])] = 100 < u(s_1)$
(b) $E[u(a_2[\![s_1]\!])] = 150 < u(s_1)$

When the focus is on the outcome of actions, we can compare action a_1 to a_2 in terms of their outcomes, but we miss the larger impact of the action, which is easily captured using the terms of net utility. It is obvious that a_2 is preferable to a_1 with regards to their outcomes. However, are we asking the right question? Our simple example shows that although the outcome of a_2 is greater than the outcome of a_1, in relative net change terms, it does not imply that we should apply either of them since keeping the current position and doing nothing, results in a better outcome than doing anything. The theorem of indifference (6.1) captures exactly this phenomena in sequential scenarios. The theorem exploits the polarity of the net change in sequential scenarios as the bound for the utility function in order to avoid the St. Petersburg Paradox. In the next section, we take a closer look at the role of net utility polarity in the rational decision-making process and reformulate the theorem of expected utility to the theorem on expected net utility.

6.5.3 *The Expected Net Utility Theorem: Net Utility Polarity in Value Rational Decision-Making Process*

The value rational decision-making process (or game/investment) has a net positive utility polarity, i.e., it leads to total net positive change. In particular, the last decision (or position/event) of any value rational decision-making process has to be of net positive polarity.

Based on Theorem 6.4, we define the expected net utility theorem as follows: The expected net utility theorem is defined in terms of **total change of utility** rather than the **outcomes** solely as in Theorem 6.4. In practice, we define the utility of action as the difference between the action's precondition state and the outcomes of the action, rather than the action's outcomes alone. Evaluation of the utility function in terms of expected net utility theorem provides a more informative picture of the real impact of the utility function of actions/decisions. The real impact of an action is not fully captured in the outcomes of the action and can vary in terms of utility depending on the state in which the action is applied.

Theorem 6.5 (The Expected Net Utility Theorem). *Given a state s_{pre} and an action a applicable in state s_{pre}, s_{eff} is the state that is obtained* *with an application of action a. It is possible to define a real-valued utility function over actions [or decisions with their implied respective possible outcomes, each with specifiable probabilities], with the following properties:*

(1) $a_1 > -a_2$ *[i.e., action 1 definitely preferred to action 2] if and only if* $u(a_1) > u(a_2)$

(2) $u(a) = E[u(a[\![s]\!]) - u(s)]$ *[i.e., equals the expected value of* **the total net change** *of utilities implied by action a].*

(3) for an action a, the **net utility** *of a is*
$u(a) = \sum_{v \in \mathcal{V}(\mathsf{eff}(a))} [u(\mathsf{eff}(a)[v]) - u(\mathsf{pre}(a)[v])]$.

The Expected Net Utility Theorem is more informative since it exploits the utility information compactly and allows us to effectively (and efficiently) put this information into practice, i.e., to conduct a more informative preference system. A preference system that is based on the Expected Net Utility Theorem takes the net utility polarity of actions into account and allows us to compare the outcomes of actions as well as the total net change achieved by the actions. The following example shows the informativeness of a preference system based on net utility. In some cases, actions with positive outcomes might bring negative utility in net terms.

(1) $u(s_1) = 75$

 (a) $E[u(a_1[\![s_1]\!]) - u(s_1)] = 25$
 (b) $E[u(a_2[\![s_1]\!]) - u(s_1)] = 75$

(2) $u(s_1) = 100$

 (a) $E[u(a_1[\![s_1]\!]) - u(s_1)] = 0$
 (b) $E[u(a_2[\![s_1]\!]) - u(s_1)] = 50$

(3) $u(s_1) = 125$

 (a) $E[u(a_1[\![s_1]\!]) - u(s_1)] = -25$
 (b) $E[u(a_2[\![s_1]\!]) - u(s_1)] = 25$

(4) $u(s_1) = 150$

 (a) $E[u(a_1[\![s_1]\!]) - u(s_1)] = -50$
 (b) $E[u(a_2[\![s_1]\!]) - u(s_1)] = 0$

(5) $u(s_1) = 175$

 (a) $E[u(a_1[\![s_1]\!]) - u(s_1)] = -75$
 (b) $E[u(a_2[\![s_1]\!]) - u(s_1)] = -25$

6.5.4 *The Theorem of Indifference in Value Rational Decision-Making Process*

Combining the boundedness (Section 6.5.2) and the net utility polarity (Section 6.5.3) conditions for utility function, we formulated the theorem of indifference (Theorem 6.1) that recognizes the suffix of a sequence of events, decisions, or changes of position that do not bring positive change (that is, they are not of net positive polarity). The theorem of indifference combines the two conditions over the utility function in a sequential decision-making process in a sequential game/investment. It puts into practice the algorithm of incremental utility improvement evaluation provided in Fig. 6.2.

6.6 The Universal Concept of Net Utility

In 1901 [Planck (1901)] published a paper that explained the black body radiation problem by assuming that energy comes in the form of little packets called quanta. In 1905 [Einstein (1905)] published a paper that explained the photoelectric effect using the concept of quanta as proposed by Max Planck. Because the theory of quanta was able to explain two different phenomena, it was assumed to be a universal theory of nature. The concept of quanta that proposed the packaging of energy gave rise to the theory of quantum mechanics. The manner in which we solved the St. Petersburg Paradox is through the use of the concept of the net utility. The same concept of the net utility was used in behavioral economics by [Kahneman and Tversky (1979)]. In prospect theory, the importance of relative utility is observed in addition to absolute utility. The concept of net utility is useful in different disciplines such as, prescriptive economics (e.g., the St. Petersburg Paradox) and descriptive economics (e.g., behavioral economics). Hence, the concept of net utility should be used as a universal concept for understanding economics in the same way as the theory of energy quanta was assumed to be a universal theory when it explained both the black body radiation problem and the photoelectric effect. In classical economics, we define a rational agent as an agent that maximizes its utility. In light of the universal concept of utility, this is the wrong approach to defining a rational agent. Rather, we define a rational agent as an agent that maximizes its net utility. Using this definition, one is able to explain people's behavior as is done in the prospect theory. One is also able to explain the St. Petersburg Paradox.

6.7 Conclusion

This chapter proposed the use of the concept of net utility to successfully explain the St. Petersburg Paradox. The concept of net utility or relative utility was first experimentally observed by Kahneman and Tversky and has had a profound impact on the field of behavioral economics. This chapter, furthermore, concludes that the concept of net utility explains value more universally than the concept of nominal utility. The remainder of the book is focused on applications of this concept.

Chapter 7

Value Rational Planning

Oversubscription planning is the problem of choosing an action (also referred to as operator) sequence that reaches a state with an as high a utility as possible, given a budget for total action cost. In this work, we address oversubscription planning generalized to arbitrary additive utility functions over a finite-domain representation. We use the concepts of the net and gross utility of an action to provide a more comprehensive context for achievement evaluation and to with negative utility values. By focusing on net utility, we can capture relationships between sets of state variables and handle negative interactions that occur in the non-negative utility setting as well. We use the notions of gross and net utility to examine the structure of plans on the level of actions and sequences of actions and prove several properties of the structure of optimal plans. To make use of these properties, we introduce a compilation of an OSP task to classical planning, which forces a plan to conform to these properties. The landmarks of this classical planning task are value driven landmarks, that is, landmarks that must occur in every plan that improve on the utility of the initial state. We also introduce a modified version of the inc-compile-and-BFBB planner [Domshlak and Mirkis (2015)], that uses our observations on additive utility functions and optimal plans. Our empirical evaluation shows that our approach allows for a substantial reduction of search effort in problems with additive utility functions. The value-driven landmarks are more informative than previous state-of-the-art methods for landmark discovery for oversubscription planning and lead to better planning performance with non-negative utilities as well.

7.1 Introduction

Oversubscription planning [Smith (2004)], also referred to as OSP, deals with achieving a state with a high utility value, given a budget on total action cost. This formulation allows us to handle situations with under-constrained resources, which do not allow us to achieve all possible goal facts. OSP objectives differ from classical planning objectives, where the objective is to find a cheap plan which achieves *all* goals. In optimal OSP and optimal classical planning, the tasks are further constrained to finding a path which achieves a state with maximal utility, and, to find the cheapest cost path to achieving the goal, respectively.

Over the years, the theory and practice of classical planning has been studied more intensively and advanced further than OSP. Recent work [Mirkis and Domshlak (2013, 2014); Domshlak and Mirkis (2015)] has made several contributions aimed at improving the scalability of OSP solvers. In particular, they developed a planner that exploits the standard landmark discovery tools of classical planning, as well as abstractions for solving OSP problems. They also showed how the standard goal-reachability landmarks of certain classical planning tasks could be generated to represent the achievements of valuable facts from the original OSP task. These landmarks compiled into the original OSP task to obtain an equivalent OSP task with a lower cost allowance, and thus with a smaller effective search space. In this research, we investigate approximation methods for OSP, aiming at extending the scope of the landmark-based approximations for OSP, as well as improving the scalability of the state-space search driven by these approximations. We propose techniques that allow us to discover more informative landmarks than previous methods. Furthermore, our techniques are applicable for OSP tasks generalized to additive utility setting.

Starting with the most basic question of what additive utility function in OSP problem is, we point out the challenges in multi-valued planning tasks with additive utility setting. We discuss the relationships between state variables and different value assignments to a variable in successive states along a plan. We closely consider negative interactions between state variables with multi-valued (non-zero binary) utility settings, and we show how these negative interactions could occur in tasks with non-negative utility settings. We introduce a novel heuristic search approach to address additive utility OSP tasks which differs from the traditional automated action planning approach in its interpretation of the objective of planning for valuable facts. We define the utility of actions as **improving** state-variables rather than **collecting** valuable facts. An investigation of planning tasks and their utility structure, with the utility of action definition on hand allowed us to discover properties of optimal plans at the level of actions and sequences of actions. A synergistic combination of these properties allows for the handling of OSP additive utility functions over multi-valued variables.

We use the concept of *the net utility of an action* to provide more detailed reasoning about valuable facts by taking the a broader context of achievements into account. The concept of the net utility of action takes intra-state dependencies between facts into account to consider the negative as well as the positive achievements of actions. Furthermore, this concept allows for reasoning in the context of inter-state dependencies of facts, which allow us to evaluate the effectiveness of an action by considering the facts that are a given away to achieve other valuable facts. In particular, considering an action's net utility will help us to set more accurate estimations of likely goal states in an OSP task, and therefore reduce the search space. We prove that an optimal plan must end with an action that has positive net utility.

By eliminating the assumption of a zero utility value in the initial state, we define a reference point, that serves as a baseline for improvement in utility. This reference point is a set of propositions with improved utility over propositions in a given state, for each state variable. This brings us to the concept of a *gross positive* action. A gross positive action is an action that improves the utility of at least one of the state variables, although possibly at the cost of a lower utility for other variables. We prove that an optimal plan must contain at least one gross positive action (which might have a negative net utility), that achieves a valuable fact which is *maintained* until the end of the plan (which must be an action with positive net utility). This approach of *improving* utility differs from previous approaches which attempted to *collect* valuable facts and it allows us to handle any additive utility function, not just non-negative additive utility functions. Based on these observations we propose a technique that is able to discover more informative landmarks than previous methods.

To leverage these properties, we propose the compilation of an OSP task through classical planning methods, which forces the plan to conform to the given properties. The landmarks of this classical planning task are value driven landmarks (called ε-landmarks by [Domshlak and Mirkis (2015)]), meaning, landmarks that must occur in every plan that improves over the utility of the initial state. We also introduce a slight modification to the inc-compile-and-BFBB planner [Domshlak and Mirkis (2015)], that utilizes our definitions of net positive actions and gross positive actions as well our observations around these concepts.

We introduce an efficient way to define the net utility of an action, based on offline analysis of the problem structure and its utility setting. Instead of calculating the net utility of the action in each state of the search, we perform a pre-processing step that includes **only** identifying and marking the net positive actions that are candidates for terminating the search. A framework for splitting actions is presented which is essential for defining the net utility of actions in SAS+ representation with redundant precondition list. We show how this splitting of actions allows for a further reduction of the search space.

The ideas developed in this work have been implemented into a new optimal OSP planner that expands on the planner developed by Mirkis and Domshlak on the basis of the Fast Downward system [Helmert (2006a)]. An empirical evaluation of this method shows that the landmarks discovered in this work are more informative than those of [Domshlak and Mirkis (2015)] and that our modified planner outperforms state-of-the-art OSP planners in non-negative utility settings. Also, to our knowledge, this implementation constitutes the first domain independent planner for optimal OSP with arbitrary additive utility functions, and we hope that more advances in this important computational problem will follow.

Recall that, in Chapter 2, we argued that in order to rationalize the decision-making planning processes, goals should be set and problem-solving approaches should be chosen in a resource-bounded manner. When resources are bounded and budget limitations are clear, a more compact problem definition and more accurate utility function definition can be created within the stated bounds. This chapter presents the budget reduction compilation approach which reduces the effective search space. It also presents a definition of the net utility of an action for planning and exploits this definition to create a more accurate utility evaluation and reduce the effective search space. This definition of the net utility of an action allows us to define and extract 'optimal plan properties' from the task. The value-driven landmark compilation (also referred to as the valuable plan compilation in this chapter) compiles the 'optimal plan properties' into the task representation. This compilation reduces the effective search space and rationalizes the search procedure by adding constraints and forcing the search to conform to optimal planning properties and resource bounds.

7.2 The Berlin Paradox

The Berlin Paradox is a paradox of globally-local value planning. The value of an action or sequence of actions can be measured from both local and global perspectives. A sequence of actions that lead to an optimum global value might involve applying some locally negative utility actions. Measuring actions in isolation and with only the local perspective can, many cases, to a paradox. The paradox can be solved by taking a global end-means perspective on the plan rather than a local perspective (sequence of actions).

This paradox can be illustrated by the example of Tesla's German factory. In November 2019, Elon Musk, Tesla CEO, announced the Berlin-Brandenburg Gigafactory (Gigafactory 4), a European electric vehicle production plant. The Berlin-Brandenburg Gigafactory was established to build batteries, power-trains, and Tesla's Model Y car. The factory was established in Berlin, the heart of Europe and the heart of the automotive market. The central location of the Gigafactory allows it to reach the European market more easily and thus increase the usage of electro-mobility in Europe. In addition, the German government is providing financial support to Tesla and encourages electro-mobility.

Many experts agree that e-mobility must be at the heart of green recovery. It impacts the economy positively and improves fuel efficiency. It also positively impacts the environment by lowering fuel emissions and reducing noise to fuel efficiency. Taking the global perspective, the Berlin-Brandenburg Gigafactory will bring a lot of value to the company and positively impact the environment, ecology, and quality of life of citizens in urban areas. Nevertheless, the announcement of establishing the new Gigafactory in Berlin invoked massive environmental objections. Local residents raised more than 400 objections to Tesla's Gigafactory. The protests raised environmental concerns such as: forest clearing, the extensive use of water by the factory, and ecological damage following the road network construction around the factory.

This chapter shows how Oversubscription planning and focusing on net utility, allows us to capture plans that involve taking actions with a local negative utility on the way to a global optimum. In the Berlin paradox, the construction of the Gigafactory brings a local (both in time and space) negative utility in the form of local (both in time and space) environmental damage. However, this local negative utility action serves a global net utility process (or plan) which, in net terms, will result in a greater ecological and economic resulting from this factory's products. In this chapter, we demonstrate a technique for planning and finding the properties of optimal plans, that allows us to create plans with global net utility while taking the different dynamics and changes in value, including negative utility actions, into account. Taking a global perspective of a plan and using net utility measures for processes (and plans) allows us to gain more insights regarding negative utility actions in a broader context and help us solve the paradox of globally-local value planning (The Berlin Paradox).

7.3 Background

We begin by laying out the necessary background for describing our work. For $k \in \mathbb{N}^+$, by $[k]$ we denote the set $\{1, 2, \ldots, k\}$. The indicator function of a subset A of a set X is a function $\mathbb{1}_A : X \to \{0, 1\}$ defined as $\mathbb{1}_A(x) = 1$ if $x \in A$ and $\mathbb{1}_A(x) = 0$ if $x \notin A$. Following [Nebel (2000)], the *size* of a well-defined mathematical object x. The size of a (reasonable) encoding of x is detonated as $||x||$.

7.3.1 *Oversubscription Planning (OSP)*

In what follows, we adopt the OSP model representation of [Domshlak and Mirkis (2015)], by adopting a language that is close to the SAS+ language for classical planning [Bäckström and Klein (1991); Bäckström and Nebel (1995)].

A deterministic **oversubscription planning (OSP) task** is given by a sextuple

$$\Pi = \langle V, s_0, u; A, c, b \rangle, \tag{7.1}$$

where

(1) $V = \{v_1, \ldots, v_n\}$ is a finite set of finite-domain *state variables*, with each complete assignment to V representing a *state*, and $S = dom(v_1) \times \cdots \times dom(v_n)$ being the *state space* of the task;
(2) $s_0 \in S$ is a designated *initial state*;
(3) u is an efficiently computable *state value* function $u : S \to \mathbb{R}^{0+}$;
(4) A is a finite set of *operators*, with each operator $a \in A$ being represented by a pair $\langle \mathsf{pre}(a), \mathsf{eff}(a) \rangle$ of partial assignments to V, called *preconditions* and *effects* of a, respectively;
(5) $c : A \to \mathbb{R}^{0+}$ is an *operator cost* function;
(6) $b \in \mathbb{R}^{0+}$ is a *cost budget* allowed for the task.

An assignment of a variable v to value d is denoted by $\langle v/d \rangle$; we often refer to such single variable assignments as *propositions*. For a partial assignment p to V, let $\mathcal{V}(p) \subseteq V$ denote the subset of variables instantiated by p, and, for $v \in \mathcal{V}(p)$, $p[v]$ denote the value provided by p to the variable v. Operator a is applicable in a state s iff $s[v] = \mathsf{pre}(a)[v]$ for all $v \in \mathcal{V}(\mathsf{pre}(a))$. Applying a changes the value of each $v \in \mathcal{V}(\mathsf{eff}(a))$ to $\mathsf{eff}(a)[v]$, and the resulting state is denoted by $s[\![a]\!]$. This notation is only defined if a is applicable in s. Denoting an empty sequence of operators by ϵ, applying a sequence of operators $\langle a_1, \ldots, a_m \rangle$ to a state s is defined inductively as $s[\![\epsilon]\!] := s$ and $s[\![a_1, \ldots, a_j]\!] := s[\![a_1, \ldots, a_{j-1}]\!][\![a_j]\!]$. An operator sequence π is called an *s-plan* if it is applicable in state s and $c(\pi) \leq b$. In our discussion, a plan that achieves a goal from state s will be referred as s-plan.

A deterministic **classical planning** task, is given by $\Pi = \langle V, s_0, G; A, c \rangle$, where the utility function and cost budget are replaced with a hard goal constraint which is a partial assignment on state variables $G \subseteq V$.

We assume an *additive utility* function with *multi-valued variables*, defined as $u(s) = \sum_{\langle v/d \rangle \in s} u_v(d)$, with $u_v(d) \in \mathbb{R}$ for all variable-value pairs $\langle v/d \rangle$. That is, negative utility values are allowed and each variable can have many value assignments with different utility values available for each variable-value pair.

Some auxiliary notation is used later on: for an OSP task $\Pi = \langle V, s_0, u; A, c, b \rangle$, by $\mathcal{D} = \bigcup_{v \in V} dom(v)$ we denote the union of the (uniquely labeled) state-variable domains. For a state s and a proposition $\langle v/d \rangle \in \mathcal{D}$, $\langle v/d \rangle \in s$ is used as a shortcut notation for $s[v] = d$.

An example from Mirkis and Domshlak of a simple OSP task in Fig. 7.1 is used to illustrate this model representation. In this example, a truck is initially at location A, and it can only drive from location A to location B and then from location B to location C. Two packages, x and y, are initially at location B. When a package and the truck are in the same location, the package can be loaded onto the truck, and when a package is on the truck, it can be unloaded at the truck's current location. Each (drive, load, and unload) operator in the task costs one unit, and the cost budget is set to four units. Finally, a value of one (value unit) is earned for each package present at location C.

This OSP task Π is described here using three state variables $V = \{t, x, y\}$, with $dom(t) = \{A, B, C\}$ and $dom(x) = dom(y) = \{A, B, C, T\}$, corresponding to the possible locations of the truck and the two packages, respectively. The operator set $A = \{a_1, \ldots, a_{10}\}$ is detailed in Fig. 7.1(b).

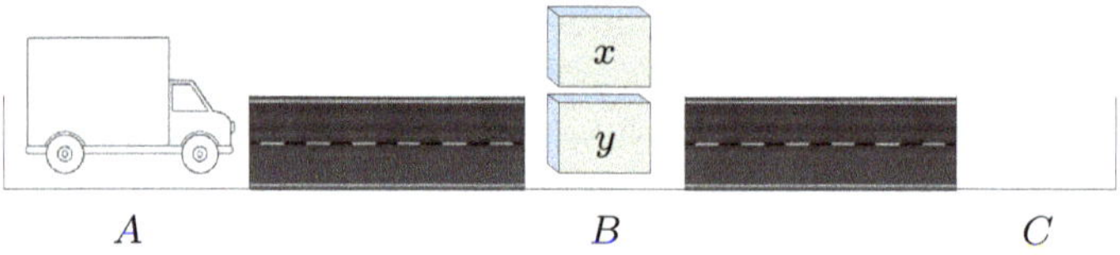

(a)

a_i	drive_{AB} $i=1$	drive_{BC} $i=2$	load_{Bx} $i=3$	load_{By} $i=4$	unload_{Cx} $i=5$
$\text{pre}(a_i)$	$\{\langle t/A\rangle\}$	$\{\langle t/B\rangle\}$	$\{\langle t/B\rangle, \langle x/B\rangle\}$	$\{\langle t/B\rangle, \langle y/B\rangle\}$	$\{\langle t/C\rangle, \langle x/T\rangle\}$
$\text{eff}(a_i)$	$\{\langle t/B\rangle\}$	$\{\langle t/C\rangle\}$	$\{\langle x/T\rangle\}$	$\{\langle y/T\rangle\}$	$\{\langle x/C\rangle\}$

a_i	unload_{Bx} $i=6$	unload_{By} $i=7$	unload_{Cy} $i=8$	load_{Cx} $i=9$	load_{Cy} $i=10$
$\text{pre}(a_i)$	$\{\langle t/B\rangle, \langle x/T\rangle\}$	$\{\langle t/B\rangle, \langle y/T\rangle\}$	$\{\langle t/C\rangle, \langle y/T\rangle\}$	$\{\langle t/C\rangle, \langle x/C\rangle\}$	$\{\langle t/C\rangle, \langle y/C\rangle\}$
$\text{eff}(a_i)$	$\{\langle x/B\rangle\}$	$\{\langle y/B\rangle\}$	$\{\langle y/C\rangle\}$	$\{\langle x/T\rangle\}$	$\{\langle y/T\rangle\}$

(b)

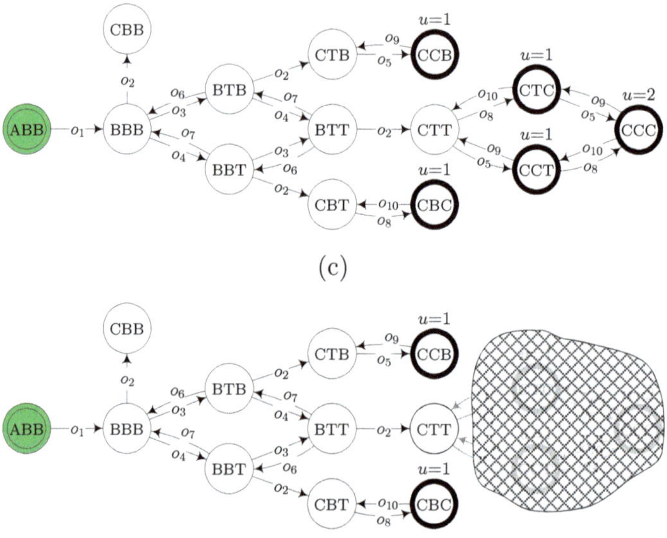

(c)

(d)

Fig. 7.1: A simple example of [Mirkis and Domshlak (2014)] for an OSP task, with (a) illustrating the story, (b) listing the operators, and (c)–(d) depicting the relevant parts of the state space; (c) shows the region of the state space that is structurally reachable from the initial state ABB, and the grayed area in (d) corresponds to the sub-region that cannot be reached from the initial state under the budget $b = 4$.

In the state model induced by this OSP task, we have $S = dom(t) \times dom(x) \times dom(y)$, the initial state $s_0 = \text{ABB}$ (with the three letters in the names of the states capturing the three components of the domain cross-product), operator cost $c(a_i) = 1$ for all operators a_i, cost budget $b = 4$, and state values

$$u(s) = \begin{cases} 1, s \in \{\star\text{AC}, \star\text{BC}, \star\text{CA}, \star\text{CB}\} \\ 2, s \in \{\star\text{CC}\} \\ 0, \text{otherwise} \end{cases} .$$

The relevant parts of the state space are depicted in Figs. 7.1(c) and 7.1(d): Figure 7.1(c) shows the region of the state space that is structurally reachable from the initial state ABB, and the grayed area in Fig. 7.1(d) corresponds to the sub-region that cannot be reached from the initial state under the budget $b = 4$.

7.3.2 *Landmarks in Heuristic Search*

In classical planning, there are two types of landmarks "fact landmarks" and "action landmarks". As stated earlier, "fact landmarks" are propositions that must be true at some point in every solution plan for a given planning task [Hoffmann *et al.* (2004)]. *s-landmark* is an assignment to variable that is true at some point in *every* plan for a state s. Similarly to landmarks over facts, an action a is an action landmark of a planning task Π iff it is taken along every plan for Π. A sufficient and efficiently testable condition for an action a being an action landmark is that a relaxed planning task without a is not solvable.

Many state-of-the-art admissible heuristics for classical planning use what are called **disjunctive action landmarks**, each corresponding to a set of operators such that every s-plan contains at least one operator from that set [Karpas and Domshlak (2009); Helmert and Domshlak (2009); Bonet and Helmert (2010); Pommerening and Helmert (2013)]. Logical *landmarks for goal reachability* [Hoffmann *et al.* (2004); Karpas and Domshlak (2009); Helmert and Domshlak (2009); Domshlak *et al.* (2012); Bonet and Helmert (2010); Pommerening and Helmert (2013)] have been found to be extremely effective in the context of optimal classical planning.

The notion **ε-landmark** [Mirkis and Domshlak (2014)] refers to disjunctive action landmarks in the context of OSP for a state s. **ε-landmark**. Introduced by [Mirkis and Domshlak (2014)] as "bring me something landmarks", they are set of actions that are applied in every plan π that achieves *something valuable.* For example, suppose $L \subseteq A$ is an ε-landmark for s, then every plan with a positive utility proposition at the end-state contains an action from L. ε-landmarks can are used to construct a **budget reduction compilation** [Mirkis and Domshlak (2014)] which is described next.

7.3.3 *Heuristic Search in OSP*

The two primary ingredients of any heuristic-search planner are its search algorithm and its heuristic function. In classical planning, the heuristic is typically a function $h : S \to \mathbb{R}^{0+} \cup \{\infty\}$, with $h(s)$ estimating the cost $h^*(s)$ of optimal s-plans. A heuristic h is **admissible** if it is *lower-bounding*, that is, $h(s) \leq h^*(s)$ for all states s. All common heuristic search algorithms for optimal classical planning, such as A^*, require admissible heuristics.

In contrast, a heuristic in OSP is a function $h : S \times \mathbb{R}^{0+} \to \mathbb{R}^{0+}$, with $h(s, b)$ estimating the value $h^*(s, b)$ of optimal s-plans under cost budget b. A heuristic h is **admissible** if it is *upper-bounding*, that is, $h(s, b) \geq h^*(s, b)$ for all states s and all cost budgets b. Here too, search algorithms for an optimal OSP, such as best-first branch-and-bound (*BFBB*), require admissible heuristics for pruning search branches without violating solution optimality. *BFBB* is also extensively used for net-benefit planning [Benton *et al.* (2007); Coles and Coles (2011); Do *et al.* (2007)], as well as for some other variants of deterministic planning [Bonet and Geffner (2008); Brafman and Chernyavsky (2005)].

Figure 7.2 depicts a pseudo-code description of *BFBB* for OSP; $s\langle n \rangle$ there denotes the state associated with search node n, and cost-so-far $g(n)$ is the total cost of the action sequence associated with n. Unlike in A^*, the order in which the nodes are selected from the OPEN list does not affect the optimality guarantee (although it may, of course, seriously affect the empirical efficiency of the search). In Fig. 7.2, the ordering of OPEN corresponds to the decreasing order of $h(s\langle n \rangle, b - g(n))$. The duplicate detection and reopening mechanisms in *BFBB* are similar to those in A^* [Pearl (1984)]. In addition, *BFBB* maintains the best solution n^* found so far and uses it to prune all generated nodes evaluated to be no higher than $u(s\langle n^* \rangle)$. Likewise, complying with the semantics of OSP, every generated node n with a cost-so-far $g(n)$ higher than the problem's budget b are immediately pruned. When the OPEN list becomes empty, or the node n selected from the list promises less than the lower bound, the plan associated with the best solution n^* is returned to. If the heuristic h is admissible and the

```
BFBB (Π = ⟨V, s_0, u; A, c, b⟩)
  open := new max-heap ordered by f(n) = h(s⟨n⟩, b − g(n))
  initialize best solution n* := make-root-node(s_0)
  open.insert(n*)
  closed:= ∅;
  best-cost:= 0
  while not open.empty()
        n := open.pop-max()
        if f(n) ≤ u(s⟨n*⟩): break
        if u(s⟨n⟩) > u(s⟨n*⟩): update n* := n
        if s⟨n⟩ ∉ closed or g(n) < best-cost(s⟨n⟩):
           closed:= closed ∪ {s⟨n⟩}
           best-cost(s⟨n⟩) := g(n)
           foreach a ∈ A(s⟨n⟩):
                    n' := make-node(s⟨n⟩[[a]], n)
                    if g(n') > b or f(n') ≤ u(s⟨n*⟩): continue
                    open.insert(n')
  return n*
```

Fig. 7.2: Best-first branch-and-bound (*BFBB*) search for OSP.

h-based pruning of the generated nodes is sound, then the plan that is returned to is guaranteed to be optimal.

inc-compile-and-BFBB [Domshlak and Mirkis (2015)], depicted in Fig. 7.3, is an OSP-customized, incremental version of the *BFBB*. In addition to the best solution so far n^*, inc-compile-and-BFBB maintains a set of reference states S_{ref}, which is updated with any new, best-so-far state that has reached n^*. For each $s_i \in S_{\text{ref}}$ and each valuable fact $g \in V \setminus s_i$ a zero cost action is added to A which indicates a valuable fact that is not in s_i. Applying all these zero cost actions verifies the achievement of a subset of *good* facts that are not included in any state from S_{ref}. With each update of S_{ref}, *BFBB* is restarted with a new set of ε-landmarks created by the *current* S_{ref}, that is derived from achieving something that has not yet been seen. These new, *ε-landmarks* are compiled back into the original task for the next iteration with a budget reduction compilation, described as follows:

- Given OSP task Π, we generate the ε-compilation Π_ε of Π, where Π_ε is a classical planning task that extends the structure of Π with a set of zero-cost actions such that applying any of them corresponds to verifying that a positive value can be achieved in Π.
- Using classical planning tools, a set of landmarks $\mathcal{L}$ is generated for Π_ε, along with an admissible landmark cost function $lcost : \mathcal{L} \rightarrow$

```
inc-compile-and-BFBB (Π = ⟨V, A; s0, c, u, b⟩)
  initialize global variables:
      n* := s0          // best solution so far
      Sref := {s0}      // current reference states
  loop:
    Π(ε,Sref) = (ε, Sref)-compilation of Π
    L := a set of landmarks for Π(ε,Sref)
    lcost := admissible landmark cost function from L
    ΠL* := budget reducing compilation of (L, lcost) into Π
    if inc-BFBB(ΠL*, Sref, n*) = done:
      return plan for Π associated with n*

inc-BFBB (Π, Sref, n*)
  open := new max-heap ordered by f(n) = h(s⟨n⟩, b − g(n))
  open.insert(make-root-node(s0))
  closed:= ∅
  best-cost:= 0
  while not open.empty()
    n := open.pop-max()
    if f(n) ≤ u(s⟨n*⟩): break
    if u(s⟨n⟩) > u(s⟨n*⟩): update n* := n
    if goods(s⟨n⟩) ⊈ goods(s′) for all s′ ∈ Sref:
      Sref := Sref ∪ {s⟨n⟩}
    if termination criterion: return updated // the rest is similar to BFBB in Fig. 7.2
    if s⟨n⟩ ∉ closed or g(n) < best-cost(s⟨n⟩):
      closed:= closed ∪ {s⟨n⟩}
      best-cost(s⟨n⟩) := g(n)
      foreach a ∈ A(s⟨n⟩):
              n′ := make-node(s⟨n⟩⟦a⟧, n)
              if g(n′) > b or f(n′) ≤ u(s⟨n*⟩): continue
              open.insert(n′)
  return done
```

Fig. 7.3: Iterative *BFBB* with landmark enhancement.

$\mathbb{R}^{0+}$ where $\sum_{L \in \mathcal{L}} lcost(L) \leq h^*(s)$ [Katz and Domshlak (2010); Karpas and Domshlak (2009); Helmert and Domshlak (2009)].

- Performing budget reducing compilation by compiling $(\mathcal{L}, lcost)$ into Π, obtaining an OSP task $\Pi_{\mathcal{L}}$, where $\Pi_{\mathcal{L}}$ extends the structure of Π by mirroring the actions of each ε-landmark L_i with their "cheaper by $lcost(L_i)$" versions. To compensate for the discounted actions, budget b is reduced by $\sum_{i=1}^{n} lcost(L_i)$. [Domshlak and Mirkis (2015)] devised two versions of polynomial and sound budget reducing compilation; A basic compilation $\Pi_{\mathcal{L}}$ applied on a pairwise disjoint landmarks and extended with auxiliary control structure, and a *generalized budget reducing compilation* applied on an arbitrary (non-disjoint) sets of ε-landmarks. This compilation can then be used within a heuristic search algorithm.

- The optimal solution for $\Pi_{\mathcal{L}}$ (and thus for Π) is then searched for using a search algorithm for optimal OSP such as a generic best-first branch-and-bound search (depicted Fig. 7.2), or the OSP-customized branch-and-bound search (depicted Fig. 7.3).

The **inc-compile-and-BFBB** framework illustrated in Fig. 7.4. Figure 7.5 depicts the general OSP framework for numerical and negative utility values, which will be described in the rest of the chapter. In the next section we take a deeper look at the concept of utility.

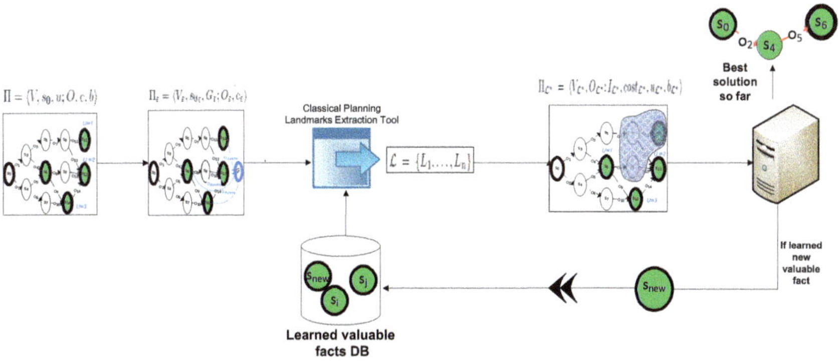

Fig. 7.4: The framework of learning based closed loops was introduced by [Mirkis and Domshlak (2014)] for the exploitation of logical *landmarks for goal reachability* in non-negative OSP problems. Given OSP task Π (1) We first generate an ε-compilation Π_{ε} of Π, (2) we then generate a set of landmarks $\mathcal{L}$ for Π_{ε}, (3) from there we obtain an OSP task $\Pi_{\mathcal{L}}$ with a budget reducing compilation by compiling $(\mathcal{L}, lcost)$ into Π, where $lcost$ is an admissible landmark cost function (4) and finally, we execute an OSP solver on $\Pi_{\mathcal{L}}$ (5). If an optimal solution is not found, update $\mathcal{L}$ and $\Pi_{\mathcal{L}}$ with any new state carrying unseen valuable fact.

7.4 General Additive Utility Functions

Deterministic automated action planning, as mentioned above, is a problem of finding trajectories in large-scale yet concisely represented state-transition systems. The solution quality measure to those planning problems vary in the ways that cost and utility functions are defined. Any trajectory $\pi \in \mathcal{P}$ is a solution for a planning task Π, with a preference towards solutions of higher quality. In what follows, $s[\![\pi]\!]$ stands for the

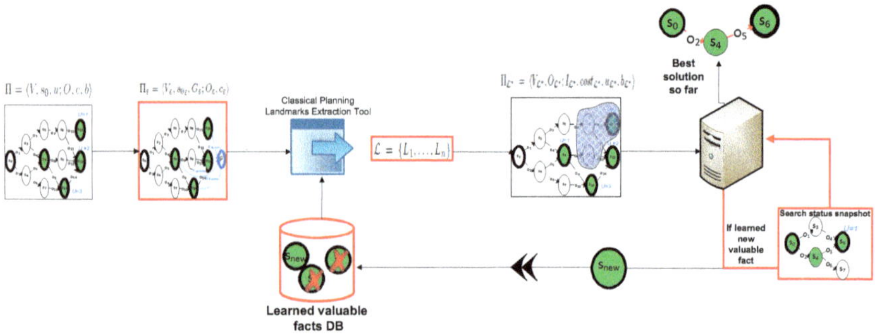

Fig. 7.5: Framework of learning based closed loop for exploitation of logical *landmarks for goal reachability* in the general OSP problem. Given an OSP task Π (1) generate ε-compilation Π_ε (2) generate a set of landmarks $\mathcal{L}$ for Π_ε (3) obtain an OSP task $\Pi_{\mathcal{L}}$ with budget reducing compilation by compiling $(\mathcal{L}, lcost)$ into Π, where $lcost$ is an admissible landmark cost function (4) execute OSP solver on $\Pi_{\mathcal{L}}$ (5) while optimal solution is not found update $\mathcal{L}$ and $\Pi_{\mathcal{L}}$ with any new information found (improved state). Marked red is our contribution to the non-negative Framework [Mirkis and Domshlak (2014)] depicted in Fig. 7.4.

end-state of a trajectory π applied at state s, and $c(\pi) = \sum_{a\in\pi} c(a)$ is the additional cost of π. The quality of the solution trajectory is measured in terms of the *cost function*, and the quality of the end-state of a trajectory is measured in terms of the *utility function.*

In classical planning, the objective is to choose one of the equally attractive goal states with the lowest total action cost possible. With this objective definition, the *utility function* captures the hard constraint of the end-state to be achieved, while the *cost function* captures the soft preference of the trajectory total action cost. Although in the classical planning problem model there is no explicit formulation of a utility function to capture the preference over plan state, it is implied from the hard constraint of goal definition and can be formulated as a binary utility measure, where

$$u(s) = \begin{cases} 1, & \text{if } G \text{ is true at state } s \\ 0, & \text{otherwise.} \end{cases} \tag{7.2}$$

On the other hand, the objective in OSP is to achieve as valuable a state as possible within a fixed allowance of the total action cost. With this objective definition, the *cost function* captures a hard constraint of the trajectory total action cost, while the *utility function* captures a soft preference for the end-state to be achieved.

In this work, we study OSP problems with an additive utility functions, which take the form

$$u(s) = \sum_{\langle v/d \rangle \in s} u_v(\langle v/d \rangle). \tag{7.3}$$

Based on [Smith (2004)], the OSP problem was mostly considered to be a problem with a large number of possible goals of different values where the planning system must choose a subset that can be accomplished within a limited budget. This, in particular, resulted in a focus on a subset of additive utility functions, namely *non-negative utility functions*, in which the additive components of the function take only non-negative values, that is, for each variable $v \in V$ and value $d \in dom(v)$, it holds that $u(\langle v/d \rangle)$. This, however, precluded the planning techniques from dealing with undesirable properties of the end states, that is, properties that the planner should try to avoid achieving. Escaping this limitation was the primary motivation of our work here.

7.4.1 *Why Negative Values Need a Special Treatment?*

With the objective of achieving a state (or a subset of goals) that is as valuable as possible, the planner should strive to achieve propositions carrying positive values while trying to avoid getting stuck with propositions carrying negative values. At the same time, because of the dependencies between the propositions, it is possible that collecting positive values might require collecting negative values along the way. In particular, it is possible that an action that achieves positive value propositions will also achieve some negative value propositions. For this reason, it would be beneficial to consider the negative achievements of the operators along with the positive achievements of the operators.

Consider a simple example in the classic Blocksworld domain in Fig. 7.6. In this example an arm is initially holding block C, blocks A and B are on the table. Three actions are applicable in the described state: stack block C on A, stack block C on block B or put block C on the table. Each operator in the task costs one unit, and the cost budget is set to one unit. Finally, a value of one utility unit is earned for each clear block (with no other blocks on top). With this utility setting, it is easy to see that all operators lead to valuable states that are all possible candidates for the goal state. Now, suppose that the utility setting for this simple example also has a penalty for not clearing blocks and a value of two utility units paid for clearing them. With this new negative utility setting, when the focus is on facts alone, all operators should be considered as leading to a goal state candidate

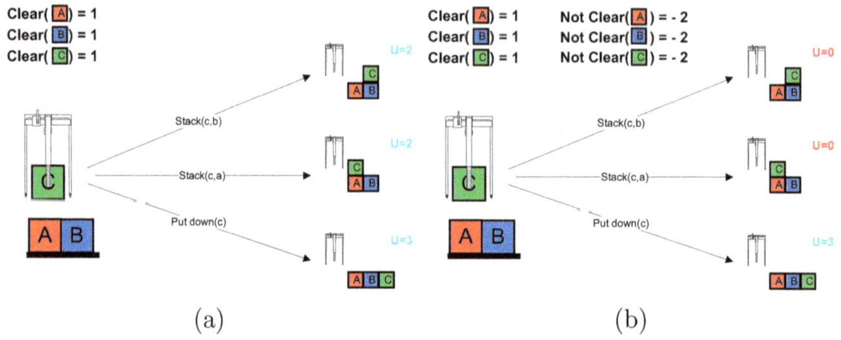

Fig. 7.6: A simple example in the classic Blocksworld domain. In this example, an arm is initially holding block C, blocks A and B are on the table. Three actions are applicable in the described state; stack block C on A, stack block C on B or put block C on the table. (a) depicts a non-negative utility setting and each operator outcome's state utility. (b) depicts each operator's total outcome utility in the general additive utility setting. When penalties are ignored the state, utilities in (b) are treated as positive, and the same is true in (a).

since they all achieve the fact *clear c* which is a valuable fact. However, when taking a broader context in which this fact has been achieved into account, we can ascertain that two of these operators lead to non-valuable states, since negative facts are acquired as well and they outbalance the utility of the valuable fact. To capture the dependencies of the entire effect list of an operator, we consider the *total outcome utility* of an operator by summarizing the total utility of newly acquired propositions. For an OSP action a, the ***total outcome utility*** of a is

$$u^{out}(a) = \sum_{v \in \mathcal{V}(\mathsf{eff}(a))} u_v(\mathsf{eff}(a)[v]). \tag{7.4}$$

If we have the *total outcome utility* of an action, we can have a better idea of the inter-state variables dependencies and capture a proposition's utility within a broader context. As we show later on, this allows us to more accurately estimate the prospective value of the states in an OSP task, and, consequently, to reduce the effective search space.

7.4.2 *Good or Better?*

At first glance, negative interactions seem to play a role in OSP when the utility setting in the task has some negative values. This, however, is not the case. In an OSP task with multi-valued utility variables, an action that

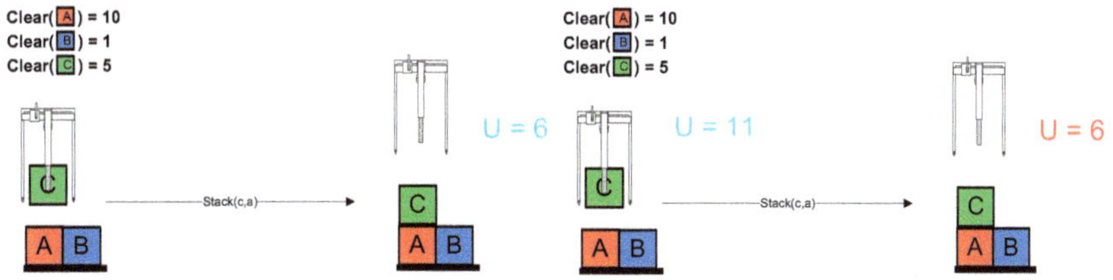

Fig. 7.7: Continuing with the schematic example from Fig. 7.6, the action of stacking block C on block A is described by both (a) fact-oriented and (b) action-oriented views: The fact-oriented view focuses only on the target state while, in action-oriented view, the origin state is taken into account as well, revealing the action in question to be less attractive.

achieves valuable propositions might lose more valuable propositions than were held at the origin state. A simple example in Fig. 7.7 illustrates how the focus on an action's target state while ignoring the action's origin state might mislead the search by treating a state as an attractive solution even though it has been achieved by giving up on a better state.

Assuming that the value of each variable affected by an operator is also specified in the preconditions of that operator, the ***net utility*** of an action is defined as follows:

Definition 7.1. For an OSP planning task operator a, the net utility of an a is

$$u(a) = \sum_{v \in \mathcal{V}(\mathsf{eff}(a))} [u_v(\mathsf{eff}(a)[v]) - u_v(\mathsf{pre}(a)[v])]. \tag{7.5}$$

The net utility of actions allows us to capture a broader context in which the achievement of a proposition is evaluated by taking into account, not only the values of the propositions and inter-state dependencies, but also intra-state dependencies since previous variable assignments are taken into account as well. In particular, the notion of an action's net utility will help us set an even more accurate estimation of likely goal states in an OSP task, and further reduce the search space. For the sake of clarity, we present the concept of the net utility of an action in SAS representation, under the assumption that for every effect variable a precondition is defined, so the notation is well defined. Later, we relax our simplifying assumption with the *selective action split* in Chapter 8.

7.4.3 *The Initial State With Additive Utility Function*

The *action-oriented approach* strives to **improve** states rather than **collect** valuable facts. Treating an OSP task as a process of improving the initial state rather than a process of collecting valuable facts is the most basic fundamental of our approach. In contrast to classical planning and partial satisfaction problems where there is one clear assignment for each variable that is defined as valuable, OSP with additive utility functions allows for each variable to be associated with a set of different utilities. Thus, in the case of additive utility, a variable assignment is valuable if its utility is better than the utility at the initial state, where an optimal solution will be the maximal utility over all variables that are *mutually consistent*. Therefore, it is easy to see that the concept of *improving states* rather than collecting valuable facts is much more suitable in most cases. Furthermore, when negative utility values are allowed, variables in solution assigned to negative utility values can be treated as "valuable" in cases where their negative value assignment *improves* from the initial state assignment.

Removing Mirkis and Domshlak's assumption that the initial state has zero utility, we define the *inf value*, which is a property of the ordinal utility function for a variable value with the least value possible over that variable.

Definition 7.2 (Inf utility). Given a state variable $v \in V$, an **inf utility** of v is a value $d_{inf} \in dom(v)$ such that there is no other $d \in dom(v)$ with $u(\langle v/d_{inf}\rangle) > u(\langle v/d\rangle)$.

The definition of *inf value* is expanded to include the lowest state utility value *inf state value* as follows.

Definition 7.3 (Inf state utility). Given an OSP task $\Pi = \langle V, s_0, u; A, c, b\rangle$, an **inf state utility** 0_{obs} is the value of a state $s_{inf} \in S$ such that for no other state $s \in S$ we have $u(s_{inf}) > u(s)$.

7.5 Landmarks in OSP with Negative Utility Values

Our first contribution to OSP generalized to arbitrary additive utility functions is to extend the landmark-based OSP approximations introduced by [Mirkis and Domshlak (2014)] to include problems with negative utility value propositions. Specifically, we present a notion v_{sum}**-compilation** that allows us to alleviate the dependence on value non-negativity, as well as to capture the relationships between state variables and different value assignments to a variable in successive states along a plan. This v_{sum}-compilation exploits the notion of actions' net utility and allows for the generation of higher quality landmarks. In turn, the budget reduction compilation, with an input of quality landmarks, produces an equivalent OSP task with more accurate and tighter groups of discounted actions, and thus with a more strictly reduced search space.

First, the v_{sum}-compilation is presented under a simplifying assumption that, each variable mentioned in the action's effects is necessarily also mentioned in the action's preconditions. We then discuss the quality of landmarks achieved by the v_{sum}-compilation, the implications on the budget reduction compilation and the search space. Next, we present a framework that expands the incremental *BFBB* algorithm for landmark discovery and incremental revelation of plans to be able to handle OSP problem with additive utility functions. Finally, we present additional observations to increase landmark and budget reduction quality. Later on, in Chapter 8, we relax our simplifying assumption by showing a compilation of a general OSP task to an equivalent OSP task with respectively constrained preconditions.

7.5.1 *The V-Sum Compilation*

The objective in deterministic OSP is to achieve a subset of goals within a fixed allowance of the total action cost that is as valuable as possible. On the one hand, this implies that we should strive to collect propositions carrying positive values while avoiding collecting propositions carrying negative values. On the other hand, because of the dependencies between the propositions, it is possible that collecting positive values might require also collecting negative values along the way. In particular, it is possible that an action that achieves positive value propositions will also achieve negative value propositions.

For this reason, considering the ε-compilation of the OSP task, it would be beneficial to not only consider positive but also negative achievements of the operators. In what follows, we assume that the initial state value is the lowest possible, that is, $u(s_0) = 0_{obs}$ as in Definition 7.3. At first glance, the net utility value of an action does not have a clear role in our reasoning. It is very much possible that optimal plans will contain numerous actions with negative net utility values because it allows for the achieving of valuable facts that outweigh the respective loss. However, Lemma 7.1 shows that operators with positive net value do play an essential role in optimal plans.

The proof of Lemma 7.1 is rather simple. In plain terms, the lemma states that; for each plan π, there is a plan π' that; (i) ends with a net positive utility value action, (ii) is at most as costly as π, and (iii) is at least as valuable as π.

Lemma 7.1. *Given an OSP task* Π *with an additive utility function* u*, for any plan* π *for* Π *such that* $u(s[\![\pi]\!]) > u(s_0)$*, there is a prefix* π' *of* π *such that:*

(1) $u(s_0[\![\pi]\!]) \leq u(s_0[\![\pi']\!])$*, and*
(2) for the last action a_{last} *along* π'*, we have* $u(a_{last}) > 0$.

Proof. The proof is by induction on the plan length n. For $n = 1$, we have $\pi = \langle a_1 \rangle$, and since $u(s[\![\pi]\!]) > u(s_0)$, the operator a_1 has a positive net utility value. Hence, $\pi' = \pi$ satisfies the claims. Assuming that the claim holds for $n \geq 1$, we now prove it for $n + 1$.

Considering a plan $\pi = \langle a_1, \ldots, a_{n+1} \rangle$, for $i \in [n + 1]$, let π_i denote the prefix of π consisting of its first i operators. If the last operator a_{n+1} along π has a positive net utility value, then we are done with $\pi' = \pi$. Otherwise, if a_{n+1} has either negative or zero net utility value, then $u(s[\![\pi]\!]) > u(s_0)$ in particular implies $u(s[\![\pi_n]\!]) > u(s_0)$. If π' is a prefix of π_n that satisfies the lemma by our assumption of induction, then π' also satisfies the lemma with respect to π since $u(\pi') \geq u(s[\![\pi_n]\!]) \geq u(s[\![\pi]\!])$. □

Definition 7.4. Given an OSP task $\Pi = \langle V, s_0, u; A, c, b \rangle$, π is a **tail gaining plan** for Π if the last operator a along π satisfies $u(a) > 0$.

Relying on Lemma 7.1, we can now extract ε-landmarks which focus on actions with positive net values as candidates for ending the search process. Specifically, we can devise a polynomial time compilation for classical planning, namely v_{sum}-compilation Π_ε, that extends the structure of Π with a goal variable g, and for any *net positive action* a, the effects are extended with the proposition $\langle g/1 \rangle$. Applying any of these actions indicates a positive value improvement in Π.

For example, let a be an operator with $\mathsf{pre}(a) = \{\langle t/B \rangle, \langle x/B \rangle\}$ and $\mathsf{eff}(a) = \{\langle x/T \rangle\}$, where $u(\langle x/B \rangle) = 1$ and $u(\langle x/T \rangle) = 2$, and thus $u_o(a) = u_x(T) - u_x(B) = 1$. We add a new operator a_ε which is equivalent to a but with $\mathsf{pre}(a) = \{\langle t/B \rangle, \langle x/B \rangle\}$ and $\mathsf{eff}(a_\varepsilon) = \{\langle x/T \rangle, \langle g/1) \rangle\}$.

With the values of different s-plans in an OSP task Π varying between 0_{obs} and the value of the optimal s-plan (which may also be 0_{obs}), let ε-**landmark** for state s be any property that is satisfied by any s-plan π that achieves *something valuable*. Considering a disjunctive action landmarks, if $L \subseteq A$ is an ε-landmark for s, then every s-plan π with $u(\pi) > 0_{obs}$ contains an operator from L.

Definition 7.5. Given an OSP task $\Pi = \langle V, s_0, u; A, c, b\rangle$, the **($\varepsilon$, V_{sum})-compilation** of Π is a classical planning task $\Pi_\varepsilon = \langle V_\varepsilon, s_{0\varepsilon}, G_\varepsilon; A_\varepsilon, c_\varepsilon\rangle$ where

$$\begin{aligned}
V_\varepsilon &= V \cup \{g\},\\
&\quad \textit{with } dom(g) = \{0,1\},\\
s_{0\varepsilon} &= s_0 \cup \{\langle g/0\rangle\},\\
G_\varepsilon &= \{\langle g/1\rangle\},\\
A_\varepsilon &= \{a_\varepsilon \mid a \in A\},\\
a_\varepsilon &= \begin{cases} \langle \mathsf{pre}(a), \mathsf{eff}(a)\rangle, & u(a) \leq 0\\ \langle \mathsf{pre}(a), \mathsf{eff}(a) \cup \langle g/1\rangle\rangle, & u(a) > 0 \end{cases}\\
c_\varepsilon(a) &= c(a).
\end{aligned}$$

To put it simply, Π_ε extends the structure of Π with a goal variable of g, and for any *net positive action* a, the effects are extended by the proposition $\langle g/1\rangle$. Applying any of these actions indicates a positive value achievement in Π. In what follows, we refer to Π_ε as the **(ε,V_{sum})-compilation** of Π. Constructing Π_ε from Π is trivially polynomial time, and it allows us to discover **ε-landmark** for Π using the standard machinery for classical planning landmark discovery.

Theorem 7.1. *For any OSP task* Π*, any landmark* L *for* Π_ε *such that* $L \subseteq A$ *is an* ε*-landmark* L *for* Π.

Proof. Let $\mathcal{P}$ be the set of all plans Π with $u(\pi) > 0_{obs}$ and $\mathcal{P}_\varepsilon$ the set of all plans for Π_ε. From Lemma 7.1 we know that for each $\pi \in \mathcal{P}$ with $u(s[\![\pi]\!]) > 0_{obs}$, there exists a prefix π' that ends with an operator $a^+ \in A$ such that $u(a^+) > 0$. Likewise, since $s_{0\varepsilon} := s_0 \cup \{\langle g/0\rangle\}$ and $A_\varepsilon \supseteq A$, π is applicable in $s_{0\varepsilon}$. By definition of A_ε, each operator a with $u(a) > 0$ is extended with additional effect $\langle g/1\rangle$, and π_ε is equivalent to π with extended net positive operators. Hence, by definition of $a_\varepsilon \in A_\varepsilon$, π_ε is applicable in $s_{0\varepsilon}$ and $\langle g/1\rangle \in s_{0\varepsilon}[\![\pi_\varepsilon]\!]$, that is, $\pi_\varepsilon \in \mathcal{P}_\varepsilon$. In turn, if L is a landmark for Π_ε, then π_ε contains an operator from L, and if $L \subseteq A$ then π contains an operator from L as well. This proves that all landmarks L for Π_ε over the extended operators of A are ε-landmarks over the operators A. □

With Theorem 7.1 in hand, we can now derive ε-landmarks for Π using any method for classical planning landmark extraction. After this compilation, we continue by performing the exact steps that developed by [Mirkis and Domshlak (2014)], that is the budget reduction and incremental BFBB, with a few optimizations that are discussed below. At the same time, the quality of the landmarks derived from the compilation (ε, V_{sum})-compilation as in Definition 7.5 can be substantially higher than those of the landmarks derived from the ε-compilation of Mirkis and Domshlak due to the refinement of the goal-achieving actions. Quite often, disjunctive landmarks contain many redundant operators, that is, operators that either don't participate in optimal plans or cannot be applied along any plan due to the unreachability of their preconditions. Still, the budget reducing compilation treats them similarly to all other operators in the landmarks, leading to redundant discounted operators and thus an increase in the effective search space.

In summary, the more the disjunctive action landmarks are refined, the better, and this is precisely what switching from ε-compilation to (ε, V_{sum})-compilation achieves.

Consider a simple example of an OSP task Π with a symmetric search space structure and with a cost budget of b = 4, depicted in Fig. 7.8(a). In this example we assume two states, s_{15} and s_{17} to include valuable propositions. The landmark extraction procedure for the assumed "goal states" provides us with four landmarks, namely

$$(a_1 \vee a_2) \wedge (a_3 \vee a_4 \vee a_5 \vee a_6) \wedge (a_8 \vee a_9 \vee a_{10}) \wedge (a_{12} \vee a_{14} \vee a_{15}). \quad (7.6)$$

Compiling $(\mathcal{L}, lcost)$ into Π using the budget reducing compilation results with a task $\Pi_{\mathcal{L}}$ with budget $b_{\mathcal{L}} = 0$ and $c(\overline{a}) = 0$ for all the discounted operators

$$\bigcup_{i=1}^{n} A_{L_i} = \{\overline{a}_1, \overline{a}_2, \overline{a}_3, \overline{a}_4, \overline{a}_5, \overline{a}_6, \overline{a}_8, \overline{a}_9, \overline{a}_{10}, \overline{a}_{12}, \overline{a}_{14}, \overline{a}_{15}\}.$$

Suppose now that s_{17} includes negative proposition as well as positive propositions, and that actions a_{14} and a_{15} achieve those valuable propositions in s_{17} along with the negative propositions. Recall the example in the classic Blocksworld in Fig. 7.6. In this case s_{15} is reachable through a plan with a net positive last action and s_{17} is only reachable through plans with net negative last actions. By using Lemma 7.1, the state s_{17} can be eliminated from the goal list. The landmark extraction procedure for the refined goal states provide us with a different set of four landmarks, namely

$$(a_1 \vee a_2) \wedge (a_5 \vee a_6) \wedge a_8 \wedge a_{13}. \quad (7.7)$$

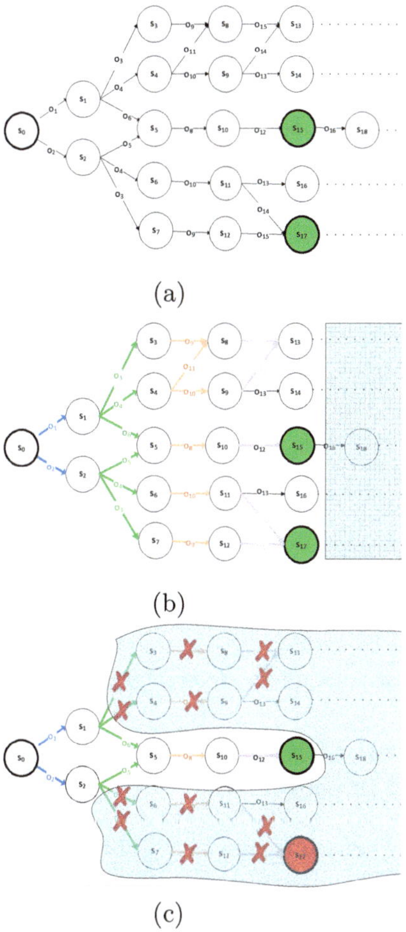

Fig. 7.8: Illustrations for our example of the landmark-based budget reducing compilation $\Pi_{\mathcal{L}}$: (a) The structurally reachable parts of the graphical skeleton of the original model induced by Π, along with a comparison between the budget-wise reachable parts of the graphical skeletons induced without (b) and with (c) the elimination of s_{17} following Lemma 7.1).

It is easy to see that the landmarks in Eq. (7.7) are much more focused than those in Eq. (7.6), leading to less discounted actions and stronger search space pruning. Indeed, compiling $(\mathcal{L}, lcost)$ into Π with the budget reducing compilation results with a task $\Pi_{\mathcal{L}}$ with budget $b_{\mathcal{L}} = 0$ and $c(\overline{a}) = 0$ for all the discounted operators

$$\bigcup_{i=1}^{n} A_{L_i} = \{\overline{a}_1, \overline{a}_2, \overline{a}_5, \overline{a}_6, \overline{a}_8, \overline{a}_{13}\}.$$

Figures 7.8(b) and 7.8(c) illustrate the effect of the budget-reducing compilation by depicting the parts of the graphical skeletons G_{M_Π} and $G_{M_{\Pi_\mathcal{L}}}$ that are actually reachable under the respective cost budgets $b = 4$ and $b_\mathcal{L} = 0$, where goals determined with (Fig. 7.8(b)) and without the elimination of the state s_{17} following Lemma 7.1. The arcs that correspond to discounted operators are colored so that each color distinguishing the landmark responsible for the respective discounted operators. While the states $\{s_3, s_4, s_6, s_7, s_8, s_9, s_{11}, s_{12}, s_{13}, s_{14}, s_{16}, s_{17}\}$ are all reachable from the initial state of Π under the budget allowance of 4, they are no longer reachable in $\Pi_\mathcal{L}$ if Lemma 7.1 is employed. The effect of the latter is a substantial reduction in the size of the search space for the next applied *BFBB*. As our empirical evaluation in Section 8.5 shows in Table 7.3 that describes the effect of budget reduction with different landmarks on the search space. Table 7.3 shows that using more informative landmarks reduce more budget and hence the search space. Furthermore as a secondary effect, within the reduced search space we have less discounted actions, which means, smaller set of applicable actions under stricter budget.

7.6 Solving OSP with Additive Utility Functions as a Process of Improvement

With the objective of increasing the quality of the derived landmarks, we refined the goal-achieving operators through characterization of the prefix of valuable plans in Lemma 7.1. At first sight, Lemma 7.1 only established one property along the prefix of plans that improve the initial state utility. However, note that Lemma 7.1 is defined for OSP tasks with an initial state of 0_{obs}. When the initial state utility is 0_{obs}, it is a special case where the occurrence of a net positive utility operator satisfies two properties of an (optimal) OSP plan that improves over the initial state utility. A solution to an optimal OSP task is,

(1) on from the perspective of efficiency, a budget preserving solution that terminates with a net positive operator, and
(2) from the perspective of effectiveness, goal reaching solution, such that improves the utility of at least one variable over its initial state assignment.

When it comes to tasks with an initial state of s_0 such that $u(s_0[\![\pi]\!]) > \theta_{obs}$, these two properties are likely to be satisfied by two separate events, that is, with an occurrence of two different operators.

As we mentioned before, in oversubscription planning, the task is to find *goal-effective* (or *valuable*) states via the most *cost-satisfying* trajectories. As illustrated by Fig. 7.9, efficiency, and effectiveness are both parts of a bigger picture, and we should focus on the top right quadrant when it comes to the objective of finding the *most* goal-effective state possible via the as *cost-effective* a trajectory as possible. From a budget perspective, when working with limited resources, the objective is to maximize the use of each of the available resources. However, by pursuing efficiency at all costs, without taking the big picture into account, the overall effectiveness may run-down. With Lemma 7.1 we tackled the efficiency aspect by pruning trajectories that are not *cost-satisfying*, and thus we moved toward the two

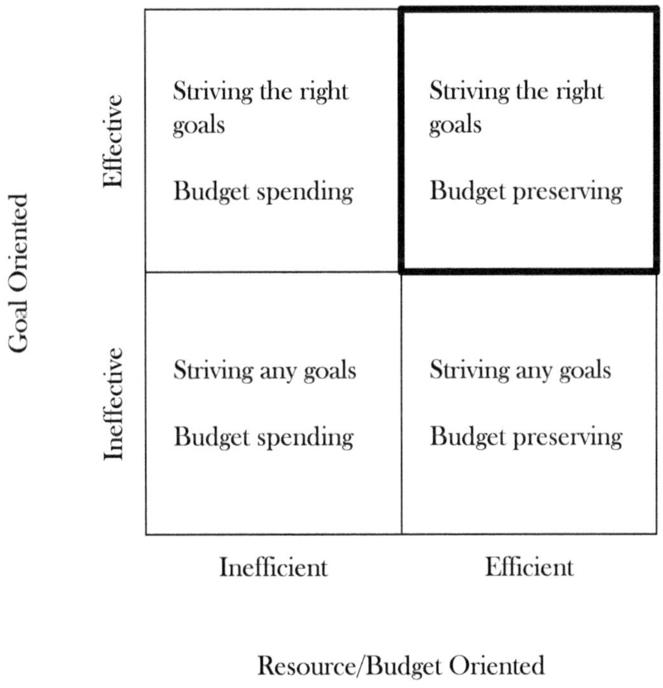

Fig. 7.9: Schematic illustration of the balance between the effectiveness and efficiency of a plan for OSP tasks. The most *goal-effective* states that are accessible via the most cost-effective trajectories, that is the optimal solutions, are in the top right quadrant.

right quadrants, as shown in Fig. 7.9. In what follows, we focus on the effectiveness aspect with a target of recognition and pruning trajectories that are not *goal-effective*.

We will refer to a state that improves over the utility of the initial state as a *valuable state* and to a sequence of actions that reaches such state as a *valuable plan*. Considering the notation of the effectiveness and the efficiency, a plan that is both efficient and effective is a *valuable plan*, that is, it improves over the initial state and is budget preserving.

In this section, we first relax the assumption of the lowest possible initial state utility. Next, we show how we refined the landmarks to reflect valuable plans, and that those refined landmarks do necessarily reduce the search effort.

7.6.1 *Relax the Assumption of the Lowest Possible Initial State Utility Value*

We now relax the simplifying assumption that we used to define the v_{sum}-compilation, that the initial state s_0 for an OSP task Π is the lowest possible state. When relaxing this assumption, the net positive utility operators may be applied in a state s such that $u(s) < u(s_0)$. Hence, such net positive utility operators may lead to a state s', yet $u(s) < u(s')$, but $u(s') < u(s_0)$. As we mentioned before, because of the dependencies between propositions, it is possible that collecting positive values might require collecting negative values along the way. In particular, it is possible that an same action that achieves positive value propositions may also achieves some negative value propositions. Accordingly, it would be beneficial not only to consider the net positive utility operators but also the operators that achieve valuable propositions, even though they might have net negative or zero utility value.

Consider a simple example of an OSP task Π with an initial state s_0 such that $u(s_0) > 0_{obs}$, depicted in Fig. 7.10. In this example the lowest possible utility in Π is $0_{obs} = -4$ and the initial state s_0 utility is $u(s_0) = -2$. The variables in Π are $V = \{v, w\}$ with $dom(v) = dom(w) = \{a, b, c\}$ and their utility setting is $u(\langle v/a \rangle) = u(\langle w/a \rangle) = -2$, $u(\langle v/b \rangle) = u(\langle w/b \rangle) = -1$ and $u(\langle v/c \rangle) = u(\langle w/c \rangle) = 0$. The initial state $s_0 = \{\langle v/b \rangle, \langle w/b \rangle\}$ can only be improved if a subset of propositions from the set $\{\langle v/c \rangle, \langle w/c \rangle\}$ is achieved, that is the set of propositions with improved utility over initial state variable assignment. Figure 7.10(a) listing the applicable operators in Π, where,

$$\mathsf{pre}(a_1) = \{\langle v/b\rangle, \langle w/b\rangle\}, \mathsf{eff} a_1 = \{\langle v/a\rangle, \langle w/a\rangle\}, u(a_1) = -2,$$
$$\mathsf{pre}(a_2) = \{\langle v/a\rangle, \langle w/a\rangle\}, \mathsf{eff} a_2 = \{\langle v/b\rangle, \langle w/a\rangle\}, u(a_2) = 1,$$
$$\mathsf{pre}(a_3) = \{\langle v/b\rangle, \langle w/a\rangle\}, \mathsf{eff} a_3 = \{\langle v/c\rangle, \langle w/b\rangle\}, u(a_3) = 2.$$

Consider a plan π for Π that improves over the initial state s_0, depicted in Fig. 7.10(b). Plan π consists of three operators, $\pi = \langle a_1, a_2, a_3\rangle$ with, a net negative utility operator a_1 followed by two net positive utility operators a_2 and a_3.

a_i	a_1	a_2	a_3
$\mathsf{pre}(a_i)$	$\{\langle v/b\rangle, \langle w/b\rangle\}$	$\{\langle v/a\rangle, \langle w/a\rangle\}$	$\{\langle v/a\rangle, \langle w/b\rangle\}$
$\mathsf{eff}(a_i)$	$\{\langle v/a\rangle, \langle w/a\rangle\}$	$\{\langle v/a\rangle, \langle w/b\rangle\}$	$\{\langle v/c\rangle\}$
$u(a_i)$	-2	1	2

(a)

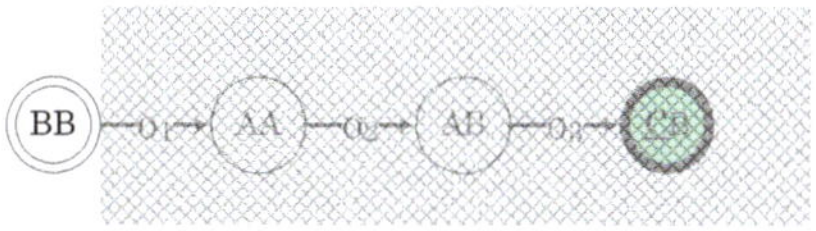

(b)

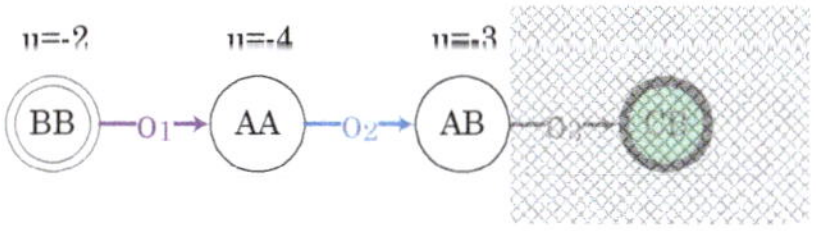

(c)

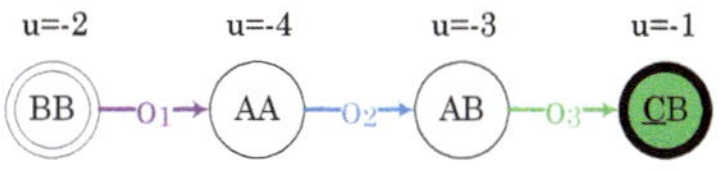

(d)

Fig. 7.10: A simple example of an OSP task, with (a) listing the operators, (b) illustrating a plan π that achieves an improvement over the initial state, (c) illustrating the "landmarks derivable" prefix of π when focus is only on net positive utility operators, and (d) illustrating the "landmarks derivable" prefix of π when focus is on operators with net positive utility and gross positive operators. The action landmarks for π are depicted in different colors, each color corresponds to a landmark.

When focus is only on the net positive utility operators, the suffix operator sequence $\langle a_3 \rangle$ of π is ignored with regards to landmark extraction. The grayed area in Fig. 7.10(c), corresponds to the suffix of π for which landmarks cannot be produced when the focus is only on net positive operators. The actions landmarks for π are depicted in different colors and each color corresponds to a landmark. In this example, where $u(s_0) \neq 0_{obs}$, we have net positive operators that clearly cannot be goal reaching operators. Treating these net positive operators as goal reaching operators is will result in the quality of the extracted landmarks being reduced. The first operator to be applied in π is a_1 with a net utility of -2, which leads to the state $s_0[\![a_1]\!]$ with $u(s_0[\![a_1]\!]) < u(s_0)$. Obviously, a net positive operator may be applied at state $s_0[\![a_1]\!]$ that will not lead to any improved state. Second operator to be applied in π is a_2 which leads to the state $s_0[\![\langle a_1, a_2 \rangle]\!]$ with $u(s_0[\![a_1]\!]) < u(s_0[\![\langle a_1, a_2 \rangle]\!]) < u(s_0)$. With a focus on the net positive utility operators only, the first occurrence of net positive utility operator, a_2, is treated as a candidate for achieving a goal state, which only allows for landmarks extraction for the prefix of π up to the occurrence of operator a_2, that is $\langle a_1, a_2 \rangle$.

The technique for relaxing the assumption of the lowest possible initial state utility is based on an expansion of the v_{sum}-compilation with additional constraints that reflect the properties (or the occurrence of events) that must happen in any plan that improves on the utility of the initial state. These constraints allow us to capture information about effective achievements of a plan, to support the decision of an efficient termination of the search procedure. In addition to the occurrence of the net positive utility operator, in what follows, we define the *gross positive operator* a_{grs}. The *gross positive operator* achieves an improvement on at least one variable in the initial state. Such an operator, as we show in Section 7.6.3, must occur in any valuable plan.

7.6.2 *High-Level Overview of the Improvement Approach*

In what follows, we present an interrelated set of properties of optimal plans, that allows us to define a pattern of valuable plans in OSP tasks. Our landmark generation method exploits these optimal plan properties at the level of actions and action sequences. This differs from the traditional "collecting" approach which generates landmarks from valuable facts, which are based on properties of the effect list of a single action. These properties are used to generate more refined and lengthier landmarks which are the input for Mirkis and Domshlak's budget reduction procedure. They also improve the pruning mechanism that is based on these landmarks. A running example in Fig. 7.11 shows all the plans for a given OSP task and will be referred to in order to demonstrate these properties. In this OSP task an additive utility function is defined over three state variables with the same domain $dom = \{A, B, C, D\}$, by $u(A) = 0, u(B) = 1, u(C) = 2$ and $u(D) = 3$ for each variable.

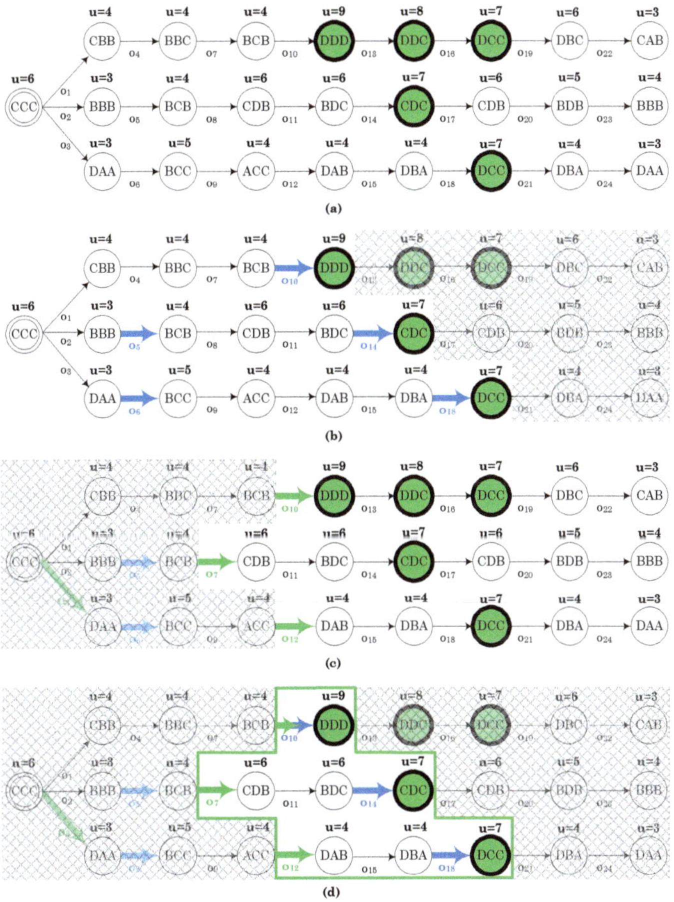

Fig. 7.11: An example of an OSP task, with (a) illustrating a search space with valuable states, depicted in green. The grayed out zone in (b) shows the pruning from Lemma 7.1 with net positive actions depicted with thick blue arrows. The region pruned by exploiting gross positive actions (Lemma 7.2) is grayed out in (c). Finally (d) shows the region that is pruned by combining both of the above.

In Lemma 7.1, we prove that any valuable plan terminates with a net positive utility action. The colored blue arrows illustrated in Fig. 7.11(b) indicate the net positive utility action candidates for finishing the search with an optimal state in hand. The green colored actions depicted in Fig. 7.11(c) are gross positive actions, whose effects improve on at least one of the variables in the initial state, but may result in total negative utility due achieving worse utility for other variables. We prove in Lemma 7.2 that such actions must occur in an optimal plan before a net positive action application that terminates the search is applied.

A special case is an action that is gross positive and has positive net utility, for example, action a_{10} in Fig. 7.11(d). In a strictly positive utility setting with a 0-binary utility function and an initial state with utility zero, the net positive actions are also gross positive. However, in the more general, additive utility settings, these actions are likely to be distinct. For example, the net positive utility actions a_5 in our running example occur before any gross positive actions occur and leads to states with lower utility than the initial state.

A maintained achievement property, which we prove in Lemma 7.3 complements Lemma 7.2 and ensures that an achieved effect of a gross positive action remains in hand when net positive actions are examined as candidates for terminating the search. For example the gross positive action a_3 and the net positive utility action a_6 (in Fig. 7.11(c)) are in the greyed-out area because the effect that is achieved by a_3 is not maintained (or is maintained for a limited subsequence of actions where net positive utility action candidates are not applicable).

The greyed-out area in Fig. 7.11(b) and Fig. 7.11(c) represents the states and actions that have been shown to be irrelevant for landmark discovery. Actions that do not add any effect with regards to net positive utility improvement are grayed-out in Fig. 7.11(b). The Grayed-out area in Fig. 7.11(c) represents actions that are not candidates for being applied last to terminate the search, which occurs before some improvement is achieved. These kinds of actions allow us to refine the set of net positive utility actions to a stricter set, excluding those that we know are not able to reach a valuable end-state, resulting in a lengthier and more informed set of landmarks.

Finally, in Theorem 7.2, we combine all these claims and define the so-called "window of opportunity" to terminate a plan with a valuable state in hand, as illustrated in Fig. 7.11(d). We construct a classical planning task, which encodes the constraints mentioned above onto the "window of opportunity". The landmarks for this classical planning task, are *value landmarks* which guide us towards a valuable state in the original OSP task.

7.6.3 *Gross Positive Actions*

Considering an OSP task $\Pi = \langle V, s_0, u; A, c, b\rangle$ with initial state $u(s_0) > 0_{obs}$, a net positive utility action might be applied during the search leading to state with a utility greater than 0_{obs} but with a lower utility than in the initial state $u(s) < u(s_0)$. Since landmarks must hold for any valuable plan, they must hold for a plan reaching state s as well. If so, then we are no longer interested in a search for plans that "achieve something", but in a search for plans that achieve an *improvement* on the initial state s_0.

Definition 7.6. Given an OSP task $\Pi = \langle V, s_0, u; A, c, b\rangle$ and a state s, let **improved**(s) be the set of all propositions $\langle v/d\rangle \in \mathcal{D}$ such that $u_v(d) > u_v(s[v])$.

Based on the definition of **improved**(s), we define a *gross positive action* as an action that improves on at least one variable from the initial state.

Definition 7.7. Given an OSP task $\Pi = \langle V, s_0, u; A, c, b\rangle$, the **gross positive actions** $A_{gPos} \subseteq A$ of Π are

$$A_{gPos} = \{a \in A, \mathsf{eff}(a) \cap \mathsf{improved}(s_0) \neq \emptyset\}.$$

For a general state s, which may be different to the initial state, we define a gross positive action relative to s;

Definition 7.8. Given an OSP task $\Pi = \langle V, s_0, u; A, c, b\rangle$ and an arbitrary state s, the **gross positive actions** relative to s $A_{gPos}(s) \subseteq A$ of Π are

$$A_{gPos}(s) = \{a \in A, \mathsf{eff}(a) \cap \mathsf{improved}(s) \neq \emptyset\}.$$

From now on, we will use the initial state s_0 as the reference state to be improved. Lemma 7.2 is based on the definition of *gross positive actions* and shows that gross positive actions play an essential role in creating optimal plans. The proof of Lemma 7.2, in simple terms, claims that, along any valuable plan π for an OSP task Π that improves over a given state, there is at least one *gross positive action*, which improves the utility of at least one of the state variables (although possibly at the cost of a lower utility for other variables).

Lemma 7.2. *Given an OSP task* $\Pi = \langle V, s_0, u; A, c, b\rangle$, *and a state* s, *for any plan* π *that improves over* s, *that is,* $u(s_0[\![\pi]\!]) > u(s)$, *it holds that:*

(1) $s_0[\![\pi]\!] \cap \mathsf{improved}(s) \neq \emptyset$, *and*

(2) $\pi \cap A_{gPos}(s) \neq \emptyset$, *that is, at least one action along* π *is gross positive.*

Proof. Assuming to the contrary that $s_0[\![\pi]\!] \cap \mathsf{improved}(s) = \emptyset$, by definition of $\mathsf{improved}(s)$ we have $u_v(s[\![\pi]\!][v]) \leq u_v(s[v])$, and thus

$$\sum_{\langle v/d\rangle \in s[\![\pi]\!]} u_v(d) \leq \sum_{\langle v/d\rangle \in s} u_v(d)$$

and, in turn, $u(s[\![\pi]\!]) \leq u(s)$, contradicting the assumption of the lemma that π improves over s.

Since $s[\![\pi]\!] \cap \mathsf{improved}(s) \neq \emptyset$, consider any proposition $\langle v/d\rangle \in s[\![\pi]\!] \cap \mathsf{improved}(s)$. By definition of $\mathsf{improved}(s)$, $\langle v/d\rangle \notin s$, π must contain an operator a achieving $\langle v/d\rangle$, and by definition of $A_{gPos}(s)$, $a \in A_{gPos}(s)$. □

Applying any of those actions indicates a valuable achievement in Π. By combining Lemma 7.1 and Lemma 7.2, we can stratify the v_{sum}-compilation by focusing on *both* operators with net positive values and gross positive operators. The number of the landmarks derived can be substantially increased with a focus on gross positive utility actions.

For instance, consider our running example of an OSP task depicted in Fig. 7.10. Since there is no gross positive operator along $\langle a_1, a_2\rangle$, we can safely determine with Lemma 7.2 that a_2 is not the last net positive operator along π and that the prefix plan $\langle a_1, a_2\rangle$ of π achieves no improvement on the initial state s_0. As illustrated in Fig. 7.10(d) in our simple example, the number of landmarks derived when focusing on both gross positive and net positive utility operators can be substantially increased, leading to better budget reduction and stronger state pruning.

7.6.4 *The Window of Opportunity to Improve*

In tasks where the initial state carries the lowest possible utility, all the constraints are satisfied by one event, that is, the last net positive action application, which makes Lemma 7.1 a sufficient condition. When it comes to tasks with an initial state utility $u(s_0)$ higher than the lowest possible utility, a set of separate events is likely to happen. When *gross positive action* and *net positive action* are different events, achievements may be lost as a result.

Furthermore, Lemma 7.1 is stated concerning the net utility of an action, which is a relative term. The decision of whether the net utility of an action is enough to improve on the initial state, depends on which state the action is applied in. When the initial state is the lowest possible utility, every net positive utility action application is a good candidate for improvement. On the other hand, gross positive actions are defined in absolute terms, and allow for the evaluation of achievements in relation to a reference state, in the context of a sequence of actions rather than a single action. The integration of these two properties to form criteria for optimal plans with any initial state utility occurs through timing. The occurrence of a gross positive action establishes a dynamic reference point. Once a reference point is established, a net positive utility improvement must occur in relation to that point. The length of the "window of opportunity" to achieve an improvement on the initial state is defined by the time that the achievement of the gross positive action is able to hold for, that is, an improved proposition (or a set of propositions) from the initial state from $\mathsf{improved}(s_0)$ holds. When there has been no achievement during the trajectory yet, or the achievement cannot be maintained, the net positive utility actions (which are not gross positive) do not bring a sustainable (global) benefit. To acquire more accurate landmarks, we have to capture information regarding the occurrence of an effective gross-positive achievement, that allows for recognition of the "zone" in which an effective search can be terminated. A net positive action that is applied outside of that "zone" can be safely treated as just an intermediate action in a plan.

7.6.5 *Maintained Achievements*

In Lemma 7.3 we define the maintained proposition property of sequential application of actions in a deterministic scenario. This notation is similar to the notion of *maintenance goals*, which is used in the context of temporal planning [Haddawy and Hanks (1993, 1998)]. The proof of Lemma 7.3 is rather simple, it finalizes the claim in Lemma 7.2 by defining the "goal area" where the plan may terminate with achievement in hand. In plain words, Lemma 7.3 states that for each improving plan π over the initial state there is a suffix plan π' such that (i) starts with a gross positive action a_{grs}, and (ii) a valuable proposition achieved by a_{grs} is maintained along π'.

Lemma 7.3. *Given an OSP task* $\Pi = \langle V, s_0, u; A, c, b\rangle$, *and a state* s, *for any plan* π *that improves over* s, *that is,* $u(s_0[\![\pi]\!]) > u(s)$, *there is a suffix* π' *of* $\pi = \pi_0 \cdot \pi'$ *such that:*

(1) π' *starts with a gross positive action* a_{grs}*, and*
(2) for some $\langle v/d\rangle \in \mathsf{eff}(a_{grs}) \cap \mathsf{improved}(s)$*,* $\langle v/d\rangle$ *is maintained along* π'*, that is, for each non-empty prefix* π'' *of* π'*,* $\langle v/d\rangle \in s_0[\![\pi_0]\!][\![\pi'']\!]$.

Proof. Let $\pi = \langle a_1, \ldots, a_n\rangle$ be a plan for Π such that $u(s_0[\![\pi]\!]) > u(s)$. By Lemma 7.2, we have $s_0[\![\pi]\!] \cap \mathsf{improved}(s) \neq \emptyset$, and for each $\langle v/d\rangle \in s_0[\![\pi]\!] \cap \mathsf{improved}(s)$, the plan π contains an operator achieving $\langle v/d\rangle$. Consider any such proposition $\langle v/d\rangle \in s_0[\![\pi]\!] \cap \mathsf{improved}(s)$, and let a_i, $i \in [n]$, be the last instance of an operator along π that achieves $\langle v/d\rangle$. Since $\langle v/d\rangle \in s_0[\![\pi]\!]$, then no operator instance along the suffix $\pi' = \langle a_i, \ldots, a_n\rangle$ of π changes the value of v, and thus π' satisfies the claim of the lemma. □

For instance, consider the OSP task depicted in Fig. 7.12, extending our running example from Fig. 7.10 with additional variable z of the same domain $dom(z) = \{a, b, c\}$ and the same utility setting $u(\langle z/a\rangle) = -2$, $u(\langle z/b\rangle) = -1$ and $u(\langle z/c\rangle) = 0$. In this example the initial state is $s_0 = \{\langle v/b\rangle, \langle w/b\rangle, \langle z/a\rangle\}$ with $u(s_0) = -4$, where $0_{obs} = -6$ in Π, that is, $u(s_0) > 0_{obs}$. The $\mathsf{improved}(s_0)$ set in Π is $\mathsf{improved}(s_0) = \{\langle v/c\rangle, \langle w/c\rangle, \langle z/b\rangle, \langle z/c\rangle\}$. Consider plan π for Π depicted in Fig. 7.12(b), plan π achieves an improvement on the initial state and consists of four actions, $\pi = \langle a_1, a_2, a_3, a_1, a_4\rangle$ where

$$\mathsf{pre}(a_1) = \{\langle w/b\rangle, \langle z/b\rangle\}, \mathsf{eff}a_1 = \{\langle w/a\rangle, \langle z/c\rangle\}, u(a_1) = 0,$$
$$\mathsf{pre}(a_2) = \{\langle z/c\rangle\}, \mathsf{eff}a_2 = \{\langle z/a\rangle\}, u(a_2) = -2,$$
$$\mathsf{pre}(a_3) = \{\langle v/b\rangle, \langle w/a\rangle, \langle z/a\rangle\}, \mathsf{eff}a_3 = \{\langle v/a\rangle, \langle w/b\rangle, \langle z/b\rangle\}, u(a_3) = 1,$$
$$\mathsf{pre}(a_4) = \{\langle v/a\rangle, \langle w/a\rangle\}, \mathsf{eff}a_4 = \{\langle v/b\rangle, \langle w/b\rangle\}, u(a_4) = 2.$$

In this utility setting, a_1 is a gross positive operator with $\langle z/c\rangle = \mathsf{improved}(s_0) \cap \mathsf{eff}(a_1)$. The operators a_3 and a_4 are of net positive utility operators, and a_2 is a net negative operator that loses the gross positive achievement, that is, $\langle z/a\rangle = \mathsf{eff}(a_2)$. Depicted in Fig. 7.12(c) is a prefix of π with gross positive operator a_1 along π, and with last net positive operator a_3. The grayed area in Fig. 7.10(c), corresponds to the suffix of π which is ignored for landmark generation. Bold and underlined letters correspond to a valuable proposition that holds in the described state, while bold, underlined and red colored corresponds to a valuable proposition from $\mathsf{improved}(s_0)$ that is lost. The action landmarks for π are depicted in different colors; each color corresponds to a different landmark.

The proposition $\langle z/c\rangle \in \mathsf{improved}(s_0)$ is achieved using by operator a_1 to satisfy a precondition of the operator a_2 (which is essential for the

a_i	a_1	a_2	a_3	a_4
$\mathsf{pre}(a_i)$	$\{\langle w/b\rangle, \langle z/b\rangle\}$	$\{\langle z/c\rangle\}$	$\{\langle v/b\rangle, \langle w/a\rangle, \langle z/a\rangle\}$	$\{\langle v/a\rangle, \langle w/a\rangle\}$
$\mathsf{eff}(a_i)$	$\{\langle w/a\rangle, \langle z/c\rangle\}$	$\{\langle z/a\rangle\}$	$\{\langle v/a\rangle, \langle w/b\rangle, \langle z/b\rangle\}$	$\{\langle v/b\rangle, \langle w/b\rangle\}$
$u(a_i)$	0	−2	1	2

(a)

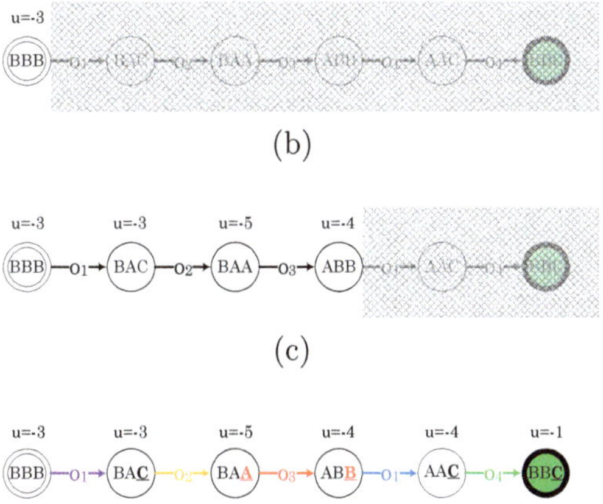

(d)

Fig. 7.12: A simple example of an OSP task, with (a) listing the operators, (b) illustrating a plan π that improves on the initial state, (c) illustrating the "landmarks derivable" path when focus is only on net positive utility operators, and (d) illustrating the "landmarks derivable" path when focus is on operators with net positive utility and gross positive operators. The actions landmarks for π are depicted in different colors, each color corresponds to a landmark.

achievement of the goal state) and is lost immediately afterwards when a_2 is applied, i.e. it is not maintained. Obviously, some propositions $\langle v/d\rangle \in \mathsf{improved}(s_0)$ must be re-acquired, and an optimal plan has to include another occurrence of gross positive operators. Using Lemma 7.2, with no *maintained proposition* in hand, we can safely determine that a_3 is not the last net positive operator in the π and that the prefix plan $\langle a_1, a_2, a_3\rangle$ of π does not improve on the initial state s_0. As depicted in Fig. 7.10(d), the action landmarks for π under the constraint of holding maintained proposition while applying last, net positive operator. The proposition $\langle z/c\rangle \in \mathsf{improved}(s_0)$ is re-acquired with the second instance of the operator a_1, where a_4 is a net positive utility operator that is applied next, and an improved state (on the initial utility) reached. This example illustrates that the number of landmarks derived under the constraint of holding maintained proposition when terminating search, in addition to the requirement of gross positive operators and net positive utility operators, can increase the number of derived landmarks. The "landmarks derivable" path is longer which allows for a higher number of derived landmarks, equal at worst to the initial state, leading to better budget reduction and stronger state pruning.

To acquire more accurate landmarks, we have to capture information regarding the occurrence of an effective gross-positive achievement, which allows for the recognition of the "zone" in which an effective search can terminate. A net positive operator that is applied outside of that "zone" can be safely treated as an intermediate operator along the plan. To compile this information into the v_{sum}-compilation, we add the gross positive achievement indicator g_{grs} to control the information regarding maintained and not-maintained achievements, which significantly improves the quality of landmarks in such domains. In what follows, the auxiliary proposition $\langle g_{grs}/1\rangle$ is used as an indicator that a gross-positive achievement has acquired and maintained.

7.6.6 *Synergistic Criteria for a Valuable Plan*

Given the OSP task Π with an additive utility function and an initial state of s_0, considering a plan π for Π with $u(s_0[\![\pi]\!]) > u(s_0)$, from Lemma 7.1, Lemma 7.2 and Lemma 7.3 we know the following properties for a valuable plan π:

(1) for the last action a along π, we have $u(a) > 0$,
(2) π contains at least one gross positive action, and
(3) an achievement of at least one gross positive action is maintained, that is, holds along a suffix of π.

Putting it all together, we are now able to devise additional constraints on valuable plans for OSP tasks. Any valuable plan π must have a valuable partial plan.

Consider a plan $\pi = \langle a_1, \ldots, a_i, \ldots, a_n\rangle$, with $i \in [n]$ where a_i is a *gross positive action*, that achieves a valuable proposition $\langle v/d\rangle \in \mathsf{improved}(s_0)$, yet with a total state utility of $u(s_0[\![\langle a_1, \ldots, a_i\rangle]\!]) < u(s_0)$. Obviously, the sequence of actions $\langle a_{i+1}, \ldots, a_n\rangle$ must include a net positive action. In this case the rest of the plan $\pi' = \langle a_i, \ldots, a_n\rangle$ is dedicated to damage reduction using the variables from $V \setminus v$ that were obtained on the way to collecting the valuable proposition $\langle v/d \rangle \in \mathsf{improved}(s_0)$. In this case, there is an *ordering constraint* on the application of a *gross positive action* and a *net positive action*, where a_i must be applied at some point before applying the net positive action a_n. Furthermore, along the execution of the partial plan $\pi' = \langle a_i, \ldots, a_n \rangle$ the proposition $\langle v/d \rangle$ must be maintained by any action a_j, where $j \in [i, n]$.

The maintained proposition property proved in Lemma 7.3 allows us to combine it with Theorem 7.2, through an *ordering constraint* on the properties provided in Lemma 7.1 and Lemma 7.2. Theorem 7.2 states that, for each valuable plan π, there is a *partial valuable plan* π'', which is the "window of opportunity" to terminate the search with an optimal end-state.

Theorem 7.2. *Given an OSP task* Π *with an additive utility function* u, *and a state* s *with* $u(s) \geq u(s_0)$, *for any plan* π *for* Π *with* $u(s_0[\![\pi]\!]) > u(s)$, *there is a suffix* π' *of* π, *such that:*

(1) *The last action* a_l *of* π' *is a net positive action, and*
(2) *The first action* a_f *of* π' *is a gross positive action relative to* s, *i.e.,* $a_f \in a_{grs}(s)$, *and*
(3) *There exists some effect* $\langle v/d \rangle$ *of* a_f, *which is maintained throughout* π'.

Proof. The proof is obtained immediately from the combination of Lemmas 7.1, 7.2, and 7.3. □

Relying on Theorem 7.2, we can define a more informative version of the compilation. The compilation is expanded by adding an auxiliary control structure of zero cost actions and zero utility propositions that restrict plans to terminating in the "window of opportunity" for improvement.

Illustrated in Fig. 7.13 is an example of the goal zone as seen from the perspective of The Window of Opportunity to Improve. The partial plans concerning goal effective achievement and efficient termination with a net positive operator, restrict the goal zone to the grayed zone and refine the landmarks through the elimination of, on the surface, false goals, that only partially obey the constraints posed by Lemma 7.2.

7.6.7 *Multiple Operator Repetitions*

Many OSP domains allow for plans with multiple operator repetitions. In particular, an optimal plan π for an OSP task Π may involve multiple

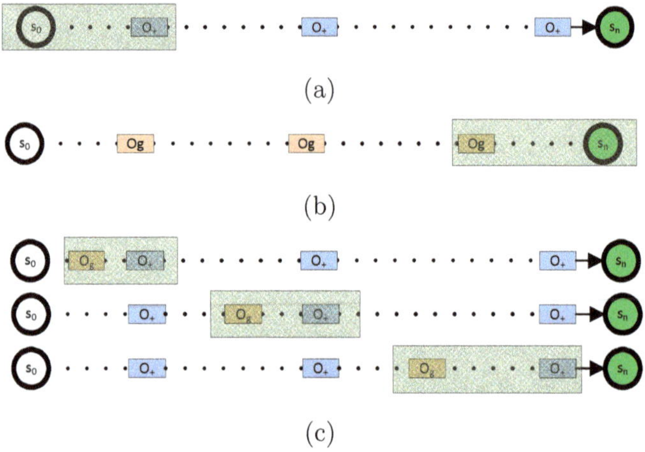

Fig. 7.13: An illustration of the length of the prefix path π' of π and suffix path π'' of π that we can now extract landmarks for, with respect to the occurrence of the first net positive operator and the last gross positive operator. The *landmark extractable* prefix path π' with Lemma 7.1 in (a), suffix path π'' Lemma 7.3 and Lemma 7.2 in (b) and the impact of their integration in Lemma 7.2 in (c).

occurrences of *net positive operators* and *gross positive operators*. Considering an optimal plan $\pi = \langle a_1, \ldots, a_i, \ldots, a_n \rangle$, with $k \in [n]$, Lemma 7.2 shows that a plan π that achieves an *improvement* on the initial state s_0 has to contain at least one *gross positive operator*. The valuable proposition that is achieved with this gross positive operator holds at the end-state of π. This necessary condition for optimal planning is beneficial for plans with a single operator repetition. As for domains in which multiple operator repetitions occur, this condition is weaker and may lead to false recognition of sub plans as valuable plans. Hence, the extracted landmarks are still admissible, but less accurate.

Consider a plan $\pi = \langle a_1, \ldots, a_i, \ldots, a_j, \ldots, a_n \rangle$, with $i, j \in [n]$, such that $i < j \leq n$ and a valuable proposition $\langle v/d \rangle \in \mathsf{eff}(a_i)$, such that $\langle v/d \rangle \in \mathsf{improved}(s_0)$, let the end-state be $s = s_0[\![\pi]\!]$ such that $u(s) > u(s_0)$. Suppose that, an action a_j is such that $\langle v/d \rangle \in \mathsf{pre}(a_j)$ and $\langle v''/d'' \rangle, \left\langle v/d' \right\rangle\} \in \mathsf{eff}(a_j)$, where $d \neq d', v \neq v'$ and $\langle v''/d'' \rangle \in \mathsf{pre}(a_n)$. In this example, the proposition $\langle v/d \rangle \in \mathsf{improved}(s_0)$ which was achieved by an intermediate operator a_i being used to satisfy a precondition for the operator a_j and being lost immediately after, i.e. it was not maintained. Obviously, the proposition $\langle v/d \rangle \in s \cap \mathsf{improved}(s_0)$ must be re-acquired, and the plan may include another occurrence of this action, that is, $\pi = \langle a_1, \ldots, a_i, \ldots, a_j, \ldots, a_i, \ldots, a_n \rangle$ so that $\langle v/d \rangle$ will hold at the end-state, that is, $\langle v/d \rangle \in s \cap \mathsf{improved}(s_0) \subseteq s$. Hence, multiple occurrence of gross positive operator a_j in the operator sequence $\pi = \langle a_i, \ldots, a_j, \ldots, a_i \rangle$, may mislead the landmark generation procedure into ignoring landmarks related to the operator of this sequence. To acquire more accurate landmarks we have to capture this information in the compiled classical planning task Π_ε. We add a gross positive achievement indicator $\langle g_{grs} \rangle$ to control the information regarding maintained and not-maintained achievements which significantly improves the quality of landmarks in such domains. We use the auxiliary proposition g_{grs} for this role, where $\langle g_{grs}/0 \rangle$ indicates a proposition that is not maintained and $\langle g_{grs}/1 \rangle$ indicates a gross positive achievement that is acquired and maintained for the rest of the plan. In our example, after first occurrence of operator a_i, the proposition $\langle g_{grs}/0 \rangle$ holds, when a_j is applied for the last time, the $\langle g_{grs}/1 \rangle$ may be achieved. Once $\langle g_{grs}/1 \rangle$ is achieved, it will be maintained until the final state of the plan. The gross positive achievement indicator $\langle g_{grs} \rangle$ in our compilation with classical planning should only be achieved once, with the last applied gross positive operator as we show in what follows.

In order to address domains such that they allow for multiple operator repetitions, we duplicate gross positive operators and extend one instance of each with an auxiliary control indicator g_{grs} as follows:

$$
\begin{aligned}
\mathsf{pre}(a_{nm}) &= \mathsf{pre}(a) \cup \langle g_{grs}/0 \rangle \\
\mathsf{eff}(a_{nm}) &= \mathsf{eff}(a) \\
c(a_{nm}) &= c(a) \\
\mathsf{pre}(a_m) &= \mathsf{pre}(a) \cup \langle g_{grs}/0 \rangle \\
\mathsf{eff}(a_m) &= \mathsf{eff}(a) \cup \langle g_{grs}/1 \rangle \\
c(a_m) &= c(a).
\end{aligned}
$$

The operator a_{nm} is associated with a not-maintained occurrence of proposition $\langle v/d \rangle$ and the operator a_m is associated with a maintained occurrence of proposition $\langle v/d \rangle$, and can only be applied once along plan π.

Using Lemma 7.3 in, we can derive ε-landmarks for an OSP task Π with multiple operator repetitions using any method for classical planning landmark extraction. We now put this observation to work and present the **maintained-proposition-compilation**. Note, it is an *OSP to OSP* compilation and will be performed before the **(ε, V_{sum})-compilation**. Operator a, being originally one action in a domain with multiple operator repetitions, will be split into a_{nm} and a_m. Hence, such operators, that may occur in two different landmarks will occur. We present a compilation that maintains one proposition, as established by Lemma 7.3. This compilation can be easily extended to maintain all propositions or subgroups of $\mathsf{improved}(s_0)$, which is beneficial for the question: Given a value x, is there a plan π for Π with initial state s_0, such that $u(s_0[\![\pi]\!]) \geq x > u(s_0)$. We will further discuss this subject in future work.

Definition 7.9. Given an OSP task $\Pi = \langle V, s_0, u; A, c, b\rangle$, the **maintained-proposition-compilation** of Π is an OSP task $\tilde{\Pi} = \langle \tilde{V}, \tilde{s_0}, \tilde{u}; \tilde{A}, \tilde{c}, \tilde{b}\rangle$ where

$$\begin{aligned}
\tilde{V} &= V \cup \{g_{grs}\}, \\
&\quad \textit{with } dom(g_{grs}) = \{0,1\}, \\
\tilde{s_0} &= s_0 \cup \{\langle g_{grs}/0\rangle\}, \\
\tilde{u} &= u, \\
\tilde{b} &= b, \\
\tilde{A} &= \{\tilde{a} \mid a \in A, \mathsf{eff}(a) \cap \mathsf{improved}(s_0) = \emptyset\} \cup \\
&\quad \{a_{\mathsf{nm}}, a_{\mathsf{m}} \mid a \in A, \mathsf{eff}(a) \cap \mathsf{improved}(s_0) \neq \emptyset\}
\end{aligned}$$

where

$$\tilde{a} = \langle \mathsf{pre}(a), \mathsf{eff}(a), c(a)\rangle$$

and

$$a_{\mathsf{nm}} = \langle \mathsf{pre}(a) \cup \langle g_{grs}/0\rangle, \mathsf{eff}(a), c(a)\rangle$$

and

$$a_{\mathsf{m}} = \langle \mathsf{pre}(a) \cup \langle g_{grs}/0\rangle, \mathsf{eff}(a) \cup \langle g_{grs}/1\rangle, c(a)\rangle.$$

7.6.8 *The Valuable Plan Compilation*

Relying on Lemma 7.2, in what follows, we focus on the **value-driven-landmarks** for OSP task Π which are generalized to additive utility function and unrestricted initial utility.

Definition 7.10. Let $\Pi = \langle V, s_0, u; A, c, b\rangle$ be an OSP task and $\mathsf{improved}(s_0)$ be the set of all propositions $\langle v/d\rangle \in \mathcal{D}$ such that $u_v(d) > u_v(s_0[v])$. The **valuable plan compilation** of Π is a classical planning task $\Pi_\uparrow = \langle V_\uparrow, s_{0\uparrow}, G_\uparrow; A_\uparrow, c_\uparrow\rangle$ where

$$
\begin{aligned}
V_{\uparrow} &= V \cup \{srch, get, ver, end, g_{grs}, g_{net}, g\} \cup Y,\\
&\quad \textit{with } dom(g) = dom(g_{grs}) = dom(g_{net}) = dom(srch) = \{1,0\},\\
&\qquad dom(get) = dom(end) = \{0,1\},\\
&\qquad Y = \{y_d^v \mid v \in V, d \in dom(v)\},\\
s_{0\uparrow} &= s_0 \cup \{\langle y_d^v/0\rangle \mid y_d^v \in Y\} \cup\\
&\quad \{\langle g/0\rangle, \langle g_{grs}/0\rangle, \langle g_{net}/0\rangle, \langle srch/1\rangle, \langle get/0\rangle, \langle end/0\rangle\},\\
G_{\uparrow} &= \{\langle g/1\rangle\},\\
A_{\uparrow} &= \{a_{\mathsf{g}} \mid a \in A, u(a) > 0, \mathsf{eff}(a) \cap \mathsf{improved}(s_0) \neq \emptyset\} \cup\\
&\quad \{a^+ \mid a \in A, u(a) > 0, \mathsf{eff}(a) \cap \mathsf{improved}(s_0) = \emptyset\} \cup\\
&\quad \{a_{\mathsf{mid}} \mid a \in A, u(a) > 0\} \cup\\
&\quad \{a_{\mathsf{nm}}, a_{\mathsf{m}} \mid a \in A, u(a) \leq 0, \mathsf{eff}(a) \cap \mathsf{improved}(s_0) \neq \emptyset\} \cup\\
&\quad \{a_{\mathsf{src}} \mid a \in A, u(a) \leq 0, \mathsf{eff}(a) \cap \mathsf{improved}(s_0) = \emptyset\} \cup\\
&\quad \{a_{ver}^{gross}, a_{ver}^{net} \mid \langle v/d\rangle \in \mathsf{improved}(s_0)\} \cup finish
\end{aligned}
$$

where

// immediate goal operators - net positive and gross positive operators

$$
a_{\mathsf{g}} = \left\langle \begin{matrix} \mathsf{pre}(a) \cup \langle g_{grs}/0\rangle \cup \langle g_{net}/0\rangle, \\ \mathsf{eff}(a) \cup \langle g_{grs}/1\rangle \cup \langle g_{net}/1\rangle, c(a) \end{matrix} \right\rangle
$$

// net positive operators (non-gross positive), not to be applied last

$$
a_{\mathsf{mid}} = \langle \mathsf{pre}(a) \cup \langle srch/1\rangle, \mathsf{eff}(a), c(a)\rangle
$$

// net positive operators (non-gross positive) to be applied last

$$
a^+ = \left\langle \begin{matrix} \mathsf{pre}(a) \cup \langle end/1\rangle \cup \langle g_{net}/0\rangle, \\ \mathsf{eff}(a) \cup \langle end/0\rangle \cup \langle g_{net}/1\rangle, c(a) \end{matrix} \right\rangle
$$

// gross positive operators (non-net positive),

// not to be applied as last gross positive achievement

// (not maintained propositions)

$$
a_{\mathsf{nm}} = \langle \mathsf{pre}(a) \cup \langle g_{grs}/0\rangle, \mathsf{eff}(a), c(a)\rangle
$$

// gross positive operators (non-net positive),

// to be applied as last gross positive achievement (maintained propositions)

$$
a_{\mathsf{m}} = \langle \mathsf{pre}(a) \cup \langle g_{grs}/0\rangle, \mathsf{eff}(a) \cup \langle g_{grs}/1\rangle, c(a)\rangle
$$

// search operators - not net positive nor gross positive operators

$$
a_{\mathsf{src}} = \langle \mathsf{pre}(a) \cup \langle srch/1\rangle, \mathsf{eff}(a), c(a)\rangle
$$

and

// *once gross positive achievement registered, finish attempts are allowed*

$$\mathsf{pre}(finish) = \langle srch/1\rangle \cup \langle g_{grs}/1\rangle$$
$$\mathsf{eff}(finish) = \langle get/1\rangle \cup \langle srch/0\rangle$$
$$c(finish) = 0$$

and

// *finish and achieve goal*

$$\mathsf{pre}(finishG) = \langle srch/1\rangle \cup \langle g_{yrs}/1\rangle \cup \langle g_{grs}/1\rangle$$
$$\mathsf{eff}(finishG) = \langle get/1\rangle \cup \langle srch/0\rangle$$
$$c(finishG) = 0$$

and

// *verify that gross positive achievement still in hand and*
// *allow net positive finalization*

$$\mathsf{pre}(a_{ver}^{gross}) = \langle v/d\rangle \cup \langle get/1\rangle \cup \langle g_{net}/0\rangle \cup \langle end/0\rangle \cup \langle y_d^v/0\rangle$$
$$\mathsf{eff}(a_{ver}^{gross}) = \langle end/1\rangle \cup \langle get/0\rangle \cup \langle y_d^v/1\rangle$$
$$c(a_{ver}^{gross}) = 0$$

and

// *verify that gross positive achievement still in hand and*
// *allow goal proposition achievement*

$$\mathsf{pre}(a_{ver}^{net}) = \langle v/d\rangle \cup \langle y_d^v/1\rangle \cup \langle g_{net}/1\rangle$$
$$\mathsf{eff}(a_{ver}^{net}) = \langle g_{net}/0\rangle \cup \langle y_d^v/0\rangle \cup \langle g/1\rangle$$
$$c(a_{ver}^{net}) = 0.$$

To put it simply, $\Pi_{\uparrow}$ extends the structure of Π with a zero cost auxiliary operator and a zero utility carrying auxiliary proposition. This auxiliary control structure allows for the transformation of an OSP task into a classical planning task, such that it reflects the original OSP task properties in a way that allows the classical planning landmarks generation procedure to consider them. A valuable state for an OSP task Π with an initial state of s_0 such that $u(s_0) > 0_{obs}$, can be acquired through a set of events. Hence, to receive landmarks of good quality, it is beneficial to provide the landmark extraction procedure with as much information as possible, that is, as accurate as possible regarding the events and the constraints that must hold in any valuable plan for an OSP task. The auxiliary control structure is constructed as follows,

- the propositions $srch, get, end, g_{grs}, g_{net}$ and g together with the operators $a_{ver}^{gross}, a_{ver}^{net}$ and $finish$ enforce the achievements with respect to timing constraints from Lemma 7.2,

- the artificial goal proposition g can be achieved directly by applying a net positive utility operator, such that it is also gross positive operator,
- the artificial goal proposition g can be achieved by applying a net positive utility operator, such that it is not a gross positive operator, only after the verification phase is terminated, that is, the operators A_{ver}^{gross}, A_{ver}^{net} and $finish$ applied. The verification phase is as follows;
  (1) the regular operators can be applied only before $finish$ operator,
  (2) the A_{ver}^{gross} operators can be applied only after $finish$ operator,
  (3) the last occurrence of net utility operators (with g_{net} verification) can be applied only after A_{ver}^{gross} operator,
  (4) the goal reaching actions can be applied only with $a_{ver}^{net} \in A_{ver}^{net}$ operator.

In this way, the first part of any plan for $\Pi_{\uparrow}$ determines a plan for Π. The second part "verifies" that the end-state of the plan achieves a subset of valuable propositions from $\mathsf{improved}(s_0)$. The third part terminates the search with net positive utility operator. Finally, the last part grantees that $\mathsf{improved}(s_0) \cap s_0[\![\pi]\!] \neq \emptyset$ by verifying that the valuable proposition that initiated the verification phase was lost during verification phase.

In what follows, we refer to $\Pi_{\uparrow}$ as the **valuable plan compilation** of Π. Constructing $\Pi_{\uparrow}$ from Π is trivially polynomial time, and it allows us to discover **value-driven-landmarks** for Π using the standard machinery for classical planning landmark discovery.

Theorem 7.3. *For any OSP task Π, any landmark L for $\Pi_{\uparrow}$ such that $L \subseteq A$ is a value-driven-landmark L for Π.*

Proof. Let $\mathcal{P}$ be the set of all plans for Π with $u(s[\![\pi]\!]) > u(s_0)$ and $\mathcal{P}_{\uparrow}$ the set of all plans for $\Pi_{\uparrow}$. The proof is obtained by showing that, for each $\pi \in \mathcal{P}$, there exists an equivalent plan $\pi_{\uparrow} \in \mathcal{P}_{\uparrow}$, and both are applicable in $s_{0\uparrow}$. Plan π is applicable in $s_{0\uparrow}$ since by the definition of $s_{0\uparrow}$, $s_0 \in s_{0\uparrow}$.

By the definition of $\Pi_{\uparrow}$, Π is extended with an auxiliary control structure based on the properties of $\mathcal{P}$ from Lemma 7.2. Each π_{ε} is equivalent to π with extended zero cost operators and zero utility propositions. We now show that each such $\pi_{\uparrow}$ is applicable in $s_{0\uparrow}$ as well. From Lemma 7.2 we know that for each $\pi \in \mathcal{P}$ with $u(s[\![\pi]\!]) > u(s_0)$, there exists a prefix

π' that ends with an operator $a^+ \in A$ such that $u(a^+) > 0$. Likewise, Lemma 7.2 guarantees the ordering of a set of events along π'. Let plan π' be $\pi' = \langle a_1, \ldots, a_i, \ldots, a_n \rangle$ where $a_n = a^+$ and $i \in [n]$. There exist an operator $a_{grs} \in A$ such that $s_0[\![\pi]\!] \cap \mathsf{improved}(s_0) \cap \mathsf{eff}(a_{grs}) \neq \emptyset$, where a_{grs} occurs before a^+ or they are both the same operator. Let $a_i = a_{grs}$ such that $i \leq n$. Furthermore, there exists a proposition $\langle v/d \rangle$ such that is a maintained proposition in the suffix of the prefix of π', that is, $s_0[\![\pi']\!] \cap \mathsf{improved}(s_0) \cap \mathsf{eff}(a_{grs}) \neq \emptyset$.

Using the definition of $A_\uparrow$ and $s_{0\uparrow}$ each operator $a \in A$ is applicable in $s_{0\uparrow}$ except for the operators A^{gross}_{ver}, A^{net}_{ver} and A^+ which are only applicable until the proposition g_{grs} holds. According to Lemma 7.2, in the first phase of any plan π, operator a_{grs} must be applied. Operator $finish$ is applicable only when the proposition g_{grs} is acquired, that is, an operator $a_{\mathsf{m}} \in A_{\mathsf{m}}$ is applied. In turn, operator $a_{\mathsf{m}} \in A_{\mathsf{m}}$ must be applied with the last occurrence of the mandatory event of achieving proposition $\langle v/d \rangle$ such that $\langle v/d \rangle \in \mathsf{improved}(s_0)$. Application of $a_{\mathsf{m}} \in A_{\mathsf{m}}$ indicate gross positive achievement and satisfy Lemma 7.2. Phase one of any $\pi_\uparrow$ is applicable in $s_{0\uparrow}$.

According to Lemma 7.2, in the second phase the net positive operator a^+ must be applied while proposition $\langle v/d \rangle$ such that $\langle v/d \rangle \in \mathsf{improved}(s_0) \cap \mathsf{eff}(a_{grs}) \neq \emptyset$ in hand. The auxiliary proposition g_{grs} holds only after the operator $finish$ have been applied. In turn, only operator $a^{gross}_{ver} \in A^{gross}_{ver}$ respective to proposition $\langle v/d \rangle$ is applicable when g_{grs} holds. Once applied only net positive operators are applicable and $\langle v/d \rangle$ verified to hold by an operator $a^{gross}_{ver} \in A^{gross}_{ver}$. Phase two of any $\pi_\uparrow$ is applicable in $s_{0\uparrow}$.

Using the definition of A^+, each net positive operator (non-gross positive) $a^+ \in A$ is extended with the additional precondition $\langle g_{net}/0 \rangle$ and $\langle end/0 \rangle$, such that for any valid plan $\pi_\uparrow \in \mathcal{P}_\uparrow$ is satisfied with an operator $a^{gross}_{ver} \in A^{gross}_{ver}$ at the initiation of phase two. Hence, any net positive operator $a^+ \in A^+$ is applicable in $s_{0\uparrow}$, making $\pi_\uparrow$ applicable in $s_{0\uparrow}$. Finally, the proposition $\langle v/d \rangle$, that initiated the verification phase to be maintained proposition with the only applicable operator, that is, a^{net}_{ver}, respective to $\langle v/d \rangle$ (and its a^{gross}_{ver}) with precondition $\langle v/d \rangle \cup \langle y^v_d/1 \rangle \cup \langle g_{net}/1 \rangle$. Same operator a^{net}_{ver} achieves the goal proposition g, and satisfies all Lemma 7.2 requirements. $\pi_\uparrow$ is applicable in $s_{0\uparrow}$, $g \in s_{0\uparrow}[\![\pi_\uparrow]\!]$ and $\pi_\uparrow \in \mathcal{P}_\uparrow$. In turn, if L is a landmark for $\Pi_\uparrow$, then $\pi_\uparrow$ contains an operator from L, and if $L \subseteq A$ then π contains an operator from L as well. This proves that all landmarks L for $\Pi_\uparrow$ over the extended operators of A are ε-landmarks over the operators A. □

With Theorem 7.3 in hand, we can derive ε-landmarks for Π using any method for classical planning landmark extraction with any initial state s_0 with $u(s_0) \neq 0_{obs}$.

7.6.9 *Incorporating the Compilation into the Planner*

We now show how the *Improving* approach and the discovery of **value-driven-landmarks** can be incorporated into the incremental *BFBB* to leverage our observations and address the generalized, additive utility functions.

Let $\Pi = \langle V, s_0, u; A, c, b\rangle$ be the OSP task of interest, and suppose we are *given* a plan π_i for Π, such that $u(\pi_i) > u(s_0)$. If so, then we are no longer interested in searching for plans that "achieve improvement", but rather in plans that achieve *improvements beyond what π_i can already achieve.* Let $s_i = s_0[\![\pi_i]\!]$ be the end-state of π_i, and for any set of propositions $s \subseteq \mathcal{D}$, let $s \cap \mathsf{improved}(s_0)$ be the set of all propositions $\langle v/d\rangle \in s$ such that $u_v(d) > u_v(s_0[v])$, and let $s \cap \mathsf{improved}(s_i)$ be the set of all propositions $\langle v/d\rangle \in s$ such that $u_v(d) > u_v(s_i[v])$. We define the **s-ref gross positive action** a^s_{gPos} as follows,

Definition 7.11. Given an OSP task $\Pi = \langle V, s_0, u; A, c, b\rangle$, the **s-ref gross positive operators** $A^s_{gPos} \subseteq A$ of Π are

$$A^s_{gPos} = \{a \in A, \mathsf{eff}(a) \cap \mathsf{improved}(s_i) \neq \emptyset\}.$$

Given a state s_i, such that $u(s_i) > u(s_0)$, Lemma 7.4 shows that any plan π for Π that improves the initial state s_0 beyond π_i such that $u(\pi) > u(s_i)$ improves at least one variable in state s_i, if so, at each increment we can focus on improving the best solution in hand, and thus on $s \cap \mathsf{improved}(s_i)$. The proof of Lemma 7.4 is rather simple and, in plain words, the lemma states that, each plan π that improves beyond best solution in hand s_i, has to contain at least one **s_i-ref gross positive action.**

Lemma 7.4. *Let s_0 be initial state for Π and let π_i be a plan for Π with the end state s_i such that $u = u(s_i) > u(s_0)$. For any plan π for Π with an end state s that improves over s_i hold*

(1) $s \cap \mathsf{improved}(s_i) \neq \emptyset$
(2) at least one operator along π is s_i-ref gross positive operator $a^{s_i}_{gPos}$
(3) $u(s) > u(s_0)$.

Proof. Let s_0 be the initial state of Π, and let π_i be a plan for Π with the end state s_i such that $u(s_i) > u(s_0)$ and let π be the plan for Π with an end state s that improves over state s_i. From Lemmas 7.2(1) and (2) are immediate. $u(s_i) > u(s_0)$ and so $u(s) > u(s_0)$ by axiom of transitivity. □

Note that, if a new plan π with an end-state s that achieves something beyond what π_i already achieves, then, Lemma 7.4 states that the initial state s_0 has improved as well. We now put this observation at work.

Definition 7.12.[1] Given an OSP task $\Pi = \langle V, s_0, u; A, c, b\rangle$, a reference state s_i of Π such that $u(s_i) > u(s_0)$ and let $\mathsf{improved}(s_i) \neq \emptyset$ be the set of all propositions $\langle v/d\rangle$ such that $u_v(d) > u_v(s_i[v])$, the $(\varepsilon, S_{\mathbf{ref}})$**-compilation** of Π is a classical planning task $\Pi_{(\varepsilon,S_{\mathrm{ref}})} = \langle V_\varepsilon, s_{0\varepsilon}, G_\varepsilon; A_\varepsilon, c_\varepsilon\rangle$ where

$$
\begin{aligned}
V_\uparrow &= V \cup \{srch, get, ver, end, g_{grs}, g_{net}, g\} \cup Y,\\
&\quad \textit{with } dom(g) = dom(g_{grs}) = dom(g_{net}) = dom(srch) = \{1,0\},\\
&\quad\quad dom(get) = dom(end) = \{0,1\},\\
&\quad\quad Y = \{y^v_d \mid v \in V, d \in dom(v)\},\\
s_{0\uparrow} &= s_0 \cup \{\langle y^v_d/0\rangle \mid y^v_d \in Y\} \cup\\
&\quad \{\langle g/0\rangle, \langle g_{grs}/0\rangle, \langle g_{net}/0\rangle, \langle srch/1\rangle, \langle get/0\rangle, \langle end/0\rangle\},\\
G_\uparrow &= \{\langle g/1\rangle\},\\
A_\uparrow &= \{a_{\mathsf{g}} \mid a \in A, u(a) > 0, \mathsf{eff}(a) \cap \mathsf{improved}(s_i) \neq \emptyset\} \cup\\
&\quad \{a^+ \mid a \in A, u(a) > 0, \mathsf{eff}(a) \cap \mathsf{improved}(s_i) = \emptyset\} \cup\\
&\quad \{a_{\mathsf{mid}} \mid a \in A, u(a) > 0, \mathsf{eff}(a)\} \cup\\
&\quad \{a_{\mathsf{nm}}, a_{\mathsf{m}} \mid a \in A, u(a) \leq 0, \mathsf{eff}(a) \cap \mathsf{improved}(s_i) \neq \emptyset\} \cup\\
&\quad \{a_{\mathsf{src}} \mid a \in A, u(a) \leq 0, \mathsf{eff}(a) \cap \mathsf{improved}(s_i) = \emptyset\} \cup\\
&\quad \{a^{gross}_{ver}, a^{net}_{ver} \mid \langle v/d\rangle \in \mathsf{improved}(s_i)\} \cup finish
\end{aligned}
$$

where

// immediate goal operators - net positive and gross positive operators

$$a_{\mathsf{g}} = \left\langle \begin{matrix} \mathsf{pre}(a) \cup \langle g_{grs}/0\rangle \cup \langle g_{net}/0\rangle, \\ \mathsf{eff}(a) \cup \langle g_{grs}/1\rangle \cup \langle g_{net}/1\rangle, c(a) \end{matrix} \right\rangle$$

// net positive operators (non-gross positive), not to be applied last

$$a_{\mathsf{mid}} = \langle \mathsf{pre}(a) \cup \langle srch/1\rangle, \mathsf{eff}(a), c(a)\rangle$$

[1] Definition 7.12 is similar to Definition 7.10 with a slight modification of the $\mathsf{improved}(s_0)$ set to represent a dynamic reference point for improvement with $\mathsf{improved}(s_i)$, rather than a fix initial state.

// net positive operators (non-gross positive) to be applied last

$$a^+ = \left\langle \begin{matrix} \mathsf{pre}(a) \cup \langle end/1 \rangle \cup \langle g_{net}/0 \rangle\,, \\ \mathsf{eff}(a) \cup \langle end/0 \rangle \cup \langle g_{net}/1 \rangle\,, c(a) \end{matrix} \right\rangle$$

// gross positive operators (non-net positive),

// not to be applied as last gross positive achievement

// (not maintained propositions)

$$a_{\mathsf{nm}} = \langle \mathsf{pre}(a) \cup \langle g_{grs}/0 \rangle\,, \mathsf{eff}(a), c(a) \rangle$$

// gross positive operators (non-net positive),

// to be applied as last gross positive achievement (maintained propositions)

$$a_{\mathsf{m}} = \langle \mathsf{pre}(a) \cup \langle g_{grs}/0 \rangle\,, \mathsf{eff}(a) \cup \langle g_{grs}/1 \rangle\,, c(a) \rangle$$

// search operators - not net positive nor gross positive operators

$$a_{\mathsf{src}} = \langle \mathsf{pre}(a) \cup \langle srch/1 \rangle\,, \mathsf{eff}(a), c(a) \rangle$$

and

// once gross positive achievement registered, finish attempts are allowed

$$\mathsf{pre}(finish) = \langle srch/1 \rangle \cup \langle g_{grs}/1 \rangle$$
$$\mathsf{eff}(finish) = \langle get/1 \rangle \cup \langle srch/0 \rangle$$
$$c(finish) = 0$$

and

// finish and achieve goal

$$\mathsf{pre}(finishG) = \langle srch/1 \rangle \cup \langle g_{grs}/1 \rangle \cup \langle g_{grs}/1 \rangle$$
$$\mathsf{eff}(finishG) = \langle get/1 \rangle \cup \langle srch/0 \rangle$$
$$c(finishG) = 0$$

and

// verify that gross positive achievement still in hand and

// allow Net Positive finalization

$$\mathsf{pre}(a_{ver}^{gross}) = \langle v/d \rangle \cup \langle get/1 \rangle \cup \langle g_{net}/0 \rangle \cup \langle end/0 \rangle \cup \langle y_d^v/0 \rangle$$
$$\mathsf{eff}(a_{ver}^{gross}) = \langle end/1 \rangle \cup \langle get/0 \rangle \cup \langle y_d^v/1 \rangle$$
$$c(a_{ver}^{gross}) = 0$$

and

// *verify that gross positive achievement still in hand and*

// *allow goal proposition achievement*

$$\mathsf{pre}(a^{net}_{ver}) = \langle v/d \rangle \cup \langle y^v_d/1 \rangle \cup \langle g_{net}/1 \rangle$$
$$\mathsf{eff}(a^{net}_{ver}) = \langle g_{net}/0 \rangle \cup \langle y^v_d/0 \rangle \cup \langle g/1 \rangle$$
$$c(a^{net}_{ver}) = 0.$$

In what follows, we refer to $\Pi_{(\varepsilon, S_{\text{ref}})}$ as the $(\varepsilon, S_{\text{ref}})$**-compilation** of Π. Constructing $\Pi_{(\varepsilon, S_{\text{ref}})}$ from Π is trivially polynomial time, and it allows us to discover ε**-landmark** for Π using the standard machinery for classical planning landmark discovery.

Lemma 7.4 and Theorem 7.3 allow us to define an efficient version of the **inc-compile-and-BFBB**, depicted in Fig. 7.14. In the context of the search procedure, our observations of optimal plans and additive utility functions are expressed with a slight modification to the **inc-compile-and-BFBB**.

Remember, the **inc-compile-and-BFBB** [Domshlak and Mirkis (2015)], depicted in Fig. 7.3, is an OSP-customized, incremental version of the *BFBB*. At each iteration of its main loop, **inc-compile-and-BFBB** uses a modified version of *BFBB*, called inc-BFBB. The latter is used in a budget-reducing compilation of Π, created on the basis of the so-called $(\varepsilon, S_{\text{ref}})$-compilation of Π that exploits a set of the valuable states S_{ref} discovered by the search routine. The $(\varepsilon, S_{\text{ref}})$-compilation is built to discover new facts that have not been seen in S_{ref}. All the non-redundant value-carrying states discovered during the search are added to the reference set S_{ref}, when a node of higher utility is discovered, n^* is updated.

With our focus on **improving** state-variables rather than on **collecting** valuable facts, we only need a reference point to indicate relative improvement. The output of standard *BFBB* procedure, the best node n^* so far represents the best state s so far. Our landmark extraction technique refers to the best solution found so far, as well. Specifically, gross positive actions a^s_{gPos} refer to an improvement relative to s, which is represented by the $\mathsf{improved}(s_i)$ set, rather than by the original initial state s_0. The modified version of inc-compile-and-BFBB depicted in Fig. 7.14, maintains a dynamic reference point of only the best solution n^* so far and eliminates the need to maintain the set of all valuable reference states. Furthermore, in optimal plans for OSP generalized to additive utility functions, the utility is not necessarily collected monotonically. There are scenarios in which facts can be achieved and lost multiple times before the optimal state is reached. The optimal state might consist of subsets of facts that have been seen in previously reached states. In such scenarios, we must rely on relative improvement to avoid unsafe pruning.

```
inc-compile-and-BFBB (Π = ⟨V, A; s0, c, u, b⟩)
  initialize n* := s0
  loop:
    Π_ε := valuable-plan-compilation(Π, n*)
    L := a set of landmarks for Π_ε
    lcost := admissible landmark cost function from L
    Π_L* := budget reducing compilation of (L, lcost) into Π
    if inc-BFBB(Π_L*, n*) = done:
      return plan for Π associated with n*

inc-BFBB (Π, n*)
  open := new max-heap ordered by f(n) = h(s⟨n⟩, b − g(n))
  open.insert(make-root-node(s0))
  closed:= ∅
  best-cost:= 0
  while not open.empty()
    n := open.pop-max()
    if f(n) ≤ u(s⟨n*⟩): break
    if u(s⟨n⟩) > u(s⟨n*⟩): update n* := n
      if termination criterion: return updated, n*
    if s⟨n⟩ ∉ closed or g(n) < best-cost(s⟨n⟩):
      closed:= closed ∪ {s⟨n⟩}
      best-cost(s⟨n⟩) := g(n)
      foreach a ∈ A(s⟨n⟩):
            n' := make-node(s⟨n⟩⟦a⟧, n)
            if g(n') > b or f(n') ≤ u(s⟨n*⟩): continue
            open.insert(n')
  return done, n*
```

Fig. 7.14: Iterative *BFBB* with landmark enhancement for OSP generalized to additive utility functions.

Theorem 7.4. *The modified* inc-compile-and-BFBB *search algorithm is sound and complete for optimal OSP.*

Proof. The proof follows directly from the soundness and completeness of *BFBB*, Lemma 7.4 and Theorem 7.3. In addition to the standard *BFBB* termination criteria, inc-BFBB modifies *BFBB* with early termination criteria which is checked after the addition of a new "best so far node" n^*. The outer loop inc-compile-and-BFBB is updated with the improved state (associated with n^*) on each iteration, which is used as a reference point for further improvement. In turn, inc-BFBB restarts with the additional pruning power of the updated value-driven-landmarks. The number of iterations of inc-compile-and-BFBB is upper-bounded by $|\mathcal{D}| = |\bigcup_{v \in V} dom(v)|$, which is the number of different possible facts, since we always want to improve the value of at least one fact. Combining Lemma 7.4 and Theorem 7.3 guarantees guidance toward a utility improvement in relation to n^*, so that the optimal solution will not be pruned. Thus, when applying the modified inc-compile-and-BFBB search algorithm with an admissible heuristic for OSP, the heuristic based pruning is sound and guarantees an optimal solution. □

7.7 Empirical Evaluation

As OSP still lacks a standard suite of benchmarks for comparative evaluation, we have cast the STRIPS classical planning tasks from the International Planning Competitions (IPC) 1998–2006 in this role. This "translation" to OSP was done by associating a separate value with each proposition in the corresponding classical IPC task.

In order to transform a classical planning task Π into a set of OSP tasks, we must first solve Π optimally using Fast Downward [Helmert (2006a)] using the admissible landmarks heuristics [Karpas and Domshlak (2009)] with a timeout of 10 minutes. Let us denote the cost of an optimal solution to Π by c^*. Similarly to [Domshlak and Mirkis (2015)] we then generate several different OSP tasks, with budgets corresponding to 25%, 50%, 75%, and 100% of c^*. To complete the process, we must assign a utility value to each proposition in Π. We used two different methods of assigning utility values to evaluate our approach: the non-negative and the negative utility setting. We now describe the results for each of these utility assignment methods.

7.7.1 *Non-Negative Utility*

In the non-negative utility setting each proposition $\langle v/d \rangle$ of multi-valued variable $v \in V$ was assigned a utility as follows:

$$u(\langle v/d \rangle) = \begin{cases} 2 & \text{if } \langle v/d \rangle \text{ is a goal proposition in } \Pi \\ 1 & \text{if } v \text{ is a goal variable in } \Pi \\ & \text{but } \langle v/d \rangle \text{ is not a goal proposition} \\ 0 & \text{otherwise.} \end{cases}$$

When using a non-negative utility setting, evaluating valuable propositions at the action level is beneficial when a search is executed. This is because an action that achieves a valuable proposition might actually result in losing a more valuable proposition. Furthermore, with this utility setting there is indifference regarding the utility of propositions of a multi-valued variable $v \in V$, where action that achieves a new valuable proposition might be otiose in terms of gained utility (recall the examples depicted in Figs. 7.6–7.7.)

For the non-negative utility assignment method, we compared our approach, referred to as the *improving* approach here, to the *collecting* approach [Domshlak and Mirkis (2015)]. In both cases we ran inc-compile-and-BFBB with the blind heuristic, using our modified version of it for the improving approach.

We begin by comparing the informativeness of the landmarks of our *improving* to the informativeness of the landmarks of the *collecting* approach. Figs. 7.15(a)–7.15(d) compare the number of expanded nodes for each problem using both collecting and improving approaches. As these figures show, the number of nodes expanded by the *improving* approach was always lower than the number of nodes expanded by the *collecting* approach. However, a closer look reveals that as the budget decreases, our approach becomes more effective.

Table 7.1 shows the total amount of time taken and the total number of problems solved by each approach for each budget. These results show that the *improving* approach is able to solve more problems than the collecting approach. Furthermore, the improving approach is able to prove that there is no way to improve upon the initial state with the given budget in more cases than with the collecting approach — this happens when the total cost of the discovered landmarks exceeds the budget. If this is the case, there is no need to perform a search. The total number of problems for each domain where this occurs is in parentheses. In total, out of the 871 tasks/budget pairs, 113 pairs were solved by the *improving* approach with no search at all, by proving that no plan could achieve a value higher than that of the initial state, while only 47 of these tasks pairs were solved with no search by the *collecting* approach.

Additionally, the table shows the total planning time for each set of commonly solved problems in each domain, where, again, the *improving* approach is faster on average.

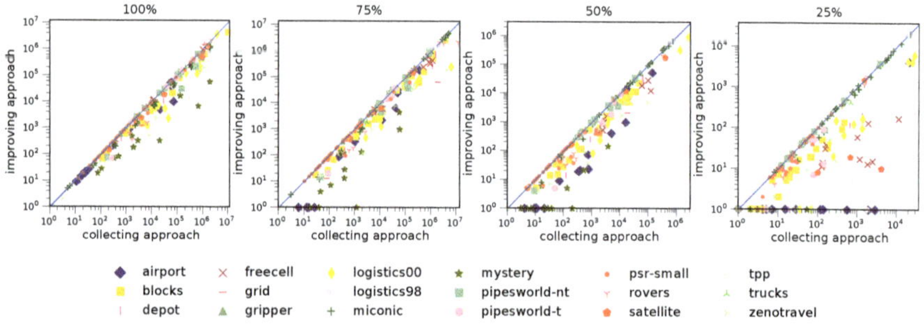

Fig. 7.15: Comparative view of the number of expanded nodes for the fact oriented *collecting* approach (x-axis) vs. the action oriented *improving* approach (y-axis) on tasks with different budgets relative to c^*.

Table 7.1: Number of problems solved and (in brackets) solved with no search at all, across the different budgets using the *improving* approach and the *collecting* approach.

	25%				50%				75%				100%			
	Improving		Collecting		Improving		Collecting		Improving		Collecting		Improving		Collecting	
	Solved	Time	Solved	Time	Solved	Time	Solved	Time	Solved	Time	Solved	Time	Solved	Time	Solved	Time
airport (17)	17(16)	44.85	17(1)	97.31	17(6)	230.08	17(0)	256.95	17(6)	248.97	17(0)	352.57	17(0)	365.72	17(0)	443.78
blocks (18)	18(3)	22.57	18(0)	24.85	18(0)	77.14	18(0)	79.90	18(0)	276.62	18(0)	343.41	18(0)	441.72	16(0)	704.34
depot (4)	4(2)	7.66	4(0)	8.17	4(0)	24.94	4(0)	28.00	4(0)	96.15	4(0)	181.27	4(0)	159.82	3(0)	543.53
freecell (11)	11(0)	457.54	11(0)	354.74	11(0)	500.99	11(0)	386.16	11(0)	1500.16	11(0)	1431.01	11(0)	2143.73	11(0)	1855.77
grid (2)	2(2)	9.58	2(2)	9.42	2(1)	20.78	2(1)	20.44	2(0)	39.67	2(0)	121.06	2(0)	317.75	2(0)	276.03
gripper (4)	4(1)	8.35	4(0)	5.96	4(0)	31.16	4(0)	21.79	4(0)	32.55	4(0)	21.75	4(0)	62.37	4(0)	46.68
logistics00 (13)	13(2)	15.49	13(0)	20.33	13(0)	103.77	12(0)	189.02	13(0)	751.91	11(0)	1087.28	13(0)	611.25	11(0)	594.93
logistics98 (3)	3(1)	2.97	3(0)	5.68	3(0)	6.58	3(0)	8.22	3(0)	518.47	3(0)	534.32	3(0)	544.24	3(0)	587.24
miconic (47)	47(15)	69.34	47(15)	58.60	47(6)	383.90	46(6)	361.32	45(1)	1852.12	45(1)	1710.02	44(0)	789.38	40(0)	963.90
mystery (11)	11(11)	50.79	11(4)	33.41	11(7)	83.40	11(0)	58.45	11(3)	95.92	11(0)	65.25	11(0)	128.36	11(0)	264.23
pipesw-nt (13)	13(2)	101.74	13(2)	89.53	12(0)	155.44	12(0)	144.90	12(0)	348.74	12(0)	362.17	12(0)	973.61	12(0)	1180.86
pipesw-t (6)	6(1)	52.67	6(0)	34.13	6(0)	102.64	6(0)	71.82	6(0)	115.44	6(0)	80.39	6(0)	182.70	6(0)	143.03
psr-small (47)	47(10)	63.38	47(1)	60.62	47(0)	131.15	47(0)	126.70	47(0)	111.84	47(0)	107.23	47(0)	364.56	47(0)	384.18
rovers (7)	7(1)	10.52	7(1)	10.20	7(0)	46.09	7(0)	61.44	7(0)	816.88	7(0)	1295.53	7(0)	938.01	6(0)	918.55
satellite (6)	6(2)	7.13	6(2)	7.80	6(0)	36.57	5(0)	63.94	5(0)	23.64	4(0)	22.60	4(0)	81.71	4(0)	101.32
tpp (6)	6(5)	3.26	6(5)	3.56	7(1)	20.30	7(1)	23.12	6(1)	151.68	6(1)	310.71	6(0)	458.78	6(0)	445.09
trucks (2)	2(1)	4.76	2(1)	3.88	2(0)	14.26	2(0)	12.78	2(0)	23.04	2(0)	20.09	2(0)	41.12	2(0)	34.52
zenotravel (8)	8(4)	8.31	8(1)	10.79	8(1)	28.68	8(1)	32.29	8(1)	36.13	8(1)	194.32	8(0)	206.90	8(0)	575.28
total (225)	225(79)	940.91	225(35)	838.98	224(22)	1997.87	221(9)	1947.24	221(12)	7039.93	218(3)	8240.98	219(0)	8811.73	209(0)	10063.26

7.7.2 *Negative Utility*

The negative utility setting is constructed as follows;

Let s be the state reached by an optimal solution of Π. Then

$$u(\langle v/d \rangle) = \begin{cases} 1 & \text{if } \langle v/d \rangle \text{ is a goal proposition in } \Pi \\ -1 & \text{if } \langle v/d \rangle \in s \text{ but} \\ & \langle v/d \rangle \text{ is not a goal proposition} \\ 0 & \text{otherwise.} \end{cases}$$

For this utility assignment method, we could not compare the improving approach to the *collecting* approach, as the collecting approach is restricted to non-negative utilities. Thus, we evaluated the *improving* approach using only our modified version of inc-compile-and-BFBB.

Table 7.2 shows the results of using the *improving* approach on these problems. While we have nothing to compare the results to, our planner does manage to optimally solve all but 1 of the tasks, and manages to solve quite a few of them with no search.

Table 7.2: Performance of the utility setting independent OSP solver across the different budgets, on domains with negative utility setting, in terms of expanded nodes. The number of problems that were solved with no search is in brackets.

	25%			50%			75%			100%		
	Expanded	*Solved*	*Time*	*Expanded*	*Solved*	*Time*	*Expanded*	*Solved*	*Time*	*Expanded*	*Solved*	*Time*
airport (15)	0	15(15)	47.76	44599	15(6)	74.02	151860	15(6)	149.11	203372	15(0)	69.38
blocks (17)	405	17(4)	21.17	24379	17(1)	32.09	1945724	17(1)	144.81	14218611	17(1)	706.26
depot (3)	25	3(2)	11.42	16928	3(1)	17.38	382154	3(0)	43.46	13900	2(0)	8.88
freecell (5)	48	5(1)	77.51	2160	5(0)	122.81	14644	5(0)	132.95	24733	5(0)	141.51
grid (2)	0	2(2)	35.49	2021	2(1)	36.76	1142555	2(0)	111.88	1409996	2(0)	399.31
gripper (3)	821	3(1)	3.27	10258	3(0)	6.84	34214	3(0)	10.25	60207	3(0)	14.25
logistics00 10)	1043	10(2)	14.41	54470	10(0)	22.84	479866	10(0)	40.51	1854165	10(0)	108.12
logistics98 (2)	9	2(1)	1.97	10957	2(0)	3.98	94961	2(0)	8.23	327929	2(0)	21.95
miconic (40)	12746	40(15)	44.23	639797	40(6)	134.43	4748596	40(1)	425.22	11337706	40(0)	933.18
mystery (11)	0	11(11)	49.48	160	11(10)	51.71	12516	11(5)	67.39	395511	11(0)	121.13
pipesw-nt 11)	250	11(2)	48.19	21490	11(0)	99.09	290079	11(0)	178.4	2248028	11(0)	677.66
pipesw-t (5)	71	5(1)	45.68	6386	5(0)	71.05	95533	5(0)	88.71	356736	5(0)	115.91
rovers (4)	15	4(1)	2.6	7563	4(0)	5.58	2637	4(0)	5.18	10181	4(0)	7.21
satellite (4)	30	4(2)	4.53	13949	4(0)	9.97	187176	4(0)	24.52	1013108	4(0)	104.54
tpp (5)	0	5(5)	2.61	1932	5(1)	3.54	14455	5(1)	3.35	28278	5(0)	4.49
trucks (2)	730	2(1)	2.92	21946	2(0)	6	77382	2(0)	9.62	82969	2(0)	10.88
zenotravel (7)	34	7(4)	11.94	10594	7(1)	19.94	229144	7(1)	30.14	1477266	7(1)	85.49
total (146)	16227	146(70)	425.18	882892	146(27)	718.03	9903496	146(15)	1473.72	35062696	145(2)	3630.15

7.7.3 *Landmarks Effectiveness Measure*

In order to evaluate the quality of the landmarks achieved by each approach we devised a measure of quality to evaluate the effectiveness of the budget reduction with generated landmarks. The effectiveness score of the landmarks calculated as the total number of discounted actions divided by the total reduced budget. This score is the average number of discounted actions needed to reduce one budget unit. Ideally, we would like this score to be as low as possible. Optimally, for each discounted action the budget should be reduced by the same cost.

To understand the measure of the landmarks effectiveness, recall the example in Fig. 7.8 illustrates the impact of redundant discounted actions on budget reduction effectiveness. Budget reduction effectiveness improves as the disjunctive action landmarks become more refined, which leads to a search space with less applicable redundant discounted actions. Disjunctive landmarks may contain redundant actions, that is, actions that either do not participate in any optimal plans or cannot be applied along any plan due to the unreachability of their preconditions. Still, the budget reducing compilation treats them in a similar manner to all other operators in the landmarks, leading to redundant discounted operators and thus an increase in the effective search space. In summary, the more the disjunctive action landmarks is refined, the better, and this is precisely what the landmarks effectiveness measure tends to examine.

The total number of reduced budget, discounted actions and the average number of discounted actions by the budget reduction compilation per a unit of budget reduction in all tasks of each domain, using the *improving* and the *collecting* approaches depicted in Table 7.3. As we expected, the *improving* approach payed less in discounted actions per budget unit than the *collecting* approach. In all domains the *improving* search approach outperformed the *collecting* search approach and reduced the budget five times more on average. On average, the *improving* approach pays three times less in discounted actions per budget unit. This effectiveness is obtained due to the use of the more refined and more accurate landmarks that are generated by using the value-driven landmarks.

7.8 Conclusion

This chapter reviewed and provided a background for the sequential decision-making and action application processes in Artificial Intelligence (AI). The sequential decision-making process in AI has been widely researched in the field of Planning AI. Our focus in this chapter was on the Oversubscription planning problem (OSP) and its recent research progress. The description of OSP captures the economic aspects of problems that

Table 7.3: The total number of reduced budget, discounted actions and the average number of discounted actions by the budget reduction compilation per a unit of budget reduction in all tasks of each domain, using the *improving* and the *collecting* approaches.

	Reduced Budget		Discounted Actions		[2]Effectiveness Score	
	Improving	*Collecting*	*Improving*	*Collecting*	*Improving*	*Collecting*
airport (17)	**484**	21	76318	**20375**	**157.68**	970.24
blocks (16)	**154**	18	215	**142**	**1.40**	7.89
depot (3)	**32**	3	569	**21**	17.78	**7.00**
freecell (11)	**54**	11	**5851**	15331	**108.35**	1393.73
grid (2)	**26**	15	2132	**1059**	82.00	**70.60**
gripper (4)	**60**	4	**172**	224	**2.87**	56.00
logistics00 (11)	**189**	11	212	**118**	**1.12**	10.73
logistics98 (3)	**40**	3	114	**40**	**2.85**	13.33
miconic (40)	**586**	121	2892	**1691**	**4.94**	13.98
mystery (11)	**49**	15	5142	**2122**	**104.94**	141.47
pipesw-nt (12)	**39**	28	**14751**	18500	**378.23**	660.71
pipesw-t (6)	**12**	6	9016	**5664**	**751.33**	944.00
psr-small (47)	**167**	55	2330	**1534**	**13.95**	27.89
rovers (6)	**44**	14	**380**	456	**8.64**	32.57
satellite (4)	**46**	10	264	**120**	**5.74**	12.00
tpp (6)	**62**	25	**155**	158	**2.50**	6.32
trucks (2)	**26**	7	**602**	931	**23.15**	133.00
zenotravel (8)	**57**	8	1213	**407**	**21.28**	50.88
total[3] (209)	**2127**	375	122328	**68893**	**57.51**	183.71

[2]For the Effectiveness Score, the average score is provided.
[3]The effectiveness score of the landmarks is calculated as the total number of discounted actions divided by the total reduced budget. This score is the average number of discounted actions needed to reduce one budget unit. Ideally this score should be as low as possible. Optimally, for each discounted action the budget should be reduced by the same cost.

deal with AI's sequential decision-making and action application processes. It allows us to module actions and decisions with different costs, values and budget restrictions over the planning process. This chapter presented the budget reduction compilation approach which reduces the effective search space. By defining the net utility of an action and gross positive action notations, we could exploit observations regarding the structure of optimal plans at the level of actions and sequences of actions. These properties are used to generate more informative landmarks. The value-driven landmark compilation (also referred to as the valuable plan compilation in this chapter) compiles the "optimal plan's" properties into the task representation. This compilation reduces the effective search space and rationalizes the search procedure by adding constraints and forcing the search to conform to the optimal plan properties and resource bounds. These landmarks and compilation can then be used in an OSP planner to obtain a state-of-the-art performance. We used the value-driven landmarks as an input for the budget reduction procedure and improved the pruning mechanism based on these landmarks. These notions are not restricted to OSP planning. For example, the notion of the net utility of an action can be adapted to classical planning, where an action has a net positive utility if it achieves certain goal facts without deleting any other goal facts.

Chapter 8

Inference of Net-Utility Polarity of Actions in Oversubscription Planning

In many real-world planning problems, an action's impact differs depending on the place, time, and the context in which the action is applied. The same action with the same effects can result in a different outcome if it is applied in a different context or state. Recent work on Oversubscription Planning (OSP) has defined the net utility of an action as the change in utility between the state before the action was applied and the state after it was applied. Identifying actions with positive net utility has been shown to be effective in solving OSP problems. However, the net utility of an action is only well defined for actions that have a precondition for each variable they modify. Previous work has proposed an offline technique for splitting an action whose net utility is not well defined into several versions of the action, such that the net utility of each version of the action is always either positive or negative. In this chapter, we present the selective action splitting technique for efficient offline detection of net utility polarity. We also introduce a different technique for identifying actions with positive net utility, which is based on splitting each action into a series of unitary effect actions, which must be applied one after another, in a way that allows us to detect whether an action has positive net utility online, during the search. We also present a hybrid technique that combines the online technique with the offline technique. The hybrid technique outperformed previous techniques in the empirical evaluation.

8.1 Introduction

Oversubscription planning (OSP) [Smith (2004)] is a problem that involves choosing an action sequence that reaches a state with a high utility, given a budget for total action cost. In optimal OSP, the task is further constrained to finding a path that achieves the state of maximum utility.

This formulation, sometimes referred to as partial satisfaction planning, allows us to handle real-world scenarios in which there is an "over-subscription" of possible achievements with limited resources [Smith (2004); Van Den Briel *et al.* (2004a); Do and Kambhampati (2004); Van Den Briel *et al.* (2004b); Nigenda and Kambhampati (2005); Benton (2006); Do *et al.* (2007); Aghighi and Jonsson (2014); Domshlak and Mirkis (2015); Muller and Karpas (2018a); Katz *et al.* (2019)].

Net-benefit planning [Van Den Briel *et al.* (2004a); Nigenda and Kambhampati (2005); Baier *et al.* (2009); Bonet and Geffner (2008); Benton *et al.* (2009a); Coles and Coles (2011); Keyder and Geffner (2009)] takes a relative estimation approach to achievements with respect to the costs of action sequences. While Net-Benefit Planning refers to problems in which state utility and action costs are comparable, the general formulation of OSP assumes that the utility of states and the cost of actions defined and measured in different terms are incomparable. Taking the incomparable costs of actions and utility of achievements in OSP into account Domshlak and Mirkis (2015) introduced a budget reduction compilation for heuristic search OSP. The budget reduction compilation exploits landmarks for goal reachability [Hoffmann *et al.* (2004); Karpas and Domshlak (2009); Helmert and Domshlak (2009); Domshlak *et al.* (2012); Bonet and Helmert (2010); Pommerening and Helmert (2013)] which has been found to be effective in the context of optimal classical planning. Domshlak and Mirkis (2015) introduced so-called "bring me something landmarks" for OSP which are a set of actions that must applied in every plan that achieves valuable facts. These landmarks are compiled into the original OSP task to obtain an equivalent OSP task with a lower budget, and thus with a smaller effective search space.

Recent work has defined the concept of the net utility of actions [Muller and Karpas (2018a)] and introduced a set of interrelated properties for plans that improve the net utility of states. When an action can be applied in many different states, the impact of the action is relative to the original state in which it was applied. Achieving the same outcome in different states can cause negative, positive, or no change in total utility terms, concerning the context and the value of the original state in which the action was applied. The net utility of an action provides a wider context for achievement evaluation by taking both the target state and its origin into account which allows it to capture the utility that "is given away" by applying an action in order to achieve a change. Incorporating the concept of net utility into a landmark discovery mechanism allows us to extract more informative landmarks and to reduce the effective search space with a budget reduction compilation. Furthermore, focusing on improving net utility rather than collecting valuable facts allows us to address negative and numerical utility values.

In this research, we address the ambiguity of actions' net utility for actions that are applicable in several different original states. To define the net utility of actions, a Simplified Action Structure (SAS) formalism [Bäckström and Klein (1991); Klein (1991)] is assumed, where for each effect of an action a specific precondition is specified. SAS+ [Bäckström and Klein (1991); Bäckström and Nebel (1995)] representation of planning tasks allows for a more flexible representation of actions. In SAS+ a list of precondition for an action specifies those state variables that must have a certain defined value in order to make the action applicable, and that will be changed to another value by the action. This representation allows for an incomplete list of preconditions which allows for a more compact representation of actions. At the same time, the obtained degree of freedom in state variables that are in the effects list but not in the preconditions list results in ambiguity of the net change in utility that is caused by the action. **Selective action splitting** [Muller and Karpas (2018a)], manages to determine the net utility of actions perfectly, without unnecessary action splitting, in most of the domains and tasks that are represented in SAS+ by representing the impact of an action compactly with regards to its net utility. The selective action split identifies and labels actions with respect to the polarity of the net change that is caused by the action. However, in problems with an incomplete precondition list, selective action splitting results in an increase in task size due to the multiplication of actions for each state variable in the effect list and each possible precondition assignment in the state variables.

This chapter proposes a two-phase, online and offline, technique for identifying the polarity of actions in SAS+ representation in the context of OSP with arbitrary additive utility functions for actions. It proposes an offline action-value structure analysis to exploit the compactly represented informativeness of the net utility of actions to extend the scope of OSP for the net utility value uncertainty scenarios during the online search procedure. The result of the offline pre-processing phase is an equivalent OSP task, with which we can determine the net utility of most of the actions offline. For actions with an ambiguous net utility, the offline pre-processing phase provides a compact decision planning model representation for local reasoning during the online search phase. Specifically, we introduce an *online* approach to action net utility polarity detection, by deducing the net utility polarity while executing the so-called "unit-effect" actions during the search. A set of unit effect actions is generated for each action with a value-structure that contains ambiguity regarding the action's net utility value (i.e. it can be applied in several different states). We then show how we can combine the online technique with the offline selective action split, resulting in better performance than either of them alone.

8.2 Background

We represent the OSP model in a language close to SAS+ language that is used for classical planning [Bäckström and Klein (1991); Bäckström and Nebel (1995)], an **OSP** task is given by a sextuple $\Pi = \langle V, s_0, u; A, c, b\rangle$, where $V = \{v_1, \ldots, v_n\}$ is a finite set of finite-domain *state variables*, with each complete assignment to V representing a *state*, and $S = dom(v_1) \times \cdots \times dom(v_n)$ being the *state space* of the task; $s_0 \in S$ is a designated *initial state*; u is an efficiently computable *state utility* function $u : S \rightarrow \mathbb{R}$; A is a finite set of *actions*, with each action $a \in A$ being represented by a pair $\langle \mathsf{pre}(a), \mathsf{eff}(a)\rangle$ of partial assignments to V, called *preconditions* and *effects* of a, respectively; $c : A \rightarrow \mathbb{R}^{0+}$ is an *action cost* function; $b \in \mathbb{R}^{0+}$ is a *cost budget* allowed for the task. An assignment of a variable v to a value d is denoted by $\langle v/d\rangle$ and referred to as a *fact*. For a partial assignment p to V, let $\mathcal{V}(p) \subseteq V$ denote the subset of variables instantiated by p, and, for $v \in \mathcal{V}(p)$, $p[v]$ denote the value provided by p to the variable v. Action a is applicable in a state s if $s[v] = \mathsf{pre}(a)[v]$ for all $v \in \mathcal{V}(\mathsf{pre}(a))$. Applying a changes the value of each $v \in \mathcal{V}(\mathsf{eff}(a))$ to $\mathsf{eff}(a)[v]$, and the resulting state is denoted by $s[\![a]\!]$. A sequence of actions $\langle a_1, \ldots, a_m\rangle$ denoted by π, called a plan for s if it is applicable in s and $c(\pi) \leq b$. We assume an *arbitrary additive utility* function with *multi-valued variables*, defined as $u(s) = \sum_{\langle v/d\rangle \in s} u_v(d)$, with $u_v(d) \in \mathbb{R}$ for all variable-value pairs $\langle v/d\rangle$.

Best-First-Branch-and-Bound (*BFBB*) heuristic searches for an optimal OSP must rely on admissible utility-upper-bounding heuristic functions (with a budget restrictions) $h : S \times \mathbb{R}^{0+} \rightarrow \mathbb{R}^{0+}$ to estimate the true utility $h^*(s, b)$. *BFBB* has been also used to solve the net-benefit planning problem [Benton *et al.* (2009b, 2012)].

Recent work has defined several ideas for increasing the informativeness and utility of actions in planning domains [Muller and Karpas (2018a)].

Definition 8.1. Given an OSP task $\Pi = \langle V, s_0, u; A, c, b \rangle$,

- for an action a, the **net utility** of a is $u(a) = \sum_{v \in \mathcal{V}(\mathsf{eff}(a))} [u(\mathsf{eff}(a)[v]) - u(\mathsf{pre}(a)[v])]$.
- let **improved**(s) be the set of all propositions $\langle v/d \rangle \in \mathcal{D}$ such that $u_v(d) > u_v(s[v])$.
- the **gross positive actions** $A_{gPos} \subseteq A$ of Π are $A_{gPos} = \{a \in A, \mathsf{eff}(a) \cap \mathsf{improved}(s) \neq \emptyset\}$.

These ideas serve to define a planning approach to interpreting the objective as a relative self *improvement* of the current state rather "achieving goals". These ideas allow us to define an interrelated set of properties in valuable plans in OSP tasks, that is, plans that improve their value in net terms. A synergistic combination of the properties define a so-called "window of opportunity" to maintain effective achievement and terminate a plan efficiently and with a valuable state in hand.

Theorem 8.1. *Given an OSP task* Π *with an additive utility function* u, *for any plan* $\pi = \langle a_1, \dots, a_n \rangle$ *for* Π *with* $u(s_0[\![\pi]\!]) > u(s_0)$, *there exists an action subsequence* $\langle a_i, \dots, a_j \rangle$, $i, j \in [n]$, *such that:*

- $u(s_0[\![\langle a_1, \dots, a_j \rangle]\!]) \geq u(s_0[\![\pi]\!])$,
- $u(s_0[\![\langle a_1, \dots, a_j \rangle]\!]) \geq u(s_0[\![\langle a_1, \dots, a_{i-1} \rangle]\!])$,
- a_j *is a net positive action, that is,* $u(a_j) > 0$, *and*
- a_i *is a gross-positive action, with some* $\langle v/d \rangle \in \mathsf{eff}(a_i) \cap \mathsf{improved}(s_0)$ *being maintained along* $\langle a_{i+1}, \dots, a_j \rangle$.

The "window of opportunity" is represented by a set of constraints within a procedure designed to extract *value landmarks* for an OSP task.

8.3 Offline Detection of the Net-Utility Polarity

In our OSP model representation, as in the SAS+ language for classical planning [Bäckström and Klein (1991); Bäckström and Nebel (1995)], a precondition list of an action specifies those state variables, which must have a certain defined value in order to execute the action and that will be changed to another other value by the action. In order to define the net utility of an action, we assumed that each variable affected by an action was also specified in the precondition list for that action. Note, there is a trade-off between the compact and unrestricted representation of actions in SAS+ language and the expressiveness of its precondition list. While SAS+

compactly represented actions are expressive enough to define action per state applicability, they are not expressive enough to define the net utility of an action. The penalty for obtaining the necessary expressiveness for defining the net utility of an action in SAS representation is the increase in the task size.

In an attempt to find an action representation that is both, as compact as possible and as expressive as necessary, we use the **selective action split** pre-processing procedure, which allows for efficient, offline, net utility of an action polarity detection.

The pre-processing procedure for detecting the net utility polarity is as follows;

<u>**Selective-Action-Split**</u> $(\Pi = \langle V, s_0, u; A, c, b\rangle)$
  mutex-Inference(Π)
  $A_{new} = \emptyset$
  for each $a \in A$;
    // explicit net utility (for all known preconditions)
    ENU := $\sum_{v \in \mathcal{V}(\mathsf{pre}(a))} [u(\mathsf{eff}(a)[v]) - u(\mathsf{pre}(a)[v])]$
    MSS := **min-split-set**(a)
    $A_{new} := A_{new} \cup$ **marked-or-splitted**(MSS,ENU)

<u>**min-split-set**</u>(a)
  return $\{v \mid v \in \mathcal{V}(\mathsf{eff}(a) \setminus \mathsf{pre}(a)),$ **refined-domain**$(v) \neq \emptyset\}$

<u>**refined-domain**</u>(v, a)
  // remove variables without utility variance
  // remove facts that are mutex with known preconditions
  return $\{d \mid d \in dom(v), u(\langle v/d\rangle) \neq u(\mathsf{eff}(a)[v]),$
      $\langle v/d\rangle \notin$ mutex-group$(\mathcal{V}(\mathsf{pre}(a)))\}$

<u>**marked-or-split**</u>(MSS,ENU)
  // max/min floating net utility (for all unknown preconditions)
  MAXFNU := $\sum_{v \in \mathrm{MSS}} [u(\mathsf{eff}(a)[v]) - \max_{\forall d \in dom(v)} u(\langle v/d\rangle)]$
  MINFNU := $\sum_{v \in \mathrm{MSS}} [u(\mathsf{eff}(a)[v]) - \min_{\forall d \in dom(v)} u(\langle v/d\rangle)]$
  if MAXFNU + ENU ≤ 0;
    return a-neg *// mark without split*
  if MINFNU + ENU > 0;
    return a-pos *// mark without split*
  return a**-classifier**(MSS, ENU)

<u>a**-classifier**</u>(MSS, ENU)
any binary multivariate classification algorithm into two groups:
 1) net-positive actions, and
 2) not net-positive actions

Fig. 8.1: Selective-Action-Split translation procedure.

(1) Perform **mutex inference** to complete the precondition list as far as possible (with standard Fast Downward mechanism [Helmert (2006b)]) to reduce the computational effort.

(2) Calculate the **explicit net utility (ENU)**

a. Actions that carry negative or zero net utility for all their instances in their normal form can remain in their compact encoding.

b. Actions that are *pure positive*, such that they carry positive net utility for all their instances in their normal form can be marked as *goal actions* and remain in their compact encoding as well.

(3) Reduce the remaining variables with **min-split-set**

a. Variables with no utility variance (regardless of the numerical utility value) are removed as they have no net utility contribution.

c. Perform mutex inference of unknown the preconditions with revealed precondition facts; remove if found.

(4) If redundant preconditions are left (net utility signum have not determined);

a. Calculate the maximal and the minimal floating net utility (**MAXFNU, MINFNU**)

b. If utility signum remains positive borders; mark the positive action,

c. otherwise, classify with **binary-multivariate-classifier**. To split such actions, we first calculate the total net utility of variables with a known precondition. Suppose we got a value of x. The next step, only for variables with an unrestricted precondition is to divide them into 2 groups, the positive group with a total sum higher than $-x$ and the appositive group with a total sum lower than (or equal to) $-x$. This split can be done using any method of binary multivariate classification.

In other words, we may recognize positive net actions offline, and then only perform SAS action encoding for actions that are ambiguous with regards to their net utility signum, such that they can be applied in several different states and yield different net utility polarities.

8.4 Online Detection of the Net Utility Polarity

We now present an approach to splitting actions that differs from the selective action split in regards to the timing of the determination of an action's net utility. The selective action split succeeds in defining net utility efficiently at the pre-processing stage, but as we mentioned before; sometimes we are left with actions that are ambiguous with regards to their net utility signum which could not be determined offline. To handle such actions we can perform SAS action encoding and define net utility for each action instance. In most of the domains the offline phase detects the net utility for all actions, but real-world scenarios can sometimes be more complex. In such cases, as provided in the example in Fig. 8.2, we can improve the selective action split further by supplying a supplementary mechanism to determine the net utility online.

When an action can be applied in several different states the definition of the action's net utility is dependent on the state in which it is applied and changes as follows.

Definition 8.2. For an OSP action a applied in state s, the net utility of a is $u_s(a) = \sum_{v \in \mathcal{V}(\mathsf{eff}(a))}[u_v(\mathsf{eff}(a)[v]) - u_v(s[v])]$.

Our approach to that is based on splitting each action into a set of actions, each responsible for achieving a single effect of the original action. For each affected variable with no specified preconditions, we create a group of actions that achieve the same single effect, where each one of them is combined with one, different, legal precondition on this variable. If a precondition is specified for the affected variable, then only one action is created which achieves a single effect with one precondition as specified in the original action.

When applying our approach, the equivalence of the original and the compiled planning tasks must be preserved, which means that for an optimal plan π for the original task Π with a solution utility of α, there exists an optimal plan $\tilde{\pi}$ for the compiled task $\tilde{\Pi}$ with the same solution utility of α, and vice versa. This equivalence is achieved by bounding the execution of the individual actions from each such created action set via dedicated auxiliary control structures that prevent actions from different action sets from mixing.

An example of a simple OSP task in Fig. 8.2 is used to illustrate our approach of splitting the original action into sets of single effect actions, and the use of the auxiliary control structure action set. In this example,

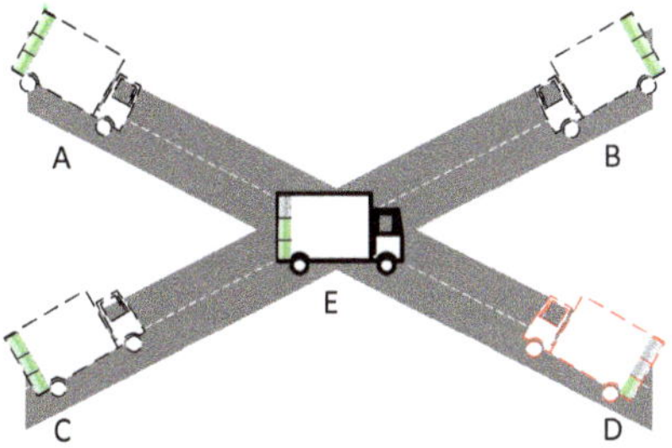

(a)

a_i	$\text{drive}_{E,2}$ $i = 1$	$\text{drive}_{E,1}$ $i = 2$	$\text{drive}_{E,0}$ $i = 3$
$\text{pre}(a_i)$	$\{\langle f/3\rangle\}$	$\{\langle f/2\rangle\}$	$\{\langle f/1\rangle\}$
$\text{eff}(a_i)$	$\{\langle t/E\rangle, \langle f/2\rangle\}$	$\{\langle t/E\rangle, \langle f/1\rangle\}$	$\{\langle t/E\rangle, \langle f/0\rangle\}$

(b)

$\text{drive}_{E,2}$ set a_i	$\text{drive}_{AE,2}$ $i = 1$	$\text{drive}_{BE,2}$ $i = 2$	$\text{drive}_{CE,2}$ $i = 3$
$\text{pre}(a_i)$	$\{\langle t/A\rangle, \langle unlock/drive_{E,2}\rangle\}$	$\{\langle t/B\rangle, \langle unlock/drive_{E,2}\rangle\}$	$\{\langle t/C\rangle, \langle unlock/drive_{E,2}\rangle\}$
$\text{eff}(a_i)$	$\{\langle t/E\rangle\}$	$\{\langle t/E\rangle\}$	$\{\langle t/E\rangle\}$

$\text{drive}_{E,2}$ set a_i	$\text{reduceFuel}_{3\to 2}$ $i = 4$	$\text{drive}^{E,2}_{unlock}$ $i = 5$	$\text{drive}^{E,2}_{lock}$ $i = 6$
$\text{pre}(a_i)$	$\{\langle f/3\rangle, \langle unlock/drive_{E,2}\rangle\}$	$\{\langle f/3\rangle\}$	$\{\langle unlock/drive_{E,2}\rangle, \langle t/E\rangle, \langle f/3\rangle\}$
$\text{eff}(a_i)$	$\{\langle f/2\rangle\}$	$\{\langle unlock/drive_{E,2}\rangle\}$	$\{\langle unlock/noOP\rangle\}$

(c)

Fig. 8.2: An example of an OSP task, with (a) illustrating the story, (b) listing the original actions, and (c) detailing a set of actions compiled from the original action $\text{drive}_{E,2}$. Each action in (c) achieves a single effect from the effects list of action $\text{drive}_{E,2}$. Actions a_5 and a_6 are auxiliary control predicates. a_5 enables the new single effect actions in the $\text{drive}_{E,2}$ set, while preventing from all other sets from being applied. a_6 approves that all effects are achieved, locking the current action set and enabling a new action set to start. Note, the truck at point D can reach point E, but since it does not meet the fuel precondition for the original action $\text{drive}_{E,2}$ it is not included in the equivalent single action set of $\text{drive}_{E,2}$ in (c).

we have a truck that can move between locations A, B, C, D and E. The truck has three levels of fuel and each step reduces the fuel by one level. As we can see in this example, a truck that is initially at one of the locations A, B, C or D, with a fuel level of three, can end up in the same location (E) with the same fuel level (two). In this case we have one specific precondition on the fuel level, but there are a few possible precondition values for the location. We create an action for each one of those possible preconditions.

The OSP task Π, described here using two state variables $V = \{t, f, unlock\}$ with $dom(t) = \{A, B, C, D, E\}$, $dom(f) = \{0, 1, 2, 3\}$ and $dom(unlock) = \{drive_{E,2}, drive_{E,1}, drive_{E,0}, noOP\}$, where t stands for the possible location of truck and f for the fuel level, *unlock* is a control predicate that enables/disables single-effect actions sets. For example when drive$_{E,2}$ set is enabled, all other sets will be disabled. In this way we avoid mixing single-effect actions from different sets and preserve equivalence. A group of available actions for this example is detailed in Fig. 8.2(b), and the created, single-effect action set for one of those actions (drive$_{E,2}$) is detailed in Fig. 8.2(c) along with their auxiliary control predicates. In the state model induced by this OSP task, we have $S = dom(t) \times dom(f) \times dom(unlock)$, and the predicate values: $u(unlock) = 0$,

$$u(t) = \begin{cases} 2, & t = E \\ 0, & \text{otherwise} \end{cases}, \; u(f) = \begin{cases} 1, & f = 1 \\ 2, & f = 2 \\ 3, & f = 3 \\ 0, & \text{otherwise.} \end{cases}$$

Now let us look at the most basic example of a single action plan, presenting our approach. Consider the OSP task Π and its compiled task $\tilde{\Pi}$, described in Fig. 8.2. The initial state $s_0 = $ A3, i.e. truck is in location A with a fuel level of 3. A valid single action plan from this initial state is: $\pi = \langle drive_{AE,2} \rangle$ using Definition 8.2 the net utility will be: $u(\pi) = u(drive_{AE,2}) = [\langle t/E \rangle - \langle t/A \rangle] + [\langle f/2 \rangle - \langle f/3 \rangle] = 1$ one of the sequences that is equivalent to the plans in the compiled task $\tilde{\Pi}$ is: $\tilde{\pi_1} = \left\langle drive^{E,2}_{unlock}, Fuel_{3\to 2}, drive_{AE,2}, drive^{E,2}_{lock} \right\rangle$ with a net utility of: $u(\tilde{\pi}) = u(drive^{E,2}_{unlock}) + u(Fuel_{3\to 2}) + u(drive_{AE,2}) + u(drive^{E,2}_{unlock}) = 0 + [\langle f/2 \rangle - \langle f/3 \rangle] + [\langle t/E \rangle - \langle t/A \rangle] + 0 = 0 - 1 + 2 + 0 = 1$. But what if we switch the order of actions $Fuel_{3\to 2}$ and $drive_{AE,2}$ in this sequence? Let us look on the following sequence; $\tilde{\pi_2} = \left\langle drive^{E,2}_{unlock}, drive_{AE,2}, Fuel_{3\to 2}, drive^{E,2}_{lock} \right\rangle$. In this case, at the end of the applied sequence we get the same net utility accumulated in a different manner, i.e. $(2 - 1 = 1)$ instead of $(-1 + 2 = 1)$. Apparently both $\tilde{\pi_1}$ and $\tilde{\pi_2}$ are equivalent to π, but while examining the action sequence in $\tilde{\pi_2}$ one can see that after applying the action $drive_{AE,2}$ the utility exceeds the optimal plan π utility reached in the original task Π, while reaching invalid utility in the original task, as illustrated in Fig. 8.3. Thus $\tilde{\pi_2}$ is not equivalent to plan π.

To preserve equivalence with the original task, we have to prevent it from exceeding the original optimal utility value during the execution of the compiled single-effect action set, as illustrated in Fig. 8.3. To promise equivalence, we expand the control structure in the compiled task

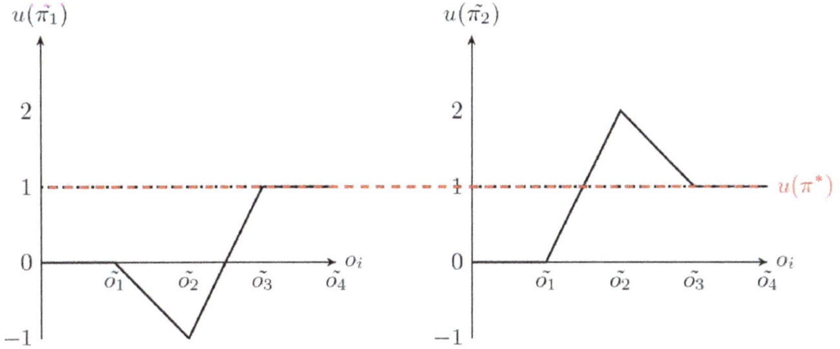

(a) sequence $\tilde{\pi_1}$ (b) sequence $\tilde{\pi_2}$

Fig. 8.3: Graphs (a), (b) presents the cumulative actions' utility of sequences $\tilde{\pi_1}$ and $\tilde{\pi_2}$, respectively. In sequence $\tilde{\pi_1}$ net-negative actions are applied prior to net-positive actions, and in sequence $\tilde{\pi_2}$ vice versa. While both $\tilde{\pi_1}$ and $\tilde{\pi_2}$ reach the same final utility, $\tilde{\pi_2}$ exceeds the optimal utility value in the original task, which violates the equivalence between Π and $\tilde{\Pi}$.

(presented in Fig. 8.2) with a set of auxiliary control predicates and actions, dedicated to verifying that the net-negative utility actions are applied before the net-positive actions, as in $\tilde{\pi_1}$.

The set of actions detailed in Fig. 8.4 is used to illustrate the expanded auxiliary control structure which is used to prevent exceeding the optimal planning π utility reached in the original task Π. We add a new group of predicates $Y_e = \{y_e^v \mid v \in V, \{e\} \in dom(v)\}$ with $dom(y_e^v) = \{0, 1\}$, where for each action a in the original task Π, we add $\{y_e^v \in Y_e \mid \langle v/e \rangle \in \mathsf{eff}(a)\}$ to a's equivalent set of single effect actions in task $\tilde{\Pi}$. The semantics of $\langle y_e^v/1 \rangle \in s$ is that, either effect e has been collected by applying a net-negative utility action, or there is no valid net-negative action that achieves effect e. When the net-positive actions in the set are defined as; $\mathsf{pre}(a^+_{p \to e}) = \{\langle v/p \rangle, \langle unlock/a_{name} \rangle\} \bigcup_{y_e^v \in Y_e \mid \langle v/e \rangle \in \mathsf{eff}(a)} \{\langle y_e^v/1 \rangle\}, \mathsf{eff}(a^+_{p \to e}) = \{\langle v/e \rangle\}$, $\tilde{c}(a^+_{p \to e}) = 0$.

This way, net-positive utility actions can be applied and positive utility values obtained only if all the net-negative actions have been applied and all negative utility carrying facts that hold in the current state and set have been collected.

To enforce the semantics of y_e^v, the action set $A_{set,o}$ contains a pair of action sets, $a^{verify}_{p \to e}$ which verifies that negative utility carrying values

$\text{drive}_{E,2}$ set a_i	$\text{reduceFuel}^{verify}_{3\to 2}$ $i=4$
$\text{pre}(a_i)$	$\{\langle f/3\rangle, \langle unlock/drive_{E,2}\rangle\}$
$\text{eff}(a_i)$	$\{\langle f/2\rangle, \langle y^{f/2}/1\rangle\}$

(a)

$\text{drive}_{E,2}$ set a_i	$\text{drive}^{verifyNO}_{AE,2}$ $i=7$	$\text{drive}^{verifyNO}_{BE,2}$ $i=8$	$\text{drive}^{verifyNO}_{CE,2}$ $i=9$
$\text{pre}(a_i)$	$\{\langle t/A\rangle, \langle unlock/drive_{E,2}\rangle\}$	$\{\langle t/B\rangle, \langle unlock/drive_{E,2}\rangle\}$	$\{\langle t/C\rangle, \langle unlock/drive_{E,2}\rangle\}$
$\text{eff}(a_i)$	$\{\langle y^{t/E}/1\rangle\}$	$\{\langle y^{t/E}/1\rangle\}$	$\{\langle y^{t/E}/1\rangle\}$

(b)

$\text{drive}_{E,2}$ set a_i	$\text{drive}^{+}_{AE,2}$ $i=1$	$\text{drive}^{+}_{BE,2}$ $i=2$
$\text{pre}(a_i)$	$\{\langle t/A\rangle, \langle unlock/drive_{E,2}\rangle, \langle y^{t/E}/1\rangle, \langle y^{f/2}/1\rangle\}$	$\{\langle t/B\rangle, \langle unlock/drive_{E,2}\rangle, \langle y^{t/E}/1\rangle, \langle y^{f/2}/1\rangle\}$
$\text{eff}(a_i)$	$\{\langle t/E\rangle\}$	$\{\langle t/E\rangle\}$

$\text{drive}_{E,2}$ set a_i	$\text{drive}^{+}_{CE,2}$ $i=3$
$\text{pre}(a_i)$	$\{\langle t/C\rangle, \langle unlock/drive_{E,2}\rangle, \langle y^{t/E}/1\rangle, \langle y^{f/2}/1\rangle\}$
$\text{eff}(a_i)$	$\{\langle t/E\rangle\}$

(c)

$\text{drive}_{E,2}$ set a_i	$\text{drive}^{E,2}_{unlock}$ $i=5$	$\text{drive}^{E,2}_{lock}$ $i=6$
$\text{pre}(a_i)$	$\{\langle f/3\rangle, \langle unlock/noOP\rangle\}$	$\{\langle unlock/drive_{E,2}\rangle, \langle t/E\rangle, \langle f/3\rangle, \langle y^{t/E}/1\rangle, \langle y^{f/2}/1\rangle\}$
$\text{eff}(a_i)$	$\{\langle unlock/drive_{E,2}\rangle\}$	$\{\langle unlock/noOP\rangle, \langle y^{t/E}/0\rangle, \langle y^{f/2}/0\rangle\}$

(d)

Fig. 8.4: A set of actions compiled for the action $\text{drive}_{E,2}$, expanded with an auxiliary control structure for preserving equivalence with the original task Π.

should be collected and are collected via a net-negative utility action, while $a^{verifyNo}_{p\to e}$ verifies that the effect cannot be achieved by net-negative utility action, where

$$\left\langle \begin{aligned} &\text{pre}(a^{verify}_{p\to e}) = \{\langle v/p\rangle, \langle unlock/a_{name}\rangle\}, \\ &\text{eff}(a^{verify}_{p\to e}) = \{\langle v/e\rangle, \langle y^v_e/1\rangle\}, \tilde{c}(a^{verify}_{p\to e}) = 0 \end{aligned} \right\rangle,$$

$$\left\langle \begin{aligned} &\text{pre}(a^{verifyNo}_{p\to e}) = \{\langle v/p\rangle, \langle unlock/a_{name}\rangle\}, \\ &\text{eff}(a^{verifyNo}_{p\to e}) = \{\langle y^v_e/1\rangle\}, \tilde{c}(a^{verifyNo}_{p\to e}) = 0 \end{aligned} \right\rangle.$$

Figure 8.4 depicts an example of the set of actions obtained by the compilation of the original action $\text{drive}_{E,2}$ with expanded, dedicated auxiliary control structures for preserving equivalence with the original task Π. The expansions beyond the action set in Fig. 8.2 are colored red, where **(a)** is a net-negative action that achieves $\langle v/e\rangle \in \text{eff}(a)$ and verifies that it has been achieved via a net-negative utility action by collecting predicate y^v_e; **(b)** are actions that verify that $\langle v/e\rangle \in \text{eff}(a)$ cannot be achieved via a net-negative utility action by collecting predicate y^v_e; **(c)** are net-positive utility actions that achieve $\langle v/e\rangle \in \text{eff}(a)$ and can be applied only after either all the net-negative utility actions have been applied, or it has been verified that there is no net-negative utility action that achieves $\langle v/e \rangle \in \mathsf{eff}(a)$ by preconditioning with $\bigcup_{y_e^v \in Y_e | \langle v/e \rangle \in \mathsf{eff}(a)} \{\langle y_e^v/1 \rangle\}$; **(d)** are control actions that enable/disable $\text{drive}_{E,2}$ set, where $\text{drive}_{lock}^{E,2}$ resets the auxiliary predicates y_e^v when finishing the sequence.

Using the extended auxiliary control structure for preserving the equivalence of plan $\tilde{\pi}$ for the compiled task $\tilde{\Pi}$ with the original task Π, $\tilde{\pi}$ will be; $\tilde{\pi_1} = \langle drive_{unlock}^{E,2}, Fuel_{3\to 2}^{verify}, drive_{AE,2}^{verifyNO}, drive_{AE,2}^{+}, drive_{lock}^{E,2} \rangle$. The net-positive utility action $drive_{AE,2}^{+}$ can only be applied after all $\langle v/e \rangle \in \mathsf{eff}(a)$ have either been collected by applying net-negative utility actions or there is no valid net-negative action that achieves them. Definition 8.3 puts together the above observations to work.

Definition 8.3. Let $\Pi = \langle V, s_0, u; A, c, b \rangle$ be an OSP task, and **unit-effect-compilation** of Π is an OSP task $\tilde{\Pi} = \langle \tilde{V}, \tilde{s_0}, \tilde{u}; \tilde{A}, \tilde{c}, \tilde{b} \rangle$ where $\tilde{V} = V \cup \{unlock\} \cup Y_e$ with $Y_e = \{y_e^v \mid v \in V, e \in dom(v)\}$, $dom(y_e^v) = \{0, 1\}$, $dom(unlock) = \{a_{name} \mid a \in A\} \cup \{noOP\}$, $\tilde{s_0} = s_0 \cup \{\langle unlock/noOP \rangle\} \cup \{\langle y/0 \rangle \mid y \in Y_e\}$, $\tilde{u} = u$, $\tilde{b} = b$, $\tilde{A} = A_{AllSets} \cup A_{unlock} \cup A_{lock}$ where $A_{AllSets} = \bigcup_{a \in A} A_{set,o}$, *with* $A_{set,o} =$

$$\{a_{p\to e}^{verify} \mid a \in A, p \in \mathsf{preSet}_v(a), \langle v/e \rangle \in \mathsf{eff}(a), u_v(e) - u_v(p) \le 0\} \cup$$
$$\{a_{p\to e}^{verifyNo} \mid a \in A, p \in \mathsf{preSet}_v(a), \langle v/e \rangle \in \mathsf{eff}(a), u_v(e) - u_v(p) > 0\} \cup$$
$$\{a_{p\to e}^{+} \mid a \in A, p \in \mathsf{preSet}_v(a), \langle v/e \rangle \in \mathsf{eff}(a), u_v(e) - u_v(p) > 0\}$$

where :

$$\mathsf{preSet}_v(a) = \begin{cases} \mathsf{pre}(a)[v], & v \in \mathcal{V}(\mathsf{pre}(a)) \\ dom(v), & v \notin \mathcal{V}(\mathsf{pre}(a)) \end{cases}$$

$$\mathsf{pre}(a_{p\to e}^{verify}) = \{\langle v/p \rangle, \langle unlock/a_{name} \rangle\}$$
$$\mathsf{eff}(a_{p\to e}^{verify}) = \{\langle v/e \rangle, \langle y_e^v/1 \rangle\}, \tilde{c}(a_{p\to e}^{verify}) = 0$$
$$\mathsf{pre}(a_{p\to e}^{verifyNo}) = \{\langle v/p \rangle, \langle unlock/a_{name} \rangle\}$$
$$\mathsf{eff}(a_{p\to e}^{verifyNo}) = \{\langle y_e^v/1 \rangle\}, \tilde{c}(a_{p\to e}^{verifyNo}) = 0$$
$$\mathsf{pre}(a_{p\to e}^{+}) = \{\langle v/p \rangle, \langle unlock/a_{name} \rangle\} \bigcup_{y_e^v \in Y_e | \langle v/e \rangle \in \mathsf{eff}(a)} \{\langle y_e^v/1 \rangle\}$$
$$\mathsf{eff}(a_{p\to e}^{+}) = \{\langle v/e \rangle\}, \tilde{c}(a_{p\to e}^{+}) = 0$$

$A_{unlock} = \{a_{unlock} \mid a \in A\}$ with $\tilde{c}(a_{unlock}) = c(a)$ and

$$\mathsf{pre}(a_{unlock}) = \mathsf{pre}(a) \cup \{\langle unlock/noOP \rangle\}$$
$$\mathsf{eff}(a_{unlock}) = \{\langle unlock/a_{name} \rangle\}$$

$A_{lock} = \{a_{lock} \mid a \in A\}$ with $\tilde{c}(a_{lock}) = 0$ and,

$$\mathsf{pre}(a_{lock}) = \mathsf{eff}(a) \cup \{\langle unlock/a_{name} \rangle\} \bigcup_{y_e^v \in Y_e \mid \langle v/e \rangle \in \mathsf{eff}(a)} \{\langle y_e^v/1 \rangle\}$$

$$\mathsf{eff}(a_{lock}) = \{\langle unlock/noOP \rangle\} \bigcup_{y_e^v \subset Y_e \mid \langle v/e \rangle \in \mathsf{eff}(a)} \{\langle y_e^v/0 \rangle\}.$$

Put simply, $\tilde{\Pi}$ extends the structure of Π by

- Converting $a \in A$ into a set of single-effect actions $A_{set,o}$.
- Adding control actions a_{unlock}. When all the preconditions for the original action $a \in A$ hold, this action permits the execution of actions $\tilde{a} \in A_{set,o}$, while locking the ability to perform any other action $\tilde{a}' \in A_{set,o'}$ such that $a' \neq a$.
- Adding control actions a_{lock}. When all the effects of action a are achieved, this action locks the current $A_{set,o}$ and allows for the starting of a new single effect actions set $A_{set,o}$, by nullifying control fact $unlock$.

Definition 8.4. For any action $a \in A$ of an OSP task Π, then actions sequence $\tilde{\pi}_o$ is defined as $\tilde{\pi}_o = \langle a_{unlock}, \tilde{a_1}, \ldots, \tilde{a_k}, a_{lock} \rangle$, where $\tilde{a_1}, \ldots, \tilde{a_k} \in A_{set,o}$ are single-effect actions.

Lemma 8.1. *Given a valid plan $\tilde{\pi}$ for an OSP task $\tilde{\Pi}$, any action sequence $\tilde{\pi}_o$ in plan $\tilde{\pi}$ is an* **atomic action sequence**, *where $\nexists \tilde{a}' \mid \tilde{a}' \in \tilde{\pi}_o, \tilde{a}' \notin A_{set,a} \cup \{a_{unlock}, a_{lock}\}, a \neq a'$.*

Proof. The proof is by case analysis. Given an OSP task Π, let $\tilde{\Pi}$ be the unit-effect-compilation of Π, where $A_{set,a_1} \ldots A_{set,a_n}$ are single-effect action sets created from the original action $a_i \in A$ in Π, respectively. Let $\tilde{\pi} = \langle \tilde{\pi}_{a_1}, \tilde{\pi}_{a_2}, \ldots, \tilde{\pi}_{a_n} \rangle$ a valid plan for an OSP task $\tilde{\Pi}$, we show that, through fact and action mutex relationships, the auxiliary control structure in task $\tilde{\Pi}$ ensures the atomic execution of action sequences in each step of the plan execution. In order to complete the proof we have to go through the following cases: **Case 1** in the initial state s_0, **Case 2** at sequence initiation, **Case 3** during sequence execution, and, **Case 4** at sequence termination. By the construction of $\tilde{\Pi}$ the following holds;

(1) For any $\tilde{a} \in \tilde{A}$ the variable $unlock \in \mathcal{V}(\mathsf{pre}(\tilde{a}))$ with a domain $dom(unlock) = \{a_{name} \mid a \in A\} \cup \{noOP\}$, the facts $\{\langle unlock/a_{name}\rangle\} \cup \{noOP\} \mid a \in A$ are pairwise mutex, hence any two actions $\tilde{a}, \tilde{a}' \in \tilde{A}$ such that $\langle unlock/p\rangle \in \mathsf{pre}(\tilde{a}), \langle unlock/p'\rangle \in \mathsf{pre}(\tilde{a}')$ where $p \neq p'$ are mutex.

(2) For any action set $A_{set,a} \in \tilde{A}$, and for any action $\tilde{a} \in A_{set,o}$ it holds that $\langle unlock/a_{name}\rangle \in \mathsf{pre}(\tilde{a})$.

(3) For any action set $A_{set,a} \in \tilde{A}$, there is a unique action a_{lock} with $\langle unlock/a_{name}\rangle \in \mathsf{pre}(a_{lock})$, and a unique action a_{unlock} with $\langle unlock/noOP\rangle \in \mathsf{pre}(a_{unlock})$.

Case 1. By the construction of $\tilde{\Pi}$, in the initial state s_0 the fact $\langle unlock/noOP\rangle$ holds. Only actions $a_{unlock} \in A_{unlock}$ contain the predicate $\langle unlock/noOP\rangle$ in their precondition list, hence, only actions $a_{unlock} \in A_{unlock}$ are applicable. Once an action $a_{unlock} \in A_{unlock}$ is applied predicate $\{\langle unlock/a_{name}\rangle\}$ is achieved, since the fact $\langle unlock/noOP\rangle$ does not hold anymore no other sequence can be initiated.

Case 2. Similar to Case 1, a new sequence can be initiated only when the fact $\langle unlock/noOP\rangle$ holds. Putting (1) and (2) together, then while $\langle unlock/noOP\rangle$ holds, no other action $\tilde{a}'$ can be applied such that $\tilde{a}' \notin A_{unlock}$. Once an action $a_{unlock} \in A_{unlock}$ is applied predicate $\{\langle unlock/a_{name}\rangle\}$ is achieved, since the fact $\langle unlock/noOP\rangle$ does not hold anymore, no other sequence can be initiated.

Case 3. Assuming that every action $a \in A$ in the original task Π is unique, putting (1), (2) and (3) together, then as long as $\langle unlock/a_{name}\rangle$ holds, no other action $\tilde{a}'$ can be applied during sequence execution, such that $\tilde{a}' \notin A_{set,a} \cup \{a_{lock}\} \mid a \neq a'$. This proves **Case 3**.

Case 4. At sequence termination. By the construction when $\langle unlock/a_{name}\rangle$ holds, new assignment to variable *unlock* is applicable only with a_{lock} action, which finalizes $\tilde{\pi}_o$, and achieves $\langle unlock/noOP\rangle$.

As shown, Lemma 8.1 holds in all cases which implies that any action sequence $\tilde{\pi}_o$ in plan $\tilde{\pi}$ is **atomic action sequence** such that $\nexists \tilde{a}' \mid \tilde{a}' \in \tilde{\pi}_o, \tilde{a}' \notin A_{set,a} \cup \{a_{unlock}, a_{lock}\}, a \neq a'$. □

Definition 8.5. Let $\Pi = \langle V, s_0, u; A, c, b\rangle$ be an OSP task and $\tilde{\Pi} = \langle \tilde{V}, \tilde{s_0}, \tilde{u}; \tilde{A}, \tilde{c}, \tilde{b}\rangle$, unit-effect-compilation of Π. The **expanding function** $\psi : S \mapsto \tilde{S}$ is defined as $\psi(s) = s \cup \{\langle unlock/noOP\rangle\} \cup \{\langle y/0\rangle \mid y \in Y_e\}$.

Lemma 8.2. *Given an OSP task* $\Pi = \langle V, s_0, u; A, c, b\rangle$, *for each action* $a \in A$ *and each state* $s \in S$ *in which* a *is applicable, there is an action sequence*

$\tilde{\pi}_o$ in task $\tilde{\Pi}$, such that: (1) $\tilde{\pi}_o$ is applicable in $\psi(s)$, (2) $\psi(s)[\![\tilde{\pi}_o]\!][v] = s[\![a]\!]$, (3) $c(a) = c(\tilde{\pi}_o)$, and (4) $u_s(a) = u_{\psi(s)}(\tilde{\pi}_o)$.

Proof. **(1)** Each action sequence $\tilde{\pi}_o$ starts with the action a_{unlock} that allows for the execution of the action sequence from action set $A_{set,o}$. By the construction of a_{unlock}, applying a_{unlock} makes only single-effect actions from action set $A_{set,o}$ applicable, while all other single-effect actions that belong to a different action sets $\tilde{a} \in A_{set,o'}$, such that $a \neq a'$, are locked. Since $\psi(s) = s \cup \{\langle unlock/noOP\rangle\} \cup \{\langle y/0\rangle \mid y \in Y_e\}$ and the preconditions for a_{unlock} are defined to be $\mathsf{pre}(a_{unlock}) = \mathsf{pre}(a) \cup \{\langle unlock/noOP\rangle\}$, the preconditions of $\tilde{\pi}_o$ are satisfied and $\tilde{\pi}_o$ is applicable in $\psi(s)$.

(2) Each action sequence $\tilde{\pi}_o$ ends with the control action a_{lock} which verifies that $\mathsf{eff}(a)$ are achieved, and finalize action sequence $\tilde{\pi}_o$. By the construction of a_{lock}, $\mathsf{pre}(a_{lock}) = \mathsf{eff}(a) \cup \{\langle unlock/a_{name}\rangle\}$ and $\mathsf{eff}(a_{lock}) = \{\langle unlock/noOP\rangle\} \bigcup_{y_e^v \in Y_e \mid \langle v/e\rangle \in \mathsf{eff}(a)} \{\langle y_e^v/0\rangle$ hence, when a_{lock} is applied, action sequence $\tilde{\pi}_o$ is terminated, and the following holds: $\psi(s)[\![\tilde{\pi}_o]\!] = \mathsf{eff}(a) \cup \{\langle unlock/noOP\rangle\} \cup \{\langle y/0\rangle \mid y \in Y_e\}$ and, $\psi(s)[\![\tilde{\pi}_o]\!][v] = s[\![a]\!]$.

(3) By the construction of $\tilde{\Pi}$, all the actions $\tilde{a} \in \tilde{A}$ have zero cost except A_{unlock} actions which carry the cost of the original action defined as $\tilde{c}(a_{unlock}) = c(a)$. Each action sequence $\tilde{\pi}_o$ is defined as starting with a unique action a_{unlock}. Hence, $c(a) = \tilde{c}(\tilde{\pi}_o)$.

(4) By Definition 8.2 of the net utility and the construction of a_{lock} it is easy to see that $u_s(a) = u(a_{lock})$. By Lemma 8.1, any actions sequence $\tilde{\pi}_o$ in plan $\tilde{\pi}$ is **atomic** in the sense that $\nexists \tilde{a}' \mid \tilde{a}' \in \tilde{\pi}_o, \tilde{a}' \notin A_{set,a} \cup \{a_{unlock}, a_{lock}\}, a \neq a'$. Hence, by the construction of $A_{set,o}$, the only utility carrying facts $\langle v/e\rangle$ that can be achieved with sequence $\tilde{\pi}_o$ are from the effect list of the original action a, such that $\langle v/e\rangle \in \mathsf{eff}(a)$. Since any action sequence $\tilde{\pi}_o$ must start with an action a_{unlock} and end with an action a_{lock} (as provided at (1) and (2) in this proof) we can infer that $u(a_{lock}) = u_{\psi(s)}(\tilde{\pi}_o)$. Hence, we have $u_s(a) = u_{\psi(s)}(\tilde{\pi}_o)$.

□

Lemma 8.3. *Let Π be an OSP task and $\tilde{\Pi}$ be the respective unit-effect-compilation of Π. Any non-empty optimal tail gaining plan $\tilde{\pi}$ for $\tilde{\Pi}$ ends with a complete action sequence $\{\tilde{\pi}_a \mid a \in A\}$.*

Proof. By the construction of $\tilde{\Pi}$, for each sequence $\{\tilde{\pi}_a \mid a \in A\}$, it holds that:

(1) Actions a_{unlock} and a_{lock} are not utility carrying facts so they do not change utility during plan execution.
(2) The cost of the entire sequence is paid at the first action executed in $\tilde{\pi_a}$, the action a_{unlock}, while any other action $\tilde{a} \in \tilde{\pi_a} \mid \tilde{a} \neq a_{unlock}$ it holds that $\tilde{c}(\tilde{a}) = 0$.
(3) Net-positive actions are applied last in the sequence after all net-negative and neutral utility actions have been applied due to the auxiliary control structure where each net-positive action is preconditioned with achieving all control predicates y_e^v, $\bigcup_{y_e^v \in Y_e \mid \langle v/e \rangle \in \mathsf{eff}(a)} \{\langle y_e^v/1 \rangle\}$.

    Each effect $e \in \mathsf{eff}(a)$ of the original action a is verified to be achieved with a net-negative/neutral utility action or it is verified that it cannot be achieved with such an action, before the net-positive utility actions become applicable and may achieve that effect. For every valid net-negative utility achievement of an effect e, such that $u_v(e) - u_v(p) \leq 0$ the action $a_{p \to e}^{verify}$ is built and verifies that the effect e has been achieved by applying a net-negative/neutral utility single-effect action, this is verified by achieving the predicate $\langle y_e^v/1 \rangle$. For every valid positive net utility achievement of an effect e, such that $u_v(e) - u_v(p) > 0$ the action $a_{p \to e}^{verifyNo}$ is built and verifies that the effect e can't be achieved by applying a net-negative/neutral action, this is verified by achieving the predicate $\langle y_e^v/1 \rangle$. Only after all the effects lists are verified with the actions $a_{p \to e}^{verify}$ or $a_{p \to e}^{verifyNo}$, the precondition $\bigcup_{y_e^v \in Y_e \mid \langle v/e \rangle \in \mathsf{eff}(a)} \{\langle y_e^v/1 \rangle\}$ for the net-positive utility single-effect action holds, and net-positive utility single-effect actions become applicable.

From (1), (2), and (3), it is easy to see that the auxiliary control structure within the action sequence $\tilde{\pi_a}$ ensures that during action sequence execution, facts that carry negative utility are collected first and then those that carry positive utility are collected. Hence, the optimal utility will be achieved with the final action being applied (before locking the sequence with action a_{lock}). At any point before the final action is applied the accumulated utility is sub-optimal. □

Theorem 8.2. *For any optimal, tail gaining plan* π *for* Π *with cost of* $c(\pi) = b$ *and utility* $u(\pi) = \alpha$, *there is an optimal, tail gaining plan* $\tilde{\pi}$

for $\tilde{\Pi}$, such that $c(\pi) = c(\tilde{\pi}) = b$ and $u(\pi) = \tilde{u}(\tilde{\pi}) = \alpha$, and vice versa. Furthermore, for any plan $\tilde{\pi}$ for $\tilde{\Pi}$, the corresponding plan π for Π can be restored.

Proof. **(1)** From the first direction, we show that, for an optimal plan π for task Π under the budget of b and solution utility of α, there exists an optimal plan $\tilde{\pi}$ for $\tilde{\Pi}$ with the same budget b and solution utility of α. Let plan $\pi = \langle a_1, a_2, \ldots, a_n \rangle$ be an optimal solution for task Π such that it is applicable at s_0, with $u(s_0[\![\pi]\!]) = \alpha$ and $c(\pi) = b$. By Lemma 8.2 we can replace each action $a_i \in \pi$ with the equivalent action sequence $\tilde{\pi}_{a_i}$ and get an equivalent plan $\tilde{\pi} = \langle \tilde{\pi}_{a_1}, \tilde{\pi}_{a_2}, \ldots, \tilde{\pi}_{a_n} \rangle$ in $\tilde{\Pi}$, where,

- for any action $a_i \in \pi$ in the original plan and the equivalent action sequence $\tilde{\pi}_{a_i} \in \tilde{\pi}$ in $\tilde{\pi}$ holds that $c(a_i) = c(\tilde{\pi}_{o_i})$, hence by accumulating all actions costs in π and accordingly action sequence costs in $\tilde{\pi}$ we get $c(\pi) = c(\tilde{\pi}) = b$.
- $\tilde{\pi}$ is applicable at $\psi(s_0)$ and ends with state $\tilde{s} = \psi(s_0[\![\pi]\!])$ such that $u(\tilde{s}) = u(s_0[\![\pi]\!]) = \alpha$.

Now we will show that there is no other plan $\tilde{\pi}$ for $\tilde{\Pi}$ that achieves utility beyond α. By Lemma 8.1 and Lemma 8.3, an optimal plan for π will be reached only after completion of full sequences (or not at all) from $\{\tilde{\pi_a} \mid a \in A\}$, i.e. an optimal plan couldn't be reached in the middle of any sequence $\tilde{\pi_a} \mid a \in A$. Furthermore, by Lemma 8.2 for each sequence $\tilde{\pi}_{a_i}$ there is a mapping to $a \in A$.

Now let assume, to the contrary, that there is a plan $\tilde{\pi}' = \langle \tilde{\pi}'_{a_1}, \tilde{\pi}'_{a_2}, \ldots, \tilde{\pi}'_{a_k} \rangle$ for $\tilde{\Pi}$ such that achieves utility β and $\beta > \alpha$. By Lemma 8.1, Lemma 8.2 and Lemma 8.3, from the optimal plan there is a mapping to a plan in the original task Π that achieves the same utility, β under the same budget. The mapping for $\tilde{\pi}'$ is $\pi' = \langle a'_1, a'_2, \ldots, a'_k \rangle$ with $u(s_0[\![\pi']\!]) = \beta$. This, however contradicts the optimality of π for Π.

(2) The proof of the other direction is similar. We show that, for an optimal plan $\tilde{\pi}$ for the compiled task $\tilde{\Pi}$ under the budget of b and a solution utility of α, there exists an optimal plan π for Π with the same budget b and a solution utility of α. Let $\tilde{\pi}$ be an optimal plan for the compiled task $\tilde{\Pi}$, then by Lemma 8.1 and Lemma 8.3 this optimal plan is made of full and separated sequences from $\{\tilde{\pi_a} \mid a \in A\}$, i.e. it is of the from, $\tilde{\pi} = \langle \tilde{\pi}_{a_1}, \tilde{\pi}_{a_2}, \ldots, \tilde{\pi}_{a_n} \rangle$. By

Lemma 8.2 (and step (1)) we can map $\tilde{\pi}$ to an equivalent solution $\pi = \langle a_1, a_2, \ldots, a_n \rangle$ in the original task Π such that it achieves the same utility α under the same budget b.

Now let us assume, to the contrary, that there is a plan $\pi' = \langle a'_1, a'_2, \ldots, a'_k \rangle$ for the original task Π such that it achieves utility β and $\beta > \alpha$. By Lemma 8.1, 8.2 and 8.3, there is a mapping from the optimal plan π' in the original task to a plan $\tilde{\pi}'$ in the compiled task $\tilde{\Pi}$ that achieves the same utility, β under the same budget. The mapping for π' is $\tilde{\pi}' = \langle \tilde{\pi}'_{a_1}, \tilde{\pi}'_{a_2}, \ldots, \tilde{\pi}'_{a_k} \rangle$ with $u(s_0[\![\tilde{\pi}']\!]) = \beta$. This, however contradicts the optimality of $\tilde{\pi}$ for $\tilde{\Pi}$.

□

8.5 Empirical Evaluation

We implemented our approach in the inc-compile-and-BFBB planner and evaluated it on a set of OSP benchmarks translated from a set of classical planning benchmarks [Domshlak and Mirkis (2015); Muller and Karpas (2018a)]. To transform a classical planning task Π into a set of OSP tasks, we first solved Π optimally using the Fast Downward method [Helmert (2006b)] with a timeout of 10 minutes. We denoted the cost of an optimal solution to be Π by c^*. We then generated several different OSP tasks, with budgets corresponding to 25%, 50%, 75%, and 100% of c^*. Each proposition $\langle v/d \rangle$ of multi-valued variable $v \in V$ in Π was associated with a separate utility;

$$u(\langle v/d \rangle) = \begin{cases} 2 & \text{if } \langle v/d \rangle \text{ is a goal proposition in } \Pi \\ 1 & \text{if } v \text{ is a goal variable in } \Pi \\ & \text{but } \langle v/d \rangle \text{ is not a goal proposition} \\ 0 & \text{otherwise.} \end{cases}$$

The unit effect action split can only be activated for a subset of actions that fit certain structural criteria such as the length of an action's precondition list or the number of possible assignments to a variable in the precondition list. In our evaluation of the unit action split approach, the unit effect split is designed to be activated for each action that is determined by the selective action split procedure (Fig. 8.1) to be a candidate for splitting into net positive and non-net positive instances. Applying the unit effect action split in the pre-processing phase of the selective action split instead of splitting the action into a set of positive and appositive actions leaves the inference of net utility polarity of action to the online phase.

Tables 8.1 and 8.2 compare the performance in terms of expanded nodes across the budgets 25%, 50%, 75%, 100% relative to c^* and the total number of problems solved within 10 minutes. We evaluated the fact-oriented (absolute) utility approach [Domshlak and Mirkis (2015)] and two versions of the net utility of an action oriented approach [Muller and Karpas (2018a)] incorporating the selective action split and the unit action split for the inference of net utility polarity. The results show that the net utility approach is an effective approach for handling the OSP problem as compared to the absolute utility approach. Both versions of the net utility approach incorporating the selective action split and unit effect split manage to solve more tasks with less expanded nodes within the time limits. The unit effect split approach outperforms the offline selective action split in terms of expansion.

Table 8.1: Performance in terms of expanded nodes across the budgets 25%, 50% relative to c^* and a total number of problems solved with the fact oriented utility approach and two versions of the net utility of action oriented approach incorporating the selective action split and the unit action split for inference of net utility polarity.

	25%							50%						
	expansion				Coverage			expansion				Coverage		
	# Tasks	Fact	ASplit	USplit	Fact	ASplit	USplit	# Tasks	Fact	ASplit	USplit	Fact	ASplit	USplit
airport (30)	21	1084176	**84451**	**84451**	21	**26**	**26**	18	896821	**605373**	**605373**	18	**19**	**19**
blocks (26)	26	17720	**9642**	**9642**	**26**	**26**	**26**	25	10604731	**6657883**	**6657883**	**25**	**25**	**25**
depot (7)	7	17830	**3191**	**3191**	**7**	**7**	**7**	7	1552274	**625564**	**625564**	**7**	**7**	**7**
driverlog (14)	14	328718	**51631**	**51631**	**14**	**14**	**14**	12	7836734	**5369555**	**5369555**	**12**	**12**	**12**
freecell (60)	50	15403222	**99054**	**99054**	50	**59**	**59**	12	2855235	**1134563**	**1134563**	15	**23**	22
grid (2)	2	**0**	**0**	0	**2**	**2**	**2**	2	17868	**2020**	**2020**	**2**	**2**	**2**
gripper (7)	7	287870	287481	**287338**	**7**	**7**	**7**	6	2217434	**2211178**	3204173	6	**7**	**7**
logistics00 (20)	20	6959508	**1554568**	**1554568**	**20**	**20**	**20**	14	21151739	**10829268**	**10829268**	14	**15**	**15**
logistics98 (6)	5	678744	**39423**	**39423**	5	**6**	**6**	2	48366	**10957**	**10957**	2	**3**	**3**
miconic (142)	75	10011481	9496351	**9151542**	75	**77**	**77**	55	31800068	30986484	**29745665**	**55**	**55**	**55**
movie (30)	30	300	300	**270**	**30**	**30**	**30**	30	3150	3150	**3120**	**30**	**30**	**30**
mprime (19)	19	203	**0**	0	**19**	**19**	**19**	19	117643	**7025**	**7025**	**19**	**19**	**19**
mystery (15)	15	105	**0**	0	**15**	**15**	**15**	15	11427	**410**	**410**	**15**	**15**	**15**
openstacks (7)	7	46120	**15194**	**15194**	**7**	**7**	**7**	7	1088268	**1000961**	**1000961**	**7**	**7**	**7**
pipes-nt (19)	19	11459	5086	**4844**	**19**	**19**	**19**	19	1963517	**712478**	880578	**19**	**19**	**19**
pipes-t (13)	13	27488	**3834**	3900	**13**	**13**	**13**	13	1694991	786404	**731596**	**13**	**13**	**13**
pipes-ns (10)	8	1525	**341**	407	**8**	**8**	**8**	7	67997	**22000**	30785	**8**	7	7
psr-small (49)	48	1418	**1274**	**1274**	**49**	**49**	48	48	70117	**30843**	**30843**	**49**	**49**	48
rovers (8)	8	114150	89760	**89291**	**8**	**8**	**8**	7	2656481	2191336	**1814358**	**7**	**7**	**7**
satellite (7)	7	359637	5321	**5319**	**7**	**7**	**7**	6	1341502	1125294	**1030810**	**6**	**6**	**6**
storage (15)	15	432	432	**401**	**15**	**15**	**15**	15	206829	206831	**162818**	**15**	**15**	**15**
tpp (6)	6	425	**329**	**329**	**6**	**6**	**6**	6	146205	**126005**	**126005**	**6**	**6**	**6**
trucks (8)	6	426851	**369828**	**369828**	6	**7**	**7**	2	274378	**126321**	**126321**	**2**	**2**	**2**
zenotravel (10)	10	43816	**7250**	**7250**	**10**	**10**	**10**	8	123047	**19815**	**19815**	8	**10**	**10**
total(530)	438	35823198	12124741	**11779147**	439	**457**	456	355	88746822	64791718	**64150466**	360	**373**	371

Table 8.2: Performance in terms of expanded nodes across the budgets 75%, 100% relative to c^* and a total number of problems solved with the fact oriented utility approach and two versions of the net utility of action oriented approach incorporating the selective action split and the unit action split for inference of net utility polarity.

	75%							100%						
	expansion				Coverage			expansion				Coverage		
	# Tasks	Fact	ASplit	USplit	Fact	ASplit	USplit	# Tasks	Fact	ASplit	USplit	Fact	ASplit	USplit
airport (30)	17	539767	**449237**	**449237**	**17**	**17**	**17**	17	646385	**582215**	**582215**	**17**	**17**	**17**
blocks (26)	18	6962323	**5216974**	**5216974**	**18**	**18**	**18**	16	12995595	**12578916**	**12578916**	**16**	**16**	**16**
depot (7)	4	2631475	**1905720**	**1905720**	4	**5**	4	3	6697010	**6494853**	**6494853**	**3**	**3**	**3**
driverlog (14)	9	20254747	**11181802**	**11181802**	**9**	**9**	**9**	5	**3446381**	3566189	3566189	5	5	**6**
freecell (60)	13	4579410	**2207048**	2755887	14	16	**18**	14	13142640	**11495984**	11496020	**14**	**14**	**14**
grid (2)	2	1854327	**131135**	**131135**	**2**	**2**	**2**	1	3947	**1267**	**1267**	1	1	1
gripper (7)	6	9875884	**9847447**	9876970	**6**	**6**	**6**	5	2775779	**2769436**	2775740	**5**	**5**	**5**
logistics00 (20)	10	1042896	**535494**	**535494**	10	10	10	10	2373434	**1710035**	**1710035**	10	10	10
logistics98 (6)	2	244011	**94152**	**94152**	**2**	**2**	**2**	2	607989	**323264**	**323264**	**2**	**2**	**2**
miconic (142)	45	25068867	24344156	**23458854**	**45**	**45**	**45**	35	2294587	2294587	**2167485**	35	**40**	**40**
movie (30)	30	9780	9780	**9750**	**30**	**30**	**30**	30	**13650**	**13650**	**13650**	**30**	**30**	**30**
mprime (19)	18	1444249	**54432**	**54432**	18	**19**	**19**	15	4180189	**160806**	**160806**	15	**18**	**18**
mystery (15)	15	332870	**22649**	**22649**	**15**	**15**	**15**	13	4153020	**453778**	**453778**	13	**15**	**15**
openstacks (7)	7	4602063	**4564016**	**4564016**	**7**	**7**	**7**	5	86142	**86033**	**86033**	5	**7**	**7**
pipes-nt (19)	13	1944267	**795164**	842251	**14**	**14**	**14**	7	1079337	**717332**	761255	**9**	**9**	**9**
pipes-t (13)	7	929426	217249	**216614**	8	**9**	**9**	6	709041	**502890**	503641	**7**	6	6
pipes-ns (10)	6	244489	127228	**126594**	**7**	6	6	6	709041	**502890**	503641	**6**	**6**	**6**
psr-small (49)	48	6988853	**393695**	**393695**	**49**	**49**	48	47	4318028	**3177126**	**3177126**	48	**49**	48
rovers (8)	5	3162058	2488569	**2481522**	**5**	**5**	**5**	4	10324	**7672**	**7672**	**4**	**4**	**4**
satellite (7)	4	202204	183388	**182979**	**4**	**4**	**4**	4	961275	898831	**897245**	**4**	**4**	**4**
storage (15)	14	1308391	1308385	**1046021**	**14**	**14**	**14**	13	3813632	3813621	**3531559**	**13**	**13**	**13**
tpp (6)	6	4942723	**3830507**	**3830507**	**6**	**6**	**6**	5	58885	**58878**	**58878**	**5**	**5**	**5**
trucks (8)	2	1136027	**947205**	**947205**	**2**	**2**	**2**	2	**3062018**	3067481	3067481	**2**	**2**	**2**
zenotravel (10)	8	4604592	**933361**	**933361**	**8**	**8**	**8**	7	1967411	**1394234**	**1394234**	**7**	**7**	**7**
total(530)	309	104905699	71788793	**71257821**	314	**318**	**318**	272	70105740	56671968	**56312983**	276	**288**	**288**

8.6 Conclusion

We introduced offline and online methods for identifying actions' net utility polarity and provided structure related decision criteria to activate the action split to unitary effects. This allows us to address real-world scenarios where the polarity of an action is detected only through interaction with the environment. We evaluated two versions of the unit-effect split in which the decision to activate the unit split is a per-task bulk decision. In future work, we will implement a machinery of per-action unit split decision to allow for better insight into and exploitation of action properties for choosing an optimal split method. This chapter demonstrates that the concept of net utility is more powerful than the concept of absolute utility.

Chapter 9

Conclusion

This book draws conclusions as to how the field of economics can be expanded to capture the concepts that are missed by focusing on absolute utility rather than net utility.

The text starts with a discussion on the value rational decision-making process (Chapter 2). We present the rational and the bounded rational decision models. We then discuss the idea of rationality in the decision-making process, focusing on bounded and flexible bounded rationality. We show some of the bounds of rationality. We present instrumental and value rational decision actions and discuss aspects of the effectiveness and efficiency of actions.

The text continues with a discussion of the context of rationality in AI and optimization (Chapters 3 and 4). The current AI paradigms, powerful, diversified, and effective are explained, focusing on how they tackle the most cumbersome real-world problems. Although some paradigms and families were left out, e.g., statistical (like Bayesian Networks), symbolic (like NLP - Natural Language Processing), and the many variations of fuzzy constructs, we focused on explaining the major underlining concepts. Fuzzy logic, although not necessarily intelligent, can be hybridized with other algorithms, greatly improving the flexibility of the interface with humans, and improving the overall performance of the produced algorithms. On that note, hybridization is another interesting possibility for improving rationality as it blends the highlights of AI and CI algorithms. The interested reader can learn much more about these families and approaches in the dedicated bestseller textbooks: on AI: "Machine Learning" by Tom Mitchel [Mitchell (1997)] and "AI: A Modern Approach" by Russel and Norvig [Russell and Norvig (2020)]; and, on CI: "Computational Intelligence: Concepts to Implementations" by Eberhart and Shi [Eberhart and

Shi (2011)], and "Computational Intelligence: An Introduction" by Andries Engelbrecht [Engelbrecht (2007)].

Chapter 4 described different optimization techniques and the extent of their rationality. The optimization approaches studied are: Broyden-Fletcher-Goldfarb-Shanno ($BFGS$), conjugate gradient approaches, Genetic Algorithms, particle swarm optimization and simulated annealing methods. The Nelder-Mead simplex approach, $BFGS$, and the conjugate gradient approach are local but more precise methods (more rational). In contrast, the Nelder-Mead simplex method, Genetic Algorithms, particle swarm optimization and simulated annealing methods are global but less precise methods (less rational). A hybrid of global and local methods is proposed to increase the extent of rationality.

Chapter 5 presented the cost-value and utility dimensions and dynamics. We discussed the terms value, utility, costs, and their hidden dimensions. We discussed how economic values are changed by applying decisions and actions. We showed negative and positive cost, value, and utility changes and discussed the term net utility and the relativity of achievements. We presented value rational actions and the value rational judgment function. We introduced the concept of landmarks in sequential decision making and planning and showed how they could represent economic values and dynamics in the decision-making process. We discussed the value of knowledge and showed the interplay between data, information, knowledge, and wisdom summarized in the DIKW hierarchy. Finally, we discussed how data is used in action and emphasized some negative aspects of so-called Big Data.

Chapter 6 proposed the use of the concept of net utility to successfully explain the St. Petersburg Paradox. The concept of net utility or relative utility was experimentally observed by Kahneman and Tversky and has had a profound impact on the field of behavioral economics. This chapter concludes that the concept of net utility explains value more universally than nominal utility. In the rest of the book we put this observation into practice.

Chapter 7 reviewed and provided a background for the sequential decision-making and action application processes in AI. The sequential decision-making process in AI has been widely researched in the field of Planning AI. Our focus in this chapter was on the Oversubscription planning problem (OSP) and its recent research progress. The OSP description captures the economic aspects of problems that deal with AI's sequential decision-making and action application processes. It allows us to module actions and decisions with different costs, values and budget restrictions over the planning process. This chapter presented a budget reduction compilation approach that reduces the effective search space. By defining the net utility of an action and gross positive action notations, we could exploit observations about the structure of optimal plans at the level of actions and action sequences. These properties are used to generate more informative landmarks. The value-driven landmark compilation (also referred to as the valuable plan compilation in this chapter) compiles the 'optimal plan properties' into the task representation. This compilation reduces the effective search space and rationalizes the search procedure by adding constraints and forcing the search to conform to optimal plan properties and resource bounds. These landmarks and compilations can then be used in an OSP planner to obtain state-of-the-art performance. We used the value-driven landmarks as an input for the budget reduction procedure and improved the pruning mechanism based on these landmarks. These notions are not restricted to OSP planning. For example, the notion of the net utility of an action can be adapted to classical planning, where the action has net positive utility if it achieves some goal facts without deleting any other goal facts.

In Chapter 8 we introduced offline and online methods to identify actions' net utility polarity and provided structure related decision criteria to activate action split to unitary effects. This allows us to address real-world scenarios where the polarity of action is detected only with interaction with the environment. We evaluated two versions of the unit-effect split in which the decision to activate the unit split is a per-task bulk decision. We showed how the online and the offline techniques for net utility detection increase the informativeness of actions in the planning and decision-making process and hence rationalize the entire process. In future work, we will implement a machinery of per-action unit split decision to allow for better insight and exploitation of action properties for choosing an optimal split method. It is noteworthy that we demonstrated that the concept of net utility is more powerful than the concept of absolute utility.

Overall, the main takeaway message of this book is that using the net utility rather than nominal utility as a measure allows us to capture a broader context of the impact of a decision's and action's possible achievement. It allows us to capture the negative and positive utilities as well as indifferent, neutral utilities of decisions and actions in human, economic, and artificial intelligence systems. Adopting problem-solving techniques like AI and optimization to exploit net utility can improve and rationalize the problem-solving process and optimize its results. Net utility increases the informativeness of actions in the planning and decision-making process and rationalizes the entire process. It allows us to increase the effectiveness and efficiency of planning and domain-independent problem-solving processes and the overall rationality of sequential decisions in the decision-making process.

Bibliography

Abdella, M. and Marwala, T. (2005). The use of genetic algorithms and neural networks to approximate missing data in database, in *IEEE 3rd International Conference on Computational Cybernetics, 2005. ICCC 2005.* (IEEE), pp. 207–212.

Ackoff, R. L. (1989). From data to wisdom, *Journal of Applied Systems Analysis* **16**, 1, pp. 3–9.

Aghighi, M. and Jonsson, P. (2014). Oversubscription planning: Complexity and compilability, in *AAAI*, pp. 2221–2227.

Arrow, K. J. (1970). Essays in the theory of risk-bearing, Tech. Rep.

Atiqullah, M. M. (2004). An efficient simple cooling schedule for simulated annealing, in A. Laganá, M. L. Gavrilova, V. Kumar, Y. Mun, C. J. K. Tan, and O. Gervasi (eds.), *Computational Science and Its Applications — ICCSA 2004* (Springer, Berlin-Heidelberg), ISBN 978-3-540-24767-8, pp. 396–404.

Aumann, R. J. (1977). The St. Petersburg Paradox: A discussion of some recent comments, *Journal of Economic Theory* **14**, 2, pp. 443–445.

Avriel, M. (2003). *Nonlinear Programming: Analysis and methods* (Courier Corporation).

Bäckström, C. and Klein, I. (1991). Planning in polynomial time: the SAS-PUBS class, *Computational Intelligence* **7**, 3, pp. 181–197.

Bäckström, C. and Nebel, B. (1995). Complexity results for SAS+ planning, *Computational Intelligence* **11**, 4, pp. 625–655.

Baier, J. A., Bacchus, F., and McIlraith, S. A. (2009). A heuristic search approach to planning with temporally extended preferences, *Artificial Intelligence* **173**, 5, p. 593.

Bassett Jr., G. W. (1987). The St. Petersburg Paradox and bounded utility, *History of Political Economy* **19**, 4, pp. 517–523.

Benton, J. (2006). Solving goal utility dependencies and simple preferences in partial satisfaction planning, *ICAPS 2006*, p. 16.

Benton, J., Coles, A. J., and Coles, A. (2012). Temporal planning with preferences and time-dependent continuous costs, in *ICAPS*, Vol. 77, p. 78.

Benton, J., Do, M., and Kambhampati, S. (2009a). Anytime heuristic search for partial satisfaction planning, *Artificial Intelligence* **173**, 5–6, pp. 562–592.

Benton, J., Do, M., and Kambhampati, S. (2009b). Anytime heuristic search for partial satisfaction planning, *Artificial Intelligence* **173**, 5–6, pp. 562–592.

Benton, J., Van Den Briel, M., and Kambhampati, S. (2007). A hybrid linear programming and relaxed plan heuristic for partial satisfaction planning problems, in *ICAPS*, pp. 34–41.

Berger, J. O. (2013). *Statistical Decision Theory and Bayesian Analysis* (Springer Science & Business Media).

Bernoulli, D. (1738). Specimen theoriae novae de mensure sortis, *Comentarii Academiae Scientarium Inperialis Petropolitanae*, p. Volume V.

Bernoulli, D. (1738/1954). Exposition of a new theory on the measurement of risk, *Econometrica* **22**, 1, pp. 23–36, `http://www.jstor.org/stable/1909829`.

Bertsekas, D., Nedic, A., and Ozdaglar, A. (2003). *Convex Analysis and Optimization* (Belmont, MA: Athena Scientific).

Bishop, C. M. *et al.* (1995). *Neural Networks for Pattern Recognition* (Oxford University Press).

Bonet, B. and Geffner, H. (2008). Heuristics for planning with penalties and rewards formulated in logic and computed through circuits, *Artificial Intelligence* **172**, 12–13, pp. 1579–1604.

Bonet, B. and Helmert, M. (2010). Strengthening landmark heuristics via hitting sets, in *ECAI*, pp. 329–334.

Bonet, B., Loerincs, G., and Geffner, H. (1997). A robust and fast action selection mechanism for planning, in *AAAI/IAAI*, pp. 714–719.

Boutilier, C., Dean, T., and Hanks, S. (1999). Decision-theoretic planning: Structural assumptions and computational leverage, *Journal of Artificial Intelligence Research* **11**, pp. 1–94.

Brafman, R. I. and Chernyavsky, Y. (2005). Planning with goal preferences and constraints, in *ICAPS*, pp. 182–191.

Breiman, L. (2001). Random forests, *Machine Learning* **45**, 1, pp. 5–32.

Breiman, L., Friedman, J. H., Olshen, R. A., and Stone, C. J. (1984). *Classification and Regression Trees. 1st Edition* (Chapman and Hall/CRC).

Brito, D. L. (1975). Becker's theory of the allocation of time and the St. Petersburg Paradox, *Journal of Economic Theory* **10**, 1, pp. 123–126.

Broyden, C. G. (1970). The convergence of a class of double-rank minimization algorithms 1. General considerations, *IMA Journal of Applied Mathematics* **6**, 1, pp. 76–90.

Bürmen, Á., Puhan, J., and Tuma, T. (2006). Grid restrained Nelder-Mead algorithm, *Computational Optimization and Applications* **34**, 3, pp. 359–375.

Cave, S. and Ó hÉigeartaigh, S. S. (2018). An AI race for strategic advantage: rhetoric and risks, in *Proceedings of the 2018 AAAI/ACM Conference on AI, Ethics, and Society*, pp. 36–40.

Coles, A. J. and Coles, A. (2011). LPRPG-P: Relaxed plan heuristics for planning with preferences, in *ICAPS*.

Cooley, M. (1980). *Architect or Bee?* (Langley Technical Services Slough).

Coope, I. D. and Price, C. J. (2002). Positive bases in numerical optimization, *Computational Optimization and Applications* **21**, 2, pp. 169–175.

Cowen, T. and High, J. (1988). Time, bounded utility, and the St. Petersburg Paradox, *Theory and Decision* **25**, 3, pp. 219–223.

Cox, J. C., Kroll, E. B., Lichters, M., Sadiraj, V., and Vogt, B. (2019). The St. Petersburg Paradox despite risk-seeking preferences: an experimental study, *Business Research* **12**, 1, pp. 27–44, doi:10.1007/s40685-018-0078-y, `https://doi.org/10.1007/s40685-018-0078-y`.

Cox, J. C., Sadiraj, V., and Vogt, B. (2011). On the empirical relevance of St. Petersburg lotteries, Petersburg Lotteries (January 1, 2011). Andrew Young School of Policy Studies Research Paper Series, 11–04.

Crossingham, B. and Marwala, T. (2008). Using genetic algorithms to optimise rough set partition sizes for HIV data analysis, in *Advances in Intelligent and Distributed Computing* (Springer), pp. 245–250.

Cunliffe, A. L. (2008). Orientations to social constructionism: Relationally responsive social constructionism and its implications for knowledge and learning, *Management Learning* **39**, 2, pp. 123–139.

Darwin, C. (1859). *The Origin of Species by Means of Natural Selection (or The Preservation of Favoured Races in the Struggle for Life)*. London: John Murray.

De Jong, K. (2006). Evolutionary computation: A unified approach. Bradford Book.

DeGroot, M. H. (2005). *Optimal statistical decisions*, Vol. 82 (John Wiley & Sons).

Dictionary, O. E. (2008). Oxford English Dictionary, Retrieved May **30**, p. 2008.

Do, M. and Kambhampati, S. (2004). Partial satisfaction (over-subscription) planning as heuristic search, *Proceedings of KBCS-04*.

Do, M. B., Benton, J., Van Den Briel, M., and Kambhampati, S. (2007). Planning with goal utility dependencies, in *IJCAI*, pp. 1872–1878.

Domshlak, C., Katz, M., and Lefler, S. (2012). Landmark-enhanced abstraction heuristics, *Artificial Intelligence* **189**, pp. 48–68.

Domshlak, C. and Mirkis, V. (2015). Deterministic oversubscription planning as heuristic search: Abstractions and reformulations, *Journal of Artificial Intelligence Research* **52**, pp. 97–169.

Dorigo, M. (1992). Optimization, learning and natural algorithms, Ph. D. Thesis, Politecnico di Milano.

Eberhart, R. C. and Shi, Y. (2011). *Computational Intelligence: Concepts to implementations* (Morgan Kaufmann).

Einstein, A. (1905). Über einen die erzeugung und verwandlung des lichtes betreffenden heuristischen gesichttspunkt (on a heuristic viewpoint concerning the production and transformation of light), *Annalen der Physik* **17**, pp. 132–148.

Eliot, T. S. (1934). *The Rock: A Pageant Play, Written for Performance at Sadler's Wells Theatre*, 28 May–9 June 1934, on Behalf of the Forty-five Churches Fund of the Dioceses of London; Book of Words by T. S. Eliot (Faber & Faber).

Empson, L. (2001). Fear of exploitation and fear of contamination: Impediments to knowledge transfer in mergers between professional service firms, *Human Relations* **54**, 7, pp. 839–862.

Engelbrecht, A. P. (2007). *Computational Intelligence: An introduction*, 2nd Ed. (John Wiley & Sons).

Farber, S. C., Costanza, R., and Wilson, M. A. (2002). Economic and ecological concepts for valuing ecosystem services, *Ecological Economics* **41**, 3, pp. 375–392.

Fechner, G. (1860). Elemente der psychophysik. breitkopf and hrtel. English edition, 1966: Elements of psychophysics, vol. 1, trans.

Fletcher, R. (1970). A new approach to variable metric algorithms, *The Computer Journal* **13**, 3, pp. 317–322.

Fletcher, R. (2000). *Practical Methods of Optimization* (John Wiley & Sons).

Garrison, L., Mestre-Ferrandiz, J., and Zamora, B. (2016). The value of knowing and knowing the value: improving the health technology assessment of complementary diagnostics, *Office of Health Economics: London, UK.*

Goldberg, D. E. (1989). *Genetic Algorithms in Search, Optimization and Machine Learning*, 1st edn. (Addison-Wesley Longman).

Goldberg, D. E. and Holland, J. H. (1988). Genetic algorithms and machine learning, *Machine Learning* **3**, 2–3, pp. 95–99.

Goldfarb, D. (1970). A family of variable metric updates derived by variational means, *Mathematics of Computation*, **24**, 109, pp. 23–26.

Goodfellow, I. J., Pouget-Abadie, J., Mirza, M., Xu, B., Warde-Farley, D., Ozair, S., Courville, A., and Bengio, Y. (2014). Generative adversarial nets, in *Proceedings of the 27th International Conference on Neural Information Processing Systems — Volume 2*, pp. 2672–2680.

Grüne-Yanoff, T. (2012). Paradoxes of rational choice theory, in *Handbook of Risk Theory* (Springer), pp. 499–516.

Guarracino, L. and Velis, D. (2007). A hybrid simulated annealing and gradient-based algorithm for the estimation of unsaturated soil parameters, *Mecánica Computacional*, **20**, pp. 2061–2071.

Haddawy, P. and Hanks, S. (1993). *Utility models for goal-directed decision-theoretic planners* (University of Washington, Department of Computer Science and Engineering).

Haddawy, P. and Hanks, S. (1998). Utility models for goal-directed, decision-theoretic planners, *Computational Intelligence* **14**, 3, pp. 392–429.

Hebb, D. O. (1949). *The Organisation of Behaviour: A neuropsychological theory* (Wiley, New York).

Helmert, M. (2006a). The fast downward planning system, *Journal of Artificial Intelligence Research* **26**, pp. 191–246.

Helmert, M. (2006b). The fast downward planning system, *Journal of Artificial Intelligence Research* **26**, pp. 191–246.

Helmert, M. and Domshlak, C. (2009). Landmarks, critical paths and abstractions: what's the difference anyway? in *ICAPS*, pp. 162–169.

Hestenes, M. R. and Stiefel, E. (1952). Methods of conjugate gradients for solving linear systems, *Journal of Research of the National Bureau of Standards* **49**, pp. 409–435.

Ho, T. K. (1995). Random decision forests, in *Proceedings of 3rd International Conference on Document Analysis and Recognition*, Vol. 1 (IEEE), pp. 278–282.

Hoffmann, J., Porteous, J., and Sebastia, L. (2004). Ordered landmarks in planning, *Journal of Artificial Intelligence Research* **22**, pp. 215–278.

Holland, J. H. (1975). *Adaptation in Natural and Artificial Systems* (University of Michigan Press, Ann Arbor, MI), second edition, 1992.

Holland, J. H. *et al.* (1992). *Adaptation in natural and artificial systems: an introductory analysis with applications to biology, control, and artificial intelligence* (MIT Press).

Jackson, P. (1986). *Introduction to Expert Systems* (Addison-Wesley).

Kahneman, D. and Tversky, A. (1979). Prospect theory: An analysis of decision under risk, *Econometrica* **47**, 2, pp. 263–292.

Karpas, E. and Domshlak, C. (2009). Cost-optimal planning with landmarks, in *IJCAI*, pp. 1728–1733.

Katz, M. and Domshlak, C. (2010). Optimal admissible composition of abstraction heuristics, *Artificial Intelligence* **174**, 12–13, pp. 767–798.

Katz, M., Keyder, E., Winterer, D., and Pommerening, F. (2019). Oversubscription planning as classical planning with multiple cost functions, in *Proceedings of the International Conference on Automated Planning and Scheduling*, Vol. 29, pp. 237–245.

Kennedy, J. (1997). The particle swarm: social adaptation of knowledge, in *Proceedings of 1997 IEEE International Conference on Evolutionary Computation* (IEEE), pp. 303–308.

Kennedy, J. and Eberhart, R. (1995). Particle swarm optimization, in *Proceedings of ICNN'95 — International Conference on Neural Networks*, Vol. 4 (IEEE), pp. 1942–1948.

Kennedy, J. and Eberhart, R. C. (2001). Swarm Intelligence.

Keyder, E. and Geffner, H. (2009). Soft goals can be compiled away, *Journal of Artificial Intelligence Research* **36**, pp. 547–556.

Kirkpatrick, S., Gelatt, C. D., and Vecchi, M. P. (1983). Optimization by simulated annealing, *Science* **220**, 4598, pp. 671–680.

Klein, I. (1991). Parallel non-binary planning in polynomial time, in *12th International Joint Conference on Artificial Intelligence*, Sydney, Australia, pp. 268–273.

Kohonen, T. (1982). Self-organized formation of topologically correct feature maps, *Biological Cybernetics* **43**, 1, pp. 59–69.

Kriger, M. P. and Barnes, L. B. (1992). Organizational decision-making as hierarchical levels of drama, *Journal of Management Studies* **29**, 4, pp. 439–457.

LeCun, Y., Bengio, Y., and Hinton, G. (2015). Deep learning, *Nature* **521**, 7553, pp. 436–444.

Libor, J. (2011). Financial and economic aspects of St. Petersburg Paradox, *Journal of Informatics and Mathematical Sciences* **3**, 3, pp. 211–220.

Luenberger, D. G. and Ye, Y. (2008). Linear and nonlinear programming, ISOR Vol. 116 (Springer).

Lunenburg, F. C. (2010). The decision making process, in *National Forum of Educational Administration & Supervision Journal*, Vol. 27.

Maniezzo, V., Boschetti, M. A., and Stützle, T. (2021). *Matheuristics: Algorithms and Implementations* (Springer Nature).

Martin-Clemente, R., Acha, J. I., and Puntonet, C. G. (2001). A conjugate gradient method and simulated annealing for blind separation of sources, in *International Work-Conference on Artificial Neural Networks* (Springer), pp. 810–817.

Marwala, T. (2002). Finite element model updating using wavelet data and genetic algorithm, *Journal of Aircraft* **39**, 4, pp. 709–711.

Marwala, T. (2007). Bayesian training of neural networks using genetic programming, *Pattern Recognition Letters* **28**, 12, pp. 1452–1458.

Marwala, T. (2009). *Computational Intelligence for Missing Data Imputation, Estimation, and Management: Knowledge Optimization Techniques: Knowledge Optimization Techniques* (IGI Global).

Marwala, T. (2010). Finite-element-model Updating Using Computional Intelligence Techniques: Applications to Structural Dynamics (Springer).

Marwala, T. (2013). Flexibly-bounded rationality and marginalization of irrationality theories for decision making, *arXiv preprint arXiv:1306.2025*.

Marwala, T. (2014). *Artificial intelligence techniques for rational decision making* (Springer).

Marwala, T. (2015). *Causality, Correlation and Artificial Intelligence for Rational Decision Making* (World Scientific).

Marwala, T. and Chakraverty, S. (2006). Fault classification in structures with incomplete measured data using autoassociative neural networks and genetic algorithm, *Current Science*, pp. 542–548.

Marwala, T. and Leke, C. A. (2019). *Handbook of Machine Learning: Volume 2: Optimization and Decision Making* (World Scientific).

McCulloch, W. S. and Pitts, W. (1943). A logical calculus of the ideas immanent in nervous activity, *The Bulletin of Mathematical Biophysics* **5**, 4, pp. 115–133.

Menger, K. (1934). Das unsicherheitsmoment in der wertlehre, *Zeitschrift für Nationalökonomie* **5**, 4, pp. 459–485.

Menger, K. (1979). The role of uncertainty in economics, in *Selected Papers in Logic and Foundations, Didactics, Economics* (Springer), pp. 259–278.

Metropolis, N., Rosenbluth, A. W., Rosenbluth, M. N., Teller, A. H., and Teller, E. (1953). Equation of state calculations by fast computing machines, *The Journal of Chemical Physics* **21**, 6, pp. 1087–1092.

Michalewicz, Z. (1992). *Genetic Algorithms + Data Structures — Evolution Programs* (Springer).

Mirkis, V. and Domshlak, C. (2013). Abstractions for oversubscription planning, in *ICAPS*.

Mirkis, V. and Domshlak, C. (2014). Landmarks in oversubscription planning, in *Proceedings of the Twenty-first European Conference on Artificial Intelligence* (IOS Press), pp. 633–638.

Mitchell, T. (1997). Machine Learning (McGraw-Hill Education).

Mitras, B. A. and Hassan, N. F. (2013). Three proposed hybrid genetic algorithms, *AL-Rafidain Journal of Computer Sciences and Mathematics* **10**, 1, pp. 53–64.

Møller, M. F. (1993). A scaled conjugate gradient algorithm for fast supervised learning, *Neural Networks* **6**, 4, pp. 525–533.

Moor, J. (2006). The Dartmouth College Artificial Intelligence Conference: The next fifty years, *AI Magazine* **27**, 4, pp. 87–87.

Muller, D. and Karpas, E. (2018a). Value driven landmarks for oversubscription planning, in *ICAPS*.

Muller, D. and Karpas, E. (2018b). Value driven landmarks for oversubscription planning, Tech. Rep. IE/IS-2018-04, Technion, Faculty of Industrial Engineering and Management.

Nebel, B. (2000). On the compilability and expressive power of propositional planning formalisms, *Journal of Artificial Intelligence Research* **12**, pp. 271–315.

Neto, F. B. D. L. and de Lacerda, M. G. P. (2014). Weight based fish school search for continuous optimization in multimodal complex problems, in *Proceedings of 2014 IEEE International Conference on Systems, Man, and Cybernetics* pp. 270–277.

Neugebauer, T. *et al.* (2010). Moral impossibility in the Petersburg Paradox: A literature survey and experimental evidence, *Luxembourg School of Finance Research Working Paper Series* **10**, 174, pp. 1–43.

Newell, A., Simon, H. A., *et al.* (1972). *Human Problem Solving*, Vol. 104 (Prentice-hall, Englewood Cliffs).

Nigenda, R. S. and Kambhampati, S. (2005). Planning graph heuristics for selecting objectives in over-subscription planning problems, in *ICAPS*, pp. 192–201.

Pan, W., Zhun, F., Shan, F., and Yun, Z. (2000). Study on a novel hybrid adaptive genetic algorithm embedding conjugate gradient algorithm, in *Proceedings of the 3rd World Congress on Intelligent Control and Automation*, Vol. 1 (IEEE), pp. 630–633.

Pearl, J. (1984). *Heuristics: Intelligent search strategies for computer problem solving* (Addison-Wesley, Reading, MA).

Planck, M. (1901). Ueber das gesetz der energieverteilung im normalspectrum (on the law of the energy distribution in the normal spectrum), *Annalen der Physik* **4**, p. 553.

Poladian, V., Butler, S., Shaw, M., and Garlan, D. (2003). Time is not money: The case for multi-dimensional accounting in value-based software engineering, in *Proceedings of 5th Int'l Workshop on Economics Driven Software Engineering Research*.

Pollock, J. (2001). The logical foundations of decision-theoretic planning in autonomous agents, *preparation*. Available from `http://www.u.arizona.edu/~pollock`.

Pollock, J. L. (2006). Against optimality: Logical foundations for decision-theoretic planning in autonomous agents, *Computational Intelligence* **22**, 1, pp. 1–25.

Pommerening, F. and Helmert, M. (2013). Incremental lm-cut, in *ICAPS*.

Qteish, A. and Hamdan, M. (2010). Hybrid particle swarm and conjugate gradient optimization algorithm, in *Advances in Swarm Intelligence*, Lecture Notes in Computer Science (Springer), pp. 582–588, doi:10.1007/978-3-642-13495-1_71.

Quinlan, J. R. (1986). Induction of decision trees, *Machine Learning* **1**, 1, pp. 81–106.

Quinlan, J. R. (1988). Decision trees and multivalued attributes, *Machine Intelligence 11*, pp. 305–318.

Quinlan, J. R. (1992). *C4.5: Programs for Machine Learning* (Morgan Kaufmann, San Francisco).

Ransome, T. M. (2006). Automatic minimisation of patient setup errors in proton beam therapy, Ph.D. thesis.

Rawlins, J. E. (1991). Proceedings of the First Workshop on Foundations of Genetic Algorithms (Morgan Kaufmann), pp. 265 283.

Rosenblatt, F. (1957). The perceptron — a perceiving and recognizing automaton, Tech. Rep. 85-460-1, Cornell Aeronautical Laboratory, Ithaca, New York.

Rowley, J. (2007). The wisdom hierarchy: representations of the DIKW hierarchy, *Journal of Information Science* **33**, 2, pp. 163–180, doi:10.1177/0165551506070706, `https://doi.org/10.1177/0165551506070706`, `https://doi.org/10.1177/0165551506070706`.

Rumelhart, D. E., Hinton, G. E., and Williams, R. J. (1986). Learning representations by back-propagating errors, *Nature* **323**, 6088, pp. 533–536.

Russell, S. J. and Norvig, P. (2020). *Artificial Intelligence: A Modern Approach (4th Edition)* (Pearson), `http://aima.cs.berkeley.edu/`.

Samuelson, P. A. (1977). St. Petersburg Paradoxes: Defanged, dissected, and historically described, *Journal of Economic Literature* **15**, 1, pp. 24–55.

Schwartz, B. (2004). The Paradox of Choice: Why More is Less (Ecco New York).

Searle, J. R. (1980). Minds, brains, and programs, *Behavioral and Brain Sciences* **3**, 3, pp. 417–424.

Seidl, C. (2013). The St. Petersburg Paradox at 300, *Journal of Risk and Uncertainty* **46**, 3, pp. 247–264, doi:10.1007/s11166-013-9165-9, `https://doi.org/10.1007/s11166-013-9165-9`.

Shanno, D. F. (1970). Conditioning of quasi-newton methods for function minimization, *Mathematics of Computation* **24**, 111, pp. 647–656.

Shi, Y. and Eberhart, R. (1998). A modified particle swarm optimizer, in *1998 IEEE International Conference on Evolutionary Computation Proceedings. IEEE World Congress on Computational Intelligence* (IEEE), pp. 69–73.

Simon, H. A. (1957). *Models of Man: Social and Rational; Mathematical Essays on Rational Human Behavior in Society Setting* (Wiley).

Simon, H. A. (1990). A mechanism for social selection and successful altruism, *Science (Washington)* **250**, 4988, pp. 1665–1668.

Simon, H. A. (1991). Bounded rationality and organizational learning, *Organization science* **2**, 1, pp. 125–134.

Smith, A. (1976). *An Inquiry into the Nature and Causes of the Wealth of Nations: Volume One*, Vol. 34 (London: printed for W. Strahan; and T. Cadell, 1776).

Smith, D. E. (2004). Choosing objectives in over-subscription planning, in *ICAPS*, Vol. 4, p. 393.

Smolensky, P. (1987). Connectionist AI, symbolic AI, and the brain, *Artificial Intelligence Review* **1**, 2, pp. 95–109.

Spender, J.-C. (1996). Organizational knowledge, learning and memory: Three concepts in search of a theory, *Journal of Organizational Change Management* **9**, 1, pp. 63–78.

Strati, A. (2007). Sensible knowledge and practice-based learning, *Management Learning* **38**, 1, pp. 61–77.

Swart, J. (2011). That's why it matters: How knowing creates value, *Management Learning* **42**, 3, pp. 319–332, doi:10.1177/1350507610391591.

Székely, G. J. and Richards, D. S. P. (2004). The St. Petersburg Paradox and the crash of high-tech stocks in 2000, *The American Statistician* **58**, 3, pp. 225–231.

Tettey, T. and Marwala, T. (2006). Controlling interstate conflict using neuro-fuzzy modeling and genetic algorithms, in *2006 International Conference on Intelligent Engineering Systems* (IEEE), pp. 30–34.

Turing, A. (1950). Computing Machinery and Intelligence Mind 49 433-460, *Also available at: http://cogprints.org/499/00/turing.html.*

Tversky, A. and Kahneman, D. (1992). Advances in prospect theory: Cumulative representation of uncertainty, *Journal of Risk and Uncertainty* **5**, 4, pp. 297–323.

Van Den Briel, M., Sanchez, R., Do, M. B., and Kambhampati, S. (2004a). Effective approaches for partial satisfaction (over-subscription) planning, in *AAAI*, pp. 562–569.

Van Den Briel, M., Sanchez, R., and Kambhampati, S. (2004b). Over-subscription in planning: A partial satisfaction problem, in *ICAPS-04 Workshop on Integrating Planning into Scheduling*, pp. 91–98.

Von Neumann, J. and Morgenstern, O. (1947). Theory of Games and Economic Behavior, 2nd ed. (Princeton Univ. Press).

Von Neumann, J., Morgenstern, O., and Kuhn, H. W. (2007). *Theory of Games and Economic Behavior (Commemorative Edition)* (Princeton University Press).

Vose, M. D. (1999). *The Simple Genetic Algorithm: Foundations and Theory* (MIT Press).

Warsito, B., Prahutama, A., Yasin, H., and Sumiyati, S. (2019). Hybrid particle swarm and conjugate gradient optimization in neural network for prediction of suspended particulate matter, in *E3S Web of Conferences*, Vol. 125 (EDP Sciences), p. 25007.

Watson, I. (1997). *Applying Case-Based Reasoning: Techniques for Enterprise Systems* (Morgan Kaufmann Publishers Inc.).

Weber, E. H. (1834). *De pulsu, resorptione, auditu et tactu: annotationes anatomicae et physiologicae, auctore* (prostat apud CF Koehler).

Weiss, P. A. (1973). *The Science of Life: The Living System — A System for Living* (Futura Publishing Co., New York).

Werner, K. M. and Zank, H. (2019). A revealed reference point for prospect theory, *Economic Theory* **67**, 4, pp. 731–773, doi:10.1007/s00199-017-1096-2, `https://doi.org/10.1007/s00199-017-1096-2`.

Widrow, B. (1960). Adaptive "adaline" neuron using chemical "memistors", Tech. Rep. 1553-2, Stanford Electronics Laboratories.

Wikipedia contributors (2021). AI winter — Wikipedia, the free encyclopedia, `https://en.wikipedia.org/w/index.php?title=AI_winter&oldid=1045100056`, [Online; accessed 20-September-2021].

Xing, B. and Marwala, T. (2018a). *Smart Computing Applications in Crowdfunding* (London: CRC Press (Taylor and Francis)).

Xing, B. and Marwala, T. (2018b). Smart maintenance for human–robot interaction, *Studies in Systems, Decision and Control*, Springer, pp. 3–19.

Yaari, M. E. (1987). The dual theory of choice under risk, *Econometrica* **55**, 1, pp. 95–115, http://www.jstor.org/stable/1911158.

Ypma, T. J. (1995). Historical development of the Newton–Raphson method, *SIAM Review* **37**, 4, pp. 531–551.

Zadeh, L. (1965). Fuzzy sets, *Information and Control* **8**, 3, pp. 338–353, doi:https://doi.org/10.1016/S0019-9958(65)90241-X, https://www.sciencedirect.com/science/article/pii/S001999586590241X.

Zadeh, L. A. (2012). *Computing with Words: Principal Concepts and Ideas*, Vol. 277 (Springer).

Zeleny, M. (1987). Management support systems: Towards integrated knowledge management, *Human Systems Management* **7**, 1, pp. 59–70.

Index

Q

R

S

W

Z